Catholic Immigrants in America

Catholic Immigrants in America

James S. Olson

Nelson-Hall nh Chicago

The author would like to acknowledge the financial support of the American Philosophical Society, the National Endowment for the Humanities, and the Cushwa Center for the Study of American Catholicism at the University of Notre Dame in the development of *Catholic Immigrants in America*.

LIBRARY OF CONGRESS CATALOGING-IN-PUBLICATION DATA

Olson, James Stuart, 1946-
Catholic immigrants in America

Bibliography: p.
Includes index.
1. Catholics—United States—History. 2. United States—Ethnic Relations. I. Title.
E184.C3025 1987 973′.08822 86-16457
ISBN 0-8304-1037-6

Manufactured in the United States of America

10 9 8 7 6 5 4 3 2 1

The paper in this book is pH neutral (acid-free).

To my friends and counselors—
Ed Red, Jerry Torgesen, Dick Shumway, and Steve Hatch

Contents

1

The Catholic Dimension in American History

Ever since the first colonists sailed up the James River in 1607, people the world over have speculated on the unique character of American society. A host of foreign observers—including St. John de Crevecoeur in the eighteenth century, Alexis de Tocqueville in the nineteenth century, and D. W. Brogan and Alistair Cooke in the twentieth century—have wondered about the "exceptional" country across the sea and its enormous vitality. Some have decided that the environment is the key to American life, seeing virtue, democracy, and equality emerging out of the wilderness. Others have focused on the lack of class consciousness, deeply rooted aristocracies, or strong revolutionary traditions. Some have seen strength in America's isolation from the politics and problems of the Old World. Virtually everyone has commented on the material prosperity of America.[1]

Ethnic diversity has recently become a popular focus for the interpretation of American life. For nearly four centuries, hundreds of racial, religious, nationality, and language groups have come to the United States to try to achieve economic security, political freedom, and social tranquility. Along with the frontier, material plenty, democratic egalitarianism, and geographic isolation, ethnic pluralism has been a major force in American history. It remains today one of the most meaningful lenses through which Americans interpret their lives.[2]

Except for skin color, nationality and religion have been the most powerful ingredients of ethnic identity. If anything set America apart from the rest of the world in the eighteenth century, it was religious diversity, the unprecedented mix of Separatists, Congregationalists, Presbyterians, Baptists, Methodists, German and Dutch

Reformed, French Huguenots, Lutherans, Quakers, Anglicans, Jews, and Roman Catholics. Because no one denomination was a majority throughout the colonies, political loyalty never became synonymous with religious affiliation, on a national scale at least. An overwhelmingly Protestant spirit imbued colonial culture, but love of country never implied love of any church; so religion and nationality never fused. In that cultural circumstance lay the roots of freedom and toleration.[3]

Few colonists had any notion of freedom of religion when they first arrived, but toleration was an inevitable consequence of New World society. Slowly, the political struggles of religious zealots, so characteristic of the Old World, disappeared in America, victims of religious pluralism. The first colonists transplanted their sectarianisms, bringing their biases, fears, and denominational rivalries with them, but those feelings had a difficult time finding political expression here. Congregationalism became the established church in New England and Anglicanism in New York and the South, but after the American Revolution, most denominations recognized their minority positions and drifted toward toleration for the most selfish of reasons—survival. To ensure its own existence, each group had to guarantee the existence of every other church. Crusades to win souls were largely voluntary affairs by the mid-1700s. Religious pluralism was a major contributing force in the development of toleration.

The road was strewn with obstacles, however, and progress was painfully slow. Roman Catholics played a conspicuous role in the emergence of toleration. From the time Lord Baltimore sent his first settlers to Maryland in 1633 to John F. Kennedy's election as president in 1960, Catholics were suspect in the United States. Freedom of religion, the philosophical centerpiece of American democracy, revolved for more than three centuries around Catholicism and its place in the social and political structure. Not until Protestants worked out an accommodation with Roman Catholicism did freedom of religion really arrive in the United States.

The misunderstanding and hostility were a legacy of the sixteenth-century Protestant rebellion against Catholicism in Germany, Switzerland, England, Scandinavia, and the Low Countries. Roman Catholicism was seen as the embodiment of evil there. It was just as suspect in the colonies, primarily because of the central, authoritative role of the church. For Catholics, the church was not a loose brotherhood of people united by the influence of "saving grace" but a living, eternal body through which God communicated to his children. There was no general "priesthood of all believers" but a hierarchy of pope, bishops, and parish priests to whom God delegated the "keys of the kingdom"—the only legitimate, earthly authority to act in his name. Eternal truths existed in the Bible as well as in the historical traditions of the church. By examining the writings of church fathers, papal decrees, and the decisions of church councils, Catholics could discover the revealed will of God. Through the church, salvation was available to the good and faithful who had been baptized and confirmed, and had regularly received the sacraments of penance and communion throughout their lives. Sanctifying grace, which cleansed the stain of original and earthly sins, was available only through the sacraments of the church. For Roman Catholics, there was only one true church.[4]

Protestant hostility toward Roman Catholics in America was the product of that theology and history. Since the beginning of the English Reformation in 1534, the animosities between Protestants and Catholics had grown more bitter as doctrinal differences evolved. Mutual persecution was common and ritualized political murder hardly unknown. During the brief reign of the Catholic Queen Mary I between 1555 and 1558, for example, almost three hundred Protestants were executed, and twenty Catholics met a similar fate in the city of York between 1588 and 1603. At first, the differences between Catholics and Protestants were insubstantial, at least in the eyes of the common English citizen. They disagreed on the role of the pope because the monarchy now presided over the new Church of England, but Anglicans had retained the bishopric system and the emphasis on ritual; so to most communicants the visible church had not really changed.

In the late sixteenth century and throughout the seventeenth century, the Church of England became more and more Protestant, rejecting the veneration of relics, priestly celibacy, and the Latin Mass; denying the efficacy of all but the sacraments of baptism and communion; and introducing the English prayer book and new liturgies. The emergence of Puritanism—with its acceptance of predestination, denial of free will, emphasis on man's sinfulness, and rejection of good works and ecclesiastical hierarchies as prerequisites to salvation—only made Roman Catholicism seem more diabolical to most English Protestants.[5]

People took their religion seriously then, and articles of faith inevitably became entwined with questions of politics and diplomacy. Pope Pius V excommunicated Queen Elizabeth in 1570, and England's imperial rivalry with Spain became a religious as well as a geopolitical struggle, remaining unresolved until the defeat of the Armada in 1588. In addition to eliminating England's growing naval power, King Philip II of Spain had hoped to reverse the Reformation and restore England to Roman Catholicism. English Protestants greatly resented his paternalistic concern. Politics and religion also mixed in the seventeenth century, erupting periodically into violence like the Thirty Years War (1618–1648), the English Civil War (1640–1660), and the expulsion of the French Huguenots in 1688. At every turn, crusades for the souls of men and women were as intense as at any time in human history. Finally, during the eighteenth century, England fought four colonial wars with "Catholic France" for control of North America: King William's War (1689–1697); Queen Anne's War (1702–1713); King George's War (1740–1748); and the French and Indian War (1754–1763). With such traditions of religious hostility, mutual antipathies between the Protestants and Catholics settling America were hardly surprising.

American society often proved inhospitable to Roman Catholics. Offering land, opportunity, and mobility, America reinforced the cult of individualism just emerging in Western Europe. The New World seemed a perfect laboratory for John Locke's philosophy of natural rights. The colonists saw government as a temporary compact protecting individual claims to life, liberty, and property. They agreed with English Whigs that political power was evil, governments dangerous, and restrictions on political power absolutely necessary since the inclination of all people was to dominate others. The colonists distrusted distant, centralized governments, preferring the "republican" rule of locally elected officials: the American Revolution was largely a struggle of "localists" to cast off the distant English monarchy. Faith in capitalism was the economic counterpart of republicanism. Property ownership was widespread, and the colonists tolerated few restrictions on their right to control personal assets.[6]

Protestantism fit perfectly into that ideological world. Devoted to a "priesthood of all believers," divided into dozens of separate churches, and locating spiritual sovereignty in individual congregations, Protestantism was the religious counterpart of democratic egalitarianism and capitalism. Roman Catholicism was just the opposite. The church was openly a theocracy; the priesthood, not local congregations, was sovereign; and the church was a highly centralized institution administered by a distant bureaucracy. In a country prizing localism, democracy, and individualism, the church seemed out of place for many people. Most American Protestants, believing firmly in their "righteous empire," viewed Catholicism as a foreign anachronism at best and a dangerous, subversive threat at worst.[7]

The hostility led to widespread discrimination. In 1642, the English Civil War, with its intense Puritan enthusiasms, generated bitter anti-Catholicism on both sides of the Atlantic. That year, in the first of a long series of "penal laws" aimed at Catholics throughout the colonies, Massachusetts Bay prohibited future Catholic immigration. In Maryland, relations between the Catholic leaders of the colony and the Protestant majority deteriorated. In 1649, the colonial assembly passed an Act of Toleration, guaranteeing freedom of religion to Christians, but in 1654, when Puritans took over the colonial government, they outlawed any public Mass for Catholics, while tolerating private worship. Later in the century, the Glorious Revolution in England brought the Protestants William and Mary of Orange into power and inspired new laws disenfranchising Catholics and restricting their property rights. The Church of England became the established church in Maryland in 1692, and by 1718, Maryland Catholics could not vote, attend Mass, or establish parochial schools. As late as 1774, when Parliament passed the Quebec Act guaranteeing toleration to French Catholicism, influential American colonial leaders bitterly protested such an accommodation with the "devil."[8]

The fear of Roman Catholicism left Catholic settlers in a tenuous position, vulnerable to social pressure and frightened about their prospects of ever being accepted and tolerated. From the first, beginning in Maryland, American Catholics were preoccupied with their image, fearful that they appeared too foreign and would thus inspire Protestant wrath. George Calvert, the first Lord Baltimore, had received a huge tract of land in Maryland from King Charles I in 1632. A convert to Catholicism in 1624, Calvert wanted to find a refuge for his persecuted brothers and sisters, and in 1633 he invited several hundred of them to settle his new colony. After only a few years Catholics were a tiny minority in Maryland, swamped by a sea of Protestant immigrants. As late as 1700 there were only twenty-seven hundred Catholics in a Maryland population of nearly thirty-three thousand.

William Penn's "holy experiment" in Quaker Pennsylvania had also attracted nearly one thousand English Catholics by 1725 and seven thousand by 1780. From those bases in Maryland and Pennsylvania, Catholic missionaries and settlers made their way into Virginia and New York.[9] They were a self-conscious group. Before his colonists set foot in Maryland in 1633, Lord Baltimore warned them to be especially circumspect and private in their religious devotions, making sure that no "offense . . . be given to any of the Protestants" and that they were "silent upon all occasions . . . concerning matters of Religion."[10] For the next three centuries Catholics retained their misgivings and insecurities, never really certain about their American identity because of the sustained animosities of so many Protestants.

Because of rampant anti-Catholicism, the church was unable to establish the usual institutions of ecclesiastical authority. Fathers Andrew White and John Altham, English Jesuits, arrived in Maryland in 1633 with the first settlers, and until 1773, when Pope Clement XIV dissolved the Jesuit order, Jesuit missionaries administered the affairs of the church. In 1774, when Parliament passed the Quebec Act, granting religious toleration to French Catholics and giving them territorial sovereignty over the Ohio valley, Protestants throughout the thirteen colonies denounced Roman Catholicism as a conspiracy to dominate the New World. Most priests then serving in America were so worried about Protestant reactions to Catholic growth that they resisted appointment of a bishop for America, especially one of French extraction. They were reassured somewhat when Father John Carroll, an American-born priest from the prominent Carroll family in Maryland, was named Superior of the Mission to the United States in 1784, but Carroll himself expressed the hope that the Holy See would allow American priests to elect their own bishop as a way of allaying Protestant suspicions about "papal interference" in American life. Carroll also condemned the religious and social proclivities of incoming Irish Catholic priests and immigrants, whom he deemed morally weak and sure to raise the ire of Anglo Protestants. In 1790 the pope responded to those fears by allowing the American priests to select their own bishop, and they promptly named Father John Carroll.[11]

Throughout the first decades of the nineteenth century, English Catholicism was the foundation of the church in America, sustained by a substantial number of French clerics in important administrative positions. The church in England since the Reformation had been primarily an upper-class institution of people willing to accommodate themselves to existing political power. English Catholic piety was simple and humble, given to tranquility and isolation rather than pomp and pageantry. Archbishop John Carroll and the French priests who administered the church in early nineteenth-century America, such as Bishops Jean Cheverus of Boston, Ambrose Maréchal of Baltimore, and John DuBois of New York, assiduously worked for acceptance from the Anglo-Protestant elites in the United States by moving carefully through upper-class social circles and mingling successfully with people in power. By the beginning of the nineteenth century, Catholics were only 1 percent of the population. Feeling vulnerable as a tiny minority and accustomed to several centuries of persecution, early American Catholics were given to cooperation and accommodation, never wanting to disturb the status quo or bring too much attention to themselves.[12]

Even though the English were the backbone of the church, early American Catholicism was still an ethnic mix. Some French Catholics had settled in northern New England, and in 1755, when England expelled the Acadians from Canada at the beginning of the French and Indian War, more than six thousand Catholics moved south and settled in the British colonies. Several decades later, thousands more made their way into Louisiana.

There were also some Irish Catholics in colonial America. Although most of the 300,000 immigrants from Ireland in the colonial period were Scots-Irish Presbyterians, thousands were Roman Catholics. As indentured servants working in the South, they had little freedom to worship and no churches. Catholic parishes were nonexistent in the South in the eighteenth century, and anti-Catholicism, inspired by the passionate hatreds of the Scots-Irish, was quite strong. After release from their service contracts, the indentured Irish Catholics, without parishes and isolated from the Old World faith, usually married Scots-Irish Presbyterians and quickly assimilated.

There were also some German Catholics in Pennsylvania, particularly around Philadelphia. In 1787 parishioners at St. Mary's Church in Philadelphia tired of their English-speaking priest. They independently hired a German-speaking priest and incorporated as Holy Trinity Church. The nationality issue, which would severely divide the church a century later, was appearing. Finally, the Louisiana Purchase of 1803 brought approximately fifteen thousand French, Cajun, and Spanish Catholics into the United States.[13]

During the next two centuries, the ethnic mix of Catholic America became more complicated. The early 1800s were years of large-scale Protestant migration from northern and western Europe. Between 1820 and 1840, perhaps 250,000 Irish settled in the United States, but because of the potato famine, the number increased to nearly 2 million during the 1840s. The number of dioceses increased from eleven to forty-three. By 1900 more than 500,000 French Canadians were living in New England and several hundred thousand more in the upper Midwest. Nearly 2 million German Catholics immigrated between 1820 and 1900. Finally, the 1848 Treaty of Guadalupe Hidalgo, which ended the Mexican War, brought 78,000 Mexican Catholics into the country. With each new wave of immigration, the problems of nationality, religion, and language grew worse.[14]

The Catholic migrations inspired nativism, especially in the 1830s and 1840s when Irish settlement increased. Anti-Irish riots, rumors of Catholic conspiracies and sexual improprieties, and campaigns against immigration and Catholic parochial schools became more and more common.[15] American culture was largely Anglo in composition, and most people of English heritage carried a strong anti-Irish bias accumulated over centuries of cultural history. Many Irish immigrants saw themselves moving from one Anglo-dominated society to another because in many American cities in the 1840s and 1850s Anglo-Protestant elites controlled governments, school districts, corporations, and social institutions. Centuries of English-Protestant cultural imperialism had left Irish Catholics defensive—afraid of seeing their faith threatened in America as it had been threatened in Ireland. For protection, they built strong Roman Catholic communities and steadfastly raised their children in the church. To most native Americans bent on assimilating immigrants, the Irish seemed stubbornly clannish, and that only aggravated existing anti-Catholic prejudice.[16]

By the late 1860s, much of the nativism inspired by the Irish, French Canadians, and Germans had dissipated, but the "new immigration" soon resurrected old fears. During the 1880s, 1890s, and early 1900s, social and economic changes swept through southern and eastern Europe and uprooted millions of people. Most of the immigrants from Spain, Portugal, Austria-Hungary, and Italy were Roman Catholics, and they made Roman Catholicism the largest denomination in the United States. Between 1776 and 1820, the number of American Catholics went from 25,000 to 60,000. In the same period of time, the number of their meeting houses doubled from fifty to one hundred. Catholics were still a small minority. But by 1850 there were nearly 2 million Catholics in the United States. They were served by six archdioceses, twenty-five dioceses, four vicariate apostolics, and nearly two thousand churches. In the late 1890s, those numbers had increased to 8 million people in seventy-five dioceses and ten thousand churches. By 1920 there were nearly 20 million Catholics, and their numbers would increase to more than 27 million by the end of World War II.[17]

American Catholics settled in large cities throughout the Northeast and Midwest, with major concentrations of Poles, Lithuanians, and Czechs in Chicago; Italians in New York; Hungarians, Slovenes, Croatians, and Slovaks in Cleveland and Pittsburgh; Ukrainians and Rusins in the mining towns of Pennsylvania; and the Irish everywhere. Poor and often unskilled, crowded into ethnic ghettoes, these Catholics inspired new fears among old-line Protestants. In the 1890s, the American Protective Association, American Super-Race Foundation, and Daughters of the American Revolution warned of a "popish conspiracy" to take over the United States. Revived in 1915 to protect America from the incoming "hordes," the Ku Klux Klan experienced remarkable growth, with its membership reaching more than 5 million people in 1926. A main target was Roman Catholics. When Al Smith, an Irish-American Catholic, ran for president in 1928 against Republican Herbert Hoover, he stood no chance because of rural nativism.[18]

The National Origins Act of 1924 imposed restrictive quotas on immigration, thereby assuaging many nativist fears. Between 1929 and 1945 the crises of depression and war distracted most Americans from ethnocultural issues. Other threats seemed far more important than the Catholic menace. Never again, except for a few months in 1960 when John F. Kennedy was running for president, would most Americans fear Roman Catholicism as an alien institution subverting American values. It was not that Catholicism had become stagnant. Indeed, between 1945 and 1985 the Catholic population grew to nearly 55 million, making it by far the largest denomination in the country. Although some European immigration continued, most post-1945 Catholic immigrants were Spanish-speaking people from Cuba, Puerto Rico, and Mexico. By 1985 there were more than 1 million Cubans, 2 million Puerto Ricans, and perhaps 15 million Mexicans in the United States. As usual, the immigrants inspired intense nativism, but the fear lacked a religious dimension and did not translate into anti-Catholicism. After more than three hundred years, Roman Catholics had finally achieved mainstream acceptance from the bulk of American Protestants.

Acceptance had not been achieved without a struggle. Like the Irish before them, the new immigrants seemed clannish and unwilling to divest themselves of the Old World. That perception was not simply an outgrowth of Protestant prejudice. The Poles, Czechs, Slovaks, Germans, Hungarians, Slovenians, Lithuanians, Croatians, Rusins, Ukrainians, French Canadians, Italians, and Portuguese tended to congregate in ethnic neighborhoods around Catholic parishes and parochial schools. They feared losing their faith and becoming just one more piece in the Protestant mosaic. But language complicated their desire for ethnic and religious continuity. By the time of the Great Famine, English had become the language in Ireland, with Gaelic spoken in only the most rural parishes. In the United States, the Irish never fused language and faith into a cultural whole. But the other Catholic immigrants often equated language and faith, and were convinced that loss of the mother tongue would inevitably lead to the loss of religion and salvation. Their commitment to language set up a struggle in the Catholic church when they demanded nationality parishes with priests fluent in the Old World tongue. The Irish Catholic establishment, afraid of losing its influence, insisted on the irrelevancy of language as a measure of faith. The Irish eventually acquiesced, but the struggle over ethnic-language parishes divided the church during much of the late nineteenth and early twentieth centuries.[19]

Most Americans did not understand the ethnic diversity of Roman Catholicism. In the Old World, where cultural traditions were often regionally confined, language did not create many difficulties for the church. But that was not true in the mixed, urban neighborhoods of America, where Catholics were quite different from one another in culture, history, and religious zeal. In the 1950s, sociologist Will Herberg described a "Catholic melting pot," where ethnic

Catholics intermarried and assimilated into a larger Catholic community.[20] It was not a simple process, for beyond language were questions of culture and tradition. The faith of Irish and French Canadian Catholics, for example, had been forged in the flames of Anglo-Protestant persecution. Religion and nationality had become one and the same. Unable to separate religion and patriotism, these Catholics were not unlike those in sixteenth-century Spain in their spiritual and patriotic zeal. German Catholics, on the other hand, had little political nationalism because the German state did not emerge until late in the nineteenth century. Catholics from the various provinces of Germany were more regional and communal in their outlook, with religious perspectives depending on whether they had been a majority or minority in a particular province. Polish Catholics were different still. Bordered on the west by Prussian Lutherans and on the east by Orthodox Russians, the faith of Polish Catholics was sharply defined, even though clerics and peasants were not as united as those in Ireland or Canada. In Italy, where the church owned land and collected rent from peasants, a bitter rivalry developed between clerics and parishioners. Peasants often resented the church and identified it with oppression.

There were also differences based on ceremonialism and local values. Each country, indeed each village in some cases, had its patron saint toward whom people directed their devotions. St. Patrick symbolized Irish Catholic culture but had little significance for Polish Catholics, just as their St. Stanislaus meant little to most Irish immigrants. There were other differences. During the nineteenth century, Irish Catholicism had been influenced by increased Roman control as well as by the puritanical values of Victorian society, and the church had become strict, emotionally demanding, sexually prudish, and scholastically rational in its approach to theology and human behavior. Southern Italian ethnoreligion, on the other hand, was quite the opposite. The immigrants enjoyed a folk religion still laced with strong pre-Christian values, including animism, polytheism, and sorcery, which the Irish considered hopelessly superstitious. In the United States, the Irish and Italians had little respect for each other, and their religious controversies were intense. Roman Catholicism was hardly the monolith most Protestants assumed it to be.[21]

Despite linguistic, cultural, and historical diversity, American Catholicism avoided major schisms because the personal meanings of the different pieties were so similar. Throughout the Middle Ages, Catholic piety had been reserved and tranquil, emphasizing the private virtues of contemplation, prayer, and meditation rather than active devotions. But in response to the Protestant Reformation, the church had changed direction from the contemplative to the active, individual devotional life. In the sixteenth century, the Council of Trent had institutionalized the active piety, centering devotional life in the parish, encouraging participation in religious confraternities and turning the faithful to "orthodox behavior": the sacraments of baptism and confirmation, weekly attendance at Mass, and annual confession and communion. Regardless of ethnic background and cultural differences, American Catholics all shared a common heritage of Tridentine Catholicism, complete with a singular view of life and death, the Latin liturgy (except for the Uniate groups), the common catechisms, and loyalty to a common pope. Until the twentieth century, Tridentine Catholicism was the foundation of individual piety, a spiritual unity amidst the ethnic diversity.[22] It was that common heritage that prevented the ethnic differences in American Catholicism from breaking up the church.

During the twentieth century, much of the church's energy was consumed in assimilating immigrants, who took low-paying, unskilled jobs in mines, foundaries, mills, and factories. Crowded into tenements, laboring in difficult jobs, often cut off from friends and family, they had difficult beginnings. But they worked hard, saved money, purchased homes, and donated money to build urban parishes. Their ghetto communities were mixed neighborhoods where other ethnic groups lived, shopped, worked, and went to school. Ethnic-language churches, parochial schools, mutual aid societies, ethnic businesses, and parish organizations circumscribed social life. For many of the immigrants, the church became the major vehicle for adjusting to life in the United States.

The challenge for Roman Catholicism was to absorb each new generation of immigrants and help these parishoners maintain spiritual identity in a strange environment. Church leaders had always feared "leakage"—losing millions of immigrants to Protestantism.[23] Over and over again they debated the issue, and the controversies over "liberalism," "Americanism," "Cahenslyism," and mixed versus nationality parishes preoccupied Catholic communities. In their efforts to absorb the newcomers, church leaders presided over the modernization, secularization, and assimilation of the immigrant masses. Over the course of two centuries, Catholic peasants had left their Old World behind, with its holistic union of work, family, village, religion, and magic, and had come to the New World, with its compartmentalization of roles, separation of religion and magic, bureaucratic and technological control of the environment, and interest group control of society. By late in the twentieth century, the transition would still not be complete, but the organized, centralized rhythms of American industrial society had all but displaced the local authority models of family, parish, and village in the peasant world.

But that very success threatened the immigrant heritage in the 1960s, 1970s, and 1980s. Although Americans would be paying a good deal of attention to the "ethnic revivals" in the 1970s, the overpowering forces of assimilation were inexorably completing the work they had begun at Castle Garden and Ellis Island. The immigrant churches gradually succumbed to the combined forces of occupational and geographic mobility, education, and acculturation, and as the descendents of the immigrants melted into the larger Roman Catholic society, their levels of institutional commitment and piety changed. During the 1960s and 1970s, the disappearance of the immigrant churches led directly to growing secularism in American Catholicism, a tremendous growth in the charismatic movement, a decline in anti-Catholicism, diminishing levels of attendance at Mass and confession, and the brief flourishing of white ethnicity in Catholic communities.

2

The Irish Background of American Catholicism

During the nineteenth century, Irish immigrants became the backbone of American Catholicism, and well into the twentieth century the church had a decidedly Irish flavor. The roots of Irish-American ethnicity were planted deep in the Gaelic past. British-born St. Patrick brought Christianity to Ireland in the fifth century, and Roman Catholicism became a mainstay of Irish society. But when King Henry II of England sent his Norman supporters across the Irish Sea in 1169, a patriotic chauvinism gradually made Roman Catholicism the essence of Irish identity.

Despite Celtic customs, Gaelic language, and Roman Catholicism, the Irish were a divided people before the Anglo invasions. Clan societies dominated by regionally powerful chieftains, fanatically jealous of their prerogatives, dominated the country. But over the course of six centuries, the Anglo presence changed all that, transforming Ireland from a land of warring, petty tyrants into a country imbued with a patriotic nationalism and a passionate hatred of foreign intruders, particularly the English.[1]

Gaelic Ireland consisted of four regions: Leinster, Munster, Connaught, and Ulster, with Leinster, blessed with fine soil, the richest and most vulnerable. Facing England from across the Irish Sea, Leinster was known as the Pale, an area extending forty miles inland from Dublin, where Anglo influence was pervasive. West and southwest of the Pale, in Munster and Connaught, English power was not nearly as great. Vastly outnumbered by the native Irish there, the English settlers often married into local families, a practice so widespread by 1366 that England passed the Statutes of Kilkenny, prohibiting intermarriage and the adoption of Irish customs by the English. Gaelic Ireland flourished in the rural countryside, and Anglo-Norman culture thrived in the larger towns and cities. In the northern region of Ulster, English influence was almost unknown until the seventeenth century, so beyond the Pale, Ireland remained overwhelmingly Gaelic.[2]

The English Reformation added a religious dimension to the Anglo-Gaelic conflict. By 1600, the Church of England had become thoroughly Protestant and was demanding that the Irish renounce Roman Catholicism as a test of loyalty to the crown. In the Pale, thousands of Irish and Anglo-Irish Catholics submitted, swearing allegiance to the monarchy and Church of England. But in Connaught, Munster, and Ulster, Irish natives refused. In resisting Anglo-Protestant imperialism, they turned to Catholic leaders in Spain, France, and Italy. The Vatican sent thousands of priests and missionaries to Ireland, men whose religious views had been shaped by the intense loyalties of the Counter-Reformation. Native Irish, instead of attending English seminaries or Oxford and Cambridge, selected Catholic universities on the Continent, where their religion became even more deeply ingrained. The English crusade to Anglicize Ireland only made the Irish more Roman Catholic.[3]

Under siege, Roman Catholicism became indelibly imprinted on Irish culture, serving not only as the vehicle for spiritual salvation but also as the agent of political resistance. Catholicism had long been an integral part of Irish life, mixing inextricably over the years with ancient Celtic tribal customs. In converting the Irish, the church had superimposed Christianity on Gaelic culture. They sainted Brigid, the Celtic patroness of poetry and fertility, annointed her sacred fire at Kildare as a holy shrine, and viewed her sun-symbol cross as representing Jesus. The Celtic god Lug became Jesus; the druids became monks; and the Celtic crosses came to stand for Jesus and Mary. Each July, Irish worshipers walked barefoot up the rocky Croagh Patrick in County Mayo to celebrate St. Patrick's destruction of the snakes, but every July at that same hill the ancient Celts had celebrated Lugnas to appease the sun-god Lug and guarantee bounteous harvests. On the eve of St. Martin's Day, Irish Catholics killed a sheep or cock, sprinkled blood around their homes, and traced out a bloody cross on the forehead of each family member to ward off evil spirits. On March 17, they celebrated St. Patrick's Day and wore the green shamrock, supposedly used by St. Patrick to explain the Holy Trinity. The Irish were quite convinced that God looked with favor on their island outpost.[4]

Under the pressure of Anglo-Protestant imperialism, religion and nationality fused in the Irish mind. An ironic consequence of England's cultural imperialism was its reinforcement of Roman Catholicism and Irish nationalism. By the mid-nineteenth century, the British had stamped out the most visible symbols of Celtic culture, especially the Gaelic language. But in their attempts to exterminate Gaelic culture and Anglicize the Irish, the English only intensified Irish political identity and loyalty to Roman Catholicism. With their ancient language and culture gone, the Irish held even more doggedly to their religion and sense of peoplehood.[5] The Gaelic word *sassenach* came to mean both Protestant and English, and the Irish could not distinguish between Anglo and Protestant. They identified with the church as the central institution of their lives. An Irish peasant described those feelings:

> Whin we luck at him there, we see our blessed Saviour, stripped a'most naked lake ourselves; whin we luck at the crown i'thorns on the head, we see the Jews mockin' him, jist the same as . . . some people mock ourselves for our religion; whin we luck at his eyes, we see they wor never dry, like our own; whin we luck at the wound in his side, why we think less of our own wounds an' bruises we got 'ithin and 'ithout, every day av our lives.[6]

The Irish Catholics' devotion to the church and their equally intense resentment of English authority frightened royal officials into even more fanatical crusades against Gaelic culture. Faced with her rivals (Catholic Spain in the sixteenth century and Catholic France in the seventeenth and eighteenth centuries) and worried that a Catholic Ireland was a dangerous source of rebellion on her western flank, England tried to Anglicize the entire island, not just the Pale. Late in the 1500s, Queen Elizabeth I began granting land in Munster to Protestant loyalists, seizing it from rebellious Catholics. In Ulster, a bitter civil war erupted after 1603 when James I invited thousands of Scots Presbyterians to settle Catholic land. As dedicated Calvinists convinced that Catholicism was evil, the Scots set out to pacify Ulster. Forty years later the war had claimed more than 600,000 lives. During the Puritan revolution of the 1640s and 1650s, Oliver Cromwell invaded Ireland, confiscated Catholic property, and pushed Catholic leaders deep into Connaught. His assault on Irish society assumed genocidal proportions, destroying the economy and reducing the Irish population by more than a third in only eleven years. Following the Glorious Revolution, William of Orange, the new Protestant king of England, turned on Ireland again. At the Battle of the Boyne in July 1690, he annihilated Catholic rebels and dissolved the native Irish parliament.[7]

After the victory of 1690, England began imposing "penal laws" aimed at crushing Gaelic culture in favor of Anglo values, suppressing Catholicism in the name of Protestant supremacy, and enslaving the Irish population on behalf of absentee English landlords. To obliterate Irish political power, Parliament declared Irish Catholics ineligible to vote, hold public office, work in government jobs, serve in the armed forces, or carry weapons. They could not work as lawyers, solicitors, or judges and were prohibited from joining municipal guilds. All court proceedings and school instruction were in English, as were all public, business, and road signs. Parliament also denied the legitimacy of Catholic weddings, exiled Catholic bishops, prohibited the monastic orders, and denied entrance visas to foreign priests. Catholic priests had to stay permanently in their own parishes, and England required that all orphans be raised as Protestants. Irish Catholics could not publish books and newspapers, hire more than two apprentices, buy land from Protestants, deed estates in their entirety, or lease land for more than thirty years. Any Protestant landowner marrying a Catholic lost his civil rights, and any Protestant woman marrying a Catholic lost her inheritance. Catholics converting to Protestantism automatically became heirs to their parents' entire estate, and Catholic women converting to Protestantism could leave their husbands and legally demand complete financial support from them. Royal officials regularly sold poor Irish peasants into slavery in the West Indies. Protestant landlords could raise rents or evict Irish peasants at will. Eventually the Irish hatred of all things English and Protestant knew few bounds.[8] Carefully exposing his own feelings, one Irish patriot candidly remarked in the 1850s that

> there was perhaps less of love in it than of hate—less of filial affection to my country than of scornful impatience at the thought that I had the misfortune, I and my children, to be born in a country which suffered itself to be oppressed and humiliated by another. . . . And hatred being the thing I chiefly cherished and cultivated, the thing which I specifically hated was the British

> system, . . . wishing always that I could strike it between wind and water, and shiver its timbers.[9]

The centuries-old cultural crisis was complicated in the nineteenth century by savage economic problems. During the Napoleonic Wars, European wheat production declined and prices rose, so Irish landlords put more land into production and raised rents for Catholic tenants. The peasants had no right or power to resist. When peace returned in 1815 and European farming revived, wheat prices collapsed and Irish peasants could not pay the higher rents. With grain prices plummeting, landlords often turned their acreage back to pasture in hopes of recouping losses by raising sheep. They evicted Catholic peasants by the thousands, and between 1815 and 1825 more than 100,000 left for the United States.[10]

At the same time, the Irish population was increasing rapidly because of high fertility and the Catholic desire to have large families. Between 1725 and 1841 the Irish population went from 3 million to more than 8 million people, and the rural standard of living simultaneously declined. More and more people crowded into fewer and fewer leaseholds, and the competition for land drove rents higher. With no tradition of primogeniture, Ireland saw family plots and tenant leaseholds subdivided again and again until, in many cases, farms were no larger than one or two acres in size. Perhaps half the Irish population lived on the edge of existence, in hovels and lean-tos, subsisting on milk and potatoes. Gustave de Beaumont, a French traveler in Ireland in the 1830s, described the mud hut of an Irish peasant family:

> One single apartment contains the father, mother, children, and sometimes a grandfather or grandmother; there is no furniture in this wretched hovel; a single bed of hay or straw serves for the entire family. Five or six half-naked children may be seen crouched near a miserable fire, the ashes of which cover a few potatoes, the sole nourishment of the family.[11]

Potatoes became the staple of Ireland because they flourished in poor, moist soil, required relatively little attention, and yielded enough from one acre to support a family. The average peasant survived on about ten pounds of potatoes per day, and sold his grain, poultry, cattle, and pigs to generate cash for rent.

The potato was a fickle crop, and with the entire population dependent on it, Ireland was vulnerable to fluctuations in yield. Regional crop failures occurred in 1817, 1822, and the early 1830s, causing thousands of deaths and sending more than 200,000 emigrants to the United States.[12]

The unthinkable occurred in 1845. Expecting a good potato harvest, the Irish were stunned when they discovered that a fungus was destroying the crop. Once they were out of the ground, the potatoes quickly turned black and soft, breaking down in a few days into a putrid, inedible mass. The fungus spread throughout most of the island in 1845, destroying much of the harvest; it spread even more in 1846, when the entire crop was lost. The Great Famine was an unmitigated disaster. More than 1.5 million people perished between 1845 and 1851, sometimes dying in such enormous numbers that they could not be buried. Dogs, cats, and rats could often be seen feeding on dead bodies, but after another year even those animals disappeared. People first ate potato supplies, then seed potatoes, then livestock, and finally roots, bark, weeds, grass, insects, leaves, and wild cabbage. One traveler on his way to the Irish coast described the social carnage:

> We saw sights that will never wholly leave the eyes that beheld them, cowering wretches almost naked in the savage weather, prowling in turnip fields, and endeavoring to grub up roots which had been left, but running to hide as the mailcoach rolled by: groups and families, sitting or wandering on the highroad, with failing steps, and dim, patient eyes, gazing hopelessly into infinite darkness and despair; parties of tall, brawny men, once the flower of Meath and Galway, stalking by with a fierce but vacant scowl; as if they realized that all this ought not to be, but knew not whom to blame, saw none whom they could rend in their wrath. Sometimes, I could see, in front of the cottages, little children leaning against a fence when the sun shone out—for they could not stand—their limbs fleshless, their bodies half-naked, their faces bloated yet wrinkled, and of a pale greenish hue—children who would never, it was too plain, grow up to be men and women.[13]

The Irish peasants faced death or migration, and millions chose to leave. The Great Famine triggered a mass emigration. Between

1820 and 1900 4 million Irish entered the United States—nearly 1.7 million between 1845 and 1860. Most of them were Roman Catholics from Munster and Connaught. Leaving Ireland was a wrenching experience for most peasants. Centuries of ethnoreligious competition with Anglo Protestantism had left them profoundly attached to Ireland, and they left reluctantly. Though its economics were harsh, Ireland had provided the peasants an identity and a Roman Catholic community circumscribing their entire existence. Leaving was a desperately painful experience.[14]

The migration reinforced ethnoreligión. In trying to explain the disaster, the Irish turned to the only culprit they had ever known—England. Throughout the 1840s, while millions of Irish starved, the great English plantations in Ireland had exported thousands of tons of meat and grain. For Irish peasants, the shipments were more than a coincidental irony. They were certain the English had conspired to magnify peasant suffering in hopes of destroying Irish nationalism. It was, of course, an exaggeration, but English leaders were certainly guilty of insensitivity and ethnocentrism during the famine. A number of them believed the Great Famine was divine punishment for Irish intransigence, while others were sure that it was a solution, albeit a painful one, for Irish overpopulation. Most English leaders could not see beyond an ideological commitment to free trade and laissez faire. After repeal of the Corn Laws in 1846, their faith in unfettered international commerce was complete. They preferred not to interfere with the famine and to let nature run its course.[15] Although many English citizens contributed to private Irish philanthropy, the English government was generally faithful to laissez faire, passively watching Irish society disintegrate. Irish emigrants accused England of genocide and of forcing them to leave their homes for America. More so than those left behind, the immigrants loved Ireland, hated England, feared Protestantism, and adored Roman Catholicism.[16]

American culture intensified those feelings. There were no tax-supported Protestant churches in the country by the 1840s, but Yankee Protestants controlled wealth and power in the United States. In New England many Americans viewed the Irish Catholic migration as a threat to Anglo-Saxon civilization. Irish immigration also coincided with the cult of democracy popular during the era of Andrew Jackson; Roman Catholicism seemed alien because it invested authoritarian power in the pope and priestly hierarchy. Many

Yankee Protestants questioned the allegiance of the Irish, doubting they could ever become "true Americans" because of their passionate loyalties to Ireland and Rome. A writer for *Harper's Weekly* summarized nativist feelings by warning Irish immigrants that when they "permit priests and demagogues to form political combinations for the overthrow of the fundamental guarantee of liberty of every kind, they must not be surprised if they forfeit the respect and confidence of all good citizens."[17] To many Irish immigrants, America did not at first seem much different from Great Britain. By midcentury, anti-Catholicism was a major social theme, resurrecting some of the older pains the immigrants had experienced in Ireland. Newspapers, books, pamphlets, and flyers ridiculing Catholics became bestsellers, and frightened Protestants avidly consumed the most sensational propaganda.[18] Many believed the Irish were sexually irresponsible alcoholics subject to the whim of the pope. Violence, ridicule, and open discrimination were common in the 1840s and 1850s, but instead of changing the Irish immigrants, the hostility only increased their devotion to Catholic Ireland.[19]

But Irish Catholicism was much more than a defensive response to persecution. For every external force driving the Irish together, there were internal bonds of faith, history, and nationality. Conscious of their tenuous status in a Protestant society, they wanted to "be in the world but not of the world," to preserve and protect their Catholicism and to achieve Irish freedom. Since they worried about the assimilative seductions of American life, they made the parish the center of their lives, straining their limited resources in the 1850s and 1860s to build chapels and rectories in their neighborhoods. Strengthened by centuries of suffering in Ireland, the relationship between the Irish clergy and parishioners survived the Atlantic crossing. Since political officials in Ireland were Anglo Protestants whom Catholics despised, the parish priests came to play important roles in Irish society. Often drawn from the lower or lower-middle classes, they identified closely with the Irish masses and shared their bitter hatred of Anglo-Protestant rule. Possessing the keys of the kingdom, the priests stood between the parishioners and hell, able to baptize children, forgive sins, and recreate the body and blood of Christ. They were also the embodiment of Irish nationalism, the leaders in the struggle for survival against English imperialism. They represented both God and country. Priests became social, political, and economic leaders, the men who helped peasants interpret their environment. Gustave de Beaumont wrote in 1839 that the Irish masses

> bear at once all the charges and all the miseries of society, oppressed by the landlord, exhausted by taxation, plundered by the protestant minister, their ruin consummated by the agents of the law. Who or what is their only support in such suffering? The priest. . . . There is but one man in Ireland that mourns with the poor man, who has so much to mourn, and that man is the priest.[20]

By the 1840s the Irish church was sponsoring special seminaries dedicated to the training of missionary priests to serve Irish Catholic communities in North America. Those priests took over the New World parishes, came to know all the families, directed their church activities, and comforted them during trouble, sorrow, sickness, and death.

Desperate poverty and the Atlantic trade routes left the Irish along the eastern seaboard. Ireland had for years imported Canadian timber, and British shippers completed the round trip carrying immigrants to the Maritime Provinces of Canada, from where the Irish moved down to New England. England also purchased large volumes of cotton, wheat, flaxseed, potash, and naval stores, and ships brought other immigrants to New York, Philadelphia, Baltimore, Charleston, and New Orleans. They became the first ghetto people occupying large ethnic enclaves in the cities.[21] It was a village existence. They disdained the isolation of rural America, preferring crowded cities filled with friends, families, neighbors, priests, and churches. Indeed, the Irish migration was a "chain migration" in which whole villages and families uprooted and transplanted themselves from Ireland to America. Not surprisingly, they immediately tried to recreate, in this new urban setting, the parish atmosphere of Ireland.[22]

St. Peter parish on Barclay Street in New York City, for example, was built in 1785 and served as the only Roman Catholic church until 1815, when St. Patrick's on Mott Street opened. There were only 15,000 Catholics in the city then. Fifty years later, under the impact of mass immigration, mostly from Ireland, the number of

Roman Catholics in New York City had grown to nearly 400,000, almost half the population. They were served by thirty-two parishes, twenty-three of which were English-speaking churches with largely Irish parishioners. By the time of the famine, more than half of the priests in the diocese were foreign-born Irish. Ulster-born John Hughes replaced the Frenchman John DuBois as bishop of New York in 1842 and actively built Roman Catholicism there until his death in 1864. By then New York Catholicism had become primarily Irish Catholicism.[23]

The Irish had not always been so devoted. Although they strongly identified with Roman Catholicism before the famine, they had not been very familiar with Catholic doctrine, or particularly devout, at least in terms of regular church attendance. Because of widespread illiteracy, a shortage of priests, extraordinary poverty, and a poor transportation system, the prefamine Irish masses had been quite irregular in attendance at Mass, communion, and confession. But in the forty years before the famine, the church built a foundation for the postfamine devotional revolution that swept through the country, making Ireland the most devout country, in terms of religious observance and institutional loyalty, in the Western world.[24] After the Act of Union of 1801, Catholic priests and parishioners waged a struggle for "Catholic Emancipation" against the Anglican tithes and penal laws. In the process both clergy and laity became highly politicized and more intense about their identity. At the same time an evangelical movement was spreading through the Anglican, Methodist, and Presbyterian churches in Great Britain, and a powerful missionary spirit aimed at converting the Irish peasantry permeated the island. The proselytizing pressure only sharpened Catholic identity.[25]

The church had also made great strides in reconstructing itself from the shambles of the Protestant crusades of the 1700s and 1800s. Road building in the 1830s throughout Ireland had linked most rural areas into a regional system, making weekly attendance at Mass possible for the vast majority of Irish Catholics. By 1840 the parochial network—a parish priest and church for each area as well as a curate and parish hall for most areas—was complete. An ethnoreligious community, founded on the ecclesiastical structure of the church, now covered the country; parish activities and weekly Masses circumscribed social life.[26] Ireland was now physically prepared for a devotional revolution that made the 2.3 million postfamine immigrants even more devout than their predecessors of the 1840s and 1850s.

The devotional revolution that swept through Ireland in the second half of the nineteenth century had a dramatic influence on American Catholicism. In 1840 there were only 2,150 priests in an Irish population of 6.5 million, or 1 priest for every 3,000 people—hardly enough to meet spiritual and temporal needs. Although peasants carefully identified themselves as Catholics in 1840 and enjoyed a strong parish structure, only 40 percent attended Mass weekly and most confined confession and communion to Easter Sunday. But in the postfamine years the number of priests climbed to 3,200 while the Irish population dropped to only 4 million. With a priest-population ratio of 1 to 1,250, clerical influence was much greater, not only because parishioners loved their priests but because individual priests were able to reach out to individual parishioners.

While the number of priests was growing, Bishop Paul Cullen of Armagh and later of Dublin transformed piety by focusing on the sacraments of penance and communion. By 1880 confession, communion, and attendance at Mass were weekly affairs for 90 percent of the Irish population; missions convened annually in every parish; and a new series of devotional exercises appeared. Usually of Roman origin, the demonstrations of piety included rosaries, Forty-Hour's devotions, perpetual adorations, benedictions, vespers, jubilees, pilgrimages, shrines, and retreats. The church promoted them in association with sodalities, confraternities, Peter's Pence, St. Vincent de Paul societies, altar societies, and temperance societies. Priests also encouraged the regular use of beads, scapulars, missals, medals, prayer books, catechisms, and holy pictures to reinforce devotional exercises.

Finally, the Irish were prepared to receive the new devotions. The psychological shock of the Great Famine had turned thousands of people to the church for consolation, and many incorporated the new spirit of Roman Catholicism as part of their cultural identity. By the late nineteenth century, hundreds of years of Anglo-Protestant imperialism had taken their toll on Gaelic culture. The public school system had raised Irish literacy rates dramatically, but it had also made English the national language, suppressing and nearly destroying Gaelic. Intense devotion to Roman Catholicism became a means not only of resisting evangelical Protestantism but also of asserting the Irish heritage. More than ever before, Irish and Roman Catholic had become synonymous. Coming to the United States after 1860, these immigrants permeated American Catholicism with a decidedly Irish piety, particularly in the intensity of their individual religious observances.[27]

That piety was unique. More than a powerful institutional loyalty, a fusion of religion and nationality, and an intense individual religiosity, Irish Catholicism was ascetic and puritanical. Throughout early Irish history, because of the rural social structure and the clannish family system, church government had revolved around a confederation of influential monasteries and abbots rather than territorial dioceses and bishoprics. The monastic tradition was an ascetic one, marked by a strong sense of sin and penance, fasting, scourging, long hours of prayer, and individual isolation. Although ninth-century Viking invasions destroyed much of monastic culture, the ascetic spirit survived in Irish Catholicism.[28] Eighteenth-century Jansenism reinforced it. During the Catholic Reformation of the sixteenth century in France, Bishop Cornelius Jansen of Ypres promoted an Augustinian revival within the church that triggered intense controversy. Jansenism emphasized the doctrine of divine predestination, the need for a personal religious experience with God, and the blessings of conscious conversion. Jansenist piety was preoccupied with the fear of damnation and convinced that the sacrament of absolution only declared sins forgiven if real repentance had already occurred. It also focused on the sinfulness of "carnal man" and the "dangers of the flesh" and argued for an undeviating, unquestioning loyalty on matters of faith. To many Catholics, especially the Jesuits, the Jansenists seemed almost Protestant, even Calvinist, and they demanded its condemnation. In 1713, the pope did condemn it, but Jansenism maintained its vitality in many clerical circles. It made its way into Irish Catholicism through French seminaries. During the "penal" exile years of the eighteenth century, most Irish clerics went to the Continent for their training, and those studying at French seminaries absorbed Jansenist doctrines and then brought them back to the parishes and parochial schools of Ireland.[29] Irish Catholicism slowly assumed an Augustinian, neo-Calvinist profile.

At the same time, the Irish economy was exaggerating the ascetic tradition and the suspicion of sexuality. Meager economic resources, a dearth of jobs, and absentee landlordism made it difficult for young people to set out on their own and begin families. The death rate of the Great Famine made it especially difficult for Irish men to support their families. Millions starved and millions of others emigrated, leaving the country a wasteland, economically and psychologically. The pain of watching wives and children suffer worked against household formation and marriage. Men postponed marriage to the later years of young adulthood, delaying the arrival of children. The ascetic tradition and Jansenism, by praising self-denial and condemning sexual pleasures, provided a cultural foundation for dealing with poverty. In weekly church sermons and in the parochial schools, priests and nuns regularly preached a morality that emphasized the virtues of celibacy for everyone, especially during adolescence and young adulthood. The Irish clergy took on a puritanical perspective that fit nicely into the Victorian Protestantism taking over England. The obsession with sexual morality, suspicion of emotional and physical familiarity, and the suppression of sexual drives became more characteristic of Irish Catholic culture than of other Western societies.[30] Sexual abstinence not only would save Catholics spiritually in the next world, but would save them temporally in this one.

The evangelical religion spreading throughout Great Britain in the nineteenth century influenced Irish Catholicism. Dependent economically as well as politically on England, the Irish could not help but be affected by major cultural trends across the Irish Sea, even religious ones. The Irish preserved their identity by rejecting Protestant theology, but they did absorb some evangelical cultural values. The English had spent much time and money improving Irish elementary schools in hope of "curing" poverty, alcoholism, violence, and political alienation. By 1845 nearly 500,000 Irish children were attending the primary schools, and although the schools were ostensibly nonsectarian, Anglo-Protestant values were inevitably passed on to Irish children, particularly the emphasis on authority, law and order, intense religiosity, and Victorian sexual mores. They all fit well into the ascetic, puritanical tradition of Irish Catholicism.[31]

The Irish transplanted their values and religious institutions to America. Parish institutions circumscribed Catholic social life in the United States and made sure that most personal relationships occurred within the faith. Worried about the impact of secular education and anti-Catholicism in American public ("Protestant") schools, a legitimate concern after their experience in Ireland, and worried about the likelihood of their children marrying Protestants, the Irish built parochial schools and attached them to the parish. There Catholic children could enjoy an excellent education as well as a variety of social activities in a proper spiritual atmosphere. For adult men and women, confraternities, sodalities, societies, and organizations like the Ancient Order of Hibernians and later the Knights of Columbus confined social life to the parish and the faith, isolating and protecting people from the secular enticements of the Protestant world. A compact, relatively close-knit community, the parish was the emotional heart of Irish-American life. The Irish immigrants constructed those parishes, parochial schools, and social organizations, as well as hospitals, orphanages, old-age homes, temperance halls, and reformatories throughout urban America. They also brought with them the devotional practices and attitudes of Catholicism in Ireland. In the process the Catholic church in the United States became, for a time, largely an Irish institution.[32]

Because the vast majority of Irish immigrants spoke English as their native tongue, they organized territorial parishes with fixed regional boundaries rather than forming nationality or language parishes serving specific ethnic clienteles. But by the 1860s territorial parishes in many cities were actually "Irish" parishes. Transfiguration parish on Mott Street in New York's Sixth Ward, for example, was a territorial parish serving all Catholics living there, but it was really an Irish parish serving an urban Irish village. In such territorial parishes, the Irish immigrants preferred the Gothic-style churches they had known in Ireland; emphasized the glories of Saints Patrick, Brigid, Brendan, and Columban; wanted a simple, ascetic piety consistent with Irish Catholic culture; expected to hear sermons on temperance and sexual morality; joined the Ancient Order of Hibernians with as much enthusiasm as they did the Archconfraternity of the Holy Rosary; continued practicing the devotions they had learned in Ireland; and demanded Irish or Irish-American priests. When they could not dominate a territorial parish, they often seceded rather than practice an unfamiliar Catholicism. Many of them, for example, left St. Joseph's parish at Galion in Cleveland and formed St. Patrick's in 1869. Or in 1865, when Bishop Amadeus Rappé of Cleveland replaced Father Michael O'Neill at St. Ann's in Fremont with a French priest, the Irish parishioners were outraged and protested bitterly.[33] Though not so designated, Irish-nationality parishes existed throughout the country.

The mass immigration of Irish peasants had a profound impact on American Catholicism. By 1860 there were 2.2 million Roman Catholics in the United States, and 1.6 million of them were Irish, dwarfing the older French, Anglo-American, and German-Catholic communities. Large numbers of priests, trained in the nineteenth-century devotional revolution, poured into the United States and began moving into important ecclesiastical offices. Between 1789 and 1935, 268 of the 464 men who served as bishops in the United States were either first- or second-generation Irish, and many of the others were third-generation Irish. Most of the major diocesan sees were under Irish or Irish-American control, as were the Roman Catholic press, educational system, charitable organizations, and parish societies. Under that ethnic influence, Irish clerics stamped American Catholicism in an Irish-Catholic mold: a sense of strict, authoritarian obedience and discipline; weekly observance of confession and communion; social isolation from the surrounding Protestant society; a militant feeling of ethnoreligious pride; strong suspicions of sexuality and equally strong feelings of guilt; celebrations of celibacy, self-denial, and moral virtue; an emphasis on daily prayer and devotions; and an attitude of reverent respect for and loyalty to the clergy. From that position of zeal, fidelity, and piety, the Irish immigrants helped build the Roman Catholic church in the United States.

3

The Triumph of Irish Catholicism

The Great Famine and subsequent arrival of millions of Irish peasants had a dramatic effect on American Catholicism, giving the church a distinctly Gaelic profile and setting the stage for an intense ethnic struggle that eventually changed the lives of millions of other Catholic immigrants. The migration of Irish Catholics proved a mixed blessing for the church, bringing new strength but triggering an intense nativism not only among Anglo-American Protestants but among Anglo and French Catholics. During the two hundred years before the famine migration, American Catholicism had developed a unique identity based on the cultural values of the English-Catholic settlers in Maryland, Kentucky, and Pennsylvania as well as on those of the French Catholic priests so common in early America. The historical experiences and cultural values of the Anglo and French Catholics created a peculiarly American religion, which collided directly with the Irish Catholicism of the famine immigrants.

Until the famine migration, American Catholicism functioned in an Anglo-Saxon cultural environment. Ever since the sixteenth century, English Catholics had walked a political tightrope between their religious loyalties and the demands of the Protestant state. Survival had required a sense of discreet caution, a quiet faith that did not develop much of a public profile. At the same time, English Catholicism had survived among significant numbers of the rich and near rich, who became accustomed to compromise, negotiation, and genteel survival. Anglo Catholicism adopted similar tactics in the United States. Concerned about questions of loyalty and acceptance, American Catholics were discreet and almost passive in their religious observances, preferring not to exacerbate the anti-Catholic nativism always so close to the surface of social life. John Carroll, the first American bishop and member of one of America's most distinguished and patriotic families, spent much of his career emphasizing toleration, acquiescence, and assimilation, asking Catholics to work at accommodating themselves to Anglo-American economic and political life. In his dealings with the Vatican and the Society for the Propagation of the Faith, Archbishop Carroll repeatedly demonstrated the independence of American Catholicism from Roman direction by ignoring church directives and using the English rather than the Latin liturgies. Carroll desperately wanted the Protestant public to see Catholicism as an American institution independent from European influence as well as every other religious and political organization in the United States. When Archbishop Carroll died in 1815, he was succeeded by Ambrose Maréchal of the Baltimore see.

Maréchal was a French Catholic who shared Carroll's insistence on an independent church and his hopes for an American Catholicism comfortable in Anglo-Saxon society. Archbishop Maréchal also carried with him the cultured gentility, upper-class mentality of the French-Catholic clergy, who placed a high premium on scholarly training, family background, aesthetic sensitivities, and political gentility. He too worked at cultivating personal relationships with the Anglo-Protestant elites in the United States.[1]

The famine migration of the Irish came as quite a shock to Anglo and French Catholics dominating the church, for it upset their two centuries of cautious accommodation. The Irish immigrants hardly fit into any Anglo-Saxon mold. To most Protestants and Catholics in the United States, they seemed a particularly strange and worrisome people, quite unlikely to "melt" into the larger society. Beyond the Catholic theology, which American Protestants had fretted about for generations, the Irish exhibited cultural traits guaranteed to intensify nativism. Fleeing the Anglo Protestantism that had oppressed them for so many years in the Old World, the Irish had no intentions of soft-pedaling their Gaelic, Catholic values. Indeed, they were quite public and vocal, ready to test the freedoms of American life by their very visibility. Despite the hopes of people like Bishops Carroll and Maréchal, the Irish had no desire to accommodate themselves to, let alone assimilate into, Anglo-Saxon society. Moreover, the priests accompanying the immigrants were anything but the scholarly, cultured, and genteel clerics Maréchal and Carroll had so appreciated. Like their parishioners, the immigrant

Irish priests were undereducated members of the peasant and lower classes and intensely aggressive in their religious identities.[2] There was no chance they would be able to function successfully, on a social level, with the Protestant elite of America.

In Boston the struggle between the Anglo Catholics and Irish Catholics lasted throughout the nineteenth century. Not until the ordination of Bishop William Henry O'Connell in 1907 did the administration of church affairs at the diocesan level pass out of the hands of its longstanding Anglo-Catholic elite. Bishops like John B. Fitzpatrick (1846–1866) and John J. Williams (1866–1907) and administrators like Fathers John Roddan, George Haskins, and Joshua Bodfish had strong Yankee sympathies and represented three generations of Anglo-American Catholics who had appreciated the friendly commercialism of Boston, been accepted by the Brahmin elite, and adopted a low-key spirit of toleration and cooperation. They resented periodic outbursts of anti-Catholicism but generally enjoyed their minority, politically insignificant status in a genteel world. By the 1840s they had successfully applied the political skills of Anglo Catholicism. The influx of the Irish frightened them, not only because the intense nationalism and militant anti-Protestantism of the immigrants threatened their comfortable relationship with Brahmin society but also because it eliminated their insignificance and rendered them too public and visible. Throughout the middle decades of the nineteenth century, as Irish priests moved in increasingly large numbers into new parishes in the diocese, a bitter struggle ensued between Irish and Yankee Catholicism.[3] In addition to the Protestant nativism the Irish inspired, the famine migration inaugurated a powerful movement within the Roman Catholic church to "Americanize" the new arrivals—to blunt their social differences and render them more acceptable to native citizens.

The famine immigrants, coming largely from the poorer regions of Munster and Connaught, left Ireland before the devotional revolution had run its course. Although intensely Catholic in a spiritual sense, they were not nearly as devoted to the institutional church as the post-1865 Irish immigrants. Theirs was a culture of poverty and oppression, one in which alcoholism and crime were far more common than they would be in the lives of subsequent Irish-Catholic immigrants. Some understood Gaelic better than English, and nearly half were illiterate. In America they occupied the poorest homes and took the hardest, lowest-paying jobs in the city slums.

Violence, crime, poverty, and alcoholism plagued the early Irish-American communities and reinforced the anti-Catholic bias of the general population.[4] Not long after the arrival of the first famine immigrants, negative stereotypes about the Irish entered popular culture; such terms as "hooligans," "shenanigans," and "paddy wagons" became part of the national vocabulary. Writing in 1868 about the character of the typical Irish immigrant, the *Chicago Post* claimed that he

> never knew an hour in civilized society. . . . He is a born savage—as brutal a ruffian as an untamed Indian. . . . Breaking heads for opinion's sake is his practice. The born criminal and pauper of the civilized world . . . a wronged, abused, and pitiful spectacle of a man . . . pushed straight to hell by that abomination against common sense called the Catholic religion. . . . Scratch a convict or a pauper, and chances are that you tickle the skin of an Irish Catholic.[5]

Even the famine priests, especially those from rural parishes, had frequently suffered from drunkenness and neglected pastoral duties, much to the chagrin of episcopal authorities in Ireland and Rome. Their social problems in the United States only reinforced the prevailing stereotypes of the "shanty" Irish.

Middle-class Protestant society, whose values became the cultural standards for the entire country, placed great value on hard work, education, genteel leisure, and a studied sense of decorum and propriety. Anglo and French Catholics shared those expectations. The famine Irish seemed to possess none of them. Their poverty and frequent unemployment contradicted the standard of hard work; their thick Gaelic brogue and frequent illiteracy were the antithesis of education and "culture"; their "love of the grape" and attachment socially and politically to the corner saloon were the opposite of genteel leisure; and their boisterous, passionate love for contention, physical activity, pugilism, and occasional violence was hardly the decorum and propriety Protestants and Anglo Catholics so highly prized. The famine immigrants recognized, and then disdained, those values as part and parcel of middle-class Protestantism. Protestants in turn had little love for the famine Irish.[6]

The rivalry between incoming Irish immigrants and their priests and the Yankee or French-Catholic bishops controlling most of the American dioceses manifested itself in the "trustee" question, a controversy that plagued the immigrant church for three generations and signified the emergence of new ethnic groups in the United States. Early in the nineteenth century, most American Catholics found themselves spread across the country in a hostile cultural climate with few priests and little contact with episcopal officials. Unlike the Old World, where the church was a given fact of life, always present historically in the community, America was a spiritual vacuum for Catholics. If they were to have their own churches, they had to start them on their own, which necessitated a kind of initiative unknown in Europe. Lay Catholics often organized themselves, elected trustees, purchased land, erected churches, recruited priests, and presided at formal prayer meetings, Bible readings, and religious instruction classes. American laws gave the lay leaders even more inclination to organize because all churches were considered voluntary associations. They had to incorporate before the law would recognize and protect their assets. The trustees, after sacrificing their time and personal resources to organize churches, expected to direct ecclesiastical affairs.[7]

That expectation brought them into direct conflict with the episcopal hierarchy. Rome looked on the United States as a mission field until 1908, and as such the American church fell under the direction of the Sacred Congregation for the Propagation of the Faith. Canon law was often inoperative, and American bishops enjoyed almost unlimited authority within each diocese. Anglo-Catholic bishops had always appreciated such freedom since it made it easier for them to demonstrate their independence from Rome and prove their loyalty to the United States. But in the struggle over trusteeism, the bishops were put in the position of authoritarians. In the environment of Jacksonian democracy, they seemed the enemies of republicanism, a position they hardly relished. The trustees looked upon themselves as adjustors of European Catholicism to the New World, and they wanted bishops to accept their right to control parish finances and select and dismiss pastors. The ethnic factor only reinforced the basic division, especially when poor Irish-Catholic immigrants found themselves aligned against conservative, aristocratic Yankee and French-Catholic bishops. Throughout the 1820s, 1830s, and 1840s, struggles for control of parish affairs raged between bishops and trustees, and church authorities viewed the controversy as a major threat to Roman Catholicism. As early as 1786, Bishop Carroll was concerned that if trusteeism "should become predominant, the unity and catholicity of our church would be at an end."[8] In the end the bishops prevailed, sometimes through use of the interdict and other times through good politics. At St. Mary's in Philadelphia in 1821, Bishop Henry Conwell, Irish-born but French-educated, excommunicated Father William Hogan after the latter joined local trustees in calling for an independent Catholic church. On the other hand, when Irish trustees in Virginia and South Carolina began protesting the authority of Archbishop Ambrose Maréchal of Baltimore, demanding their own diocese with Irish bishops, Rome went along, creating new sees in 1820 at Richmond and Charleston with Patrick Kelly and John England as the new bishops. The trustees were satisfied, but church power still rested in episcopal hands.[9]

The trustee controversy was symptomatic of a much larger problem between Anglo and Irish Catholics in the nineteenth century. When the Irish immigrants had aggressively tried to assert their power in local parishes by maintaining control of finances, property titles, and pastoral appointments, Anglo Catholics had resented their presumptuousness. While the previous five generations of immigrant Catholics had tried to be discreet, accommodating, and cooperative, the Irish appeared just the opposite, too interested in asserting their ethnic and religious distinctiveness. Not only were the famine Irish a socially and economically disadvantaged people, at least as far as the Anglo Catholics were concerned, they were also proud of themselves and bent on publicly expressing their collective identity. In the 1840s, 1850s, 1860s, and 1870s, the controversies over parochial schools and Irish-American nationalism only reinforced prevailing stereotypes about the Irish and made the Catholic church seem alien and foreign oriented. For Anglo Catholics smugly satisfied with their minority status and their general invisibility, the famine migration, parochial school debates, and excesses of Irish-American nationalism were especially disconcerting.

The parochial school issue precipitated a major controversy that enraged Anglo Protestants in the United States and led them to lump all Catholics together, exactly what Yankee Catholics had feared would happen. It alienated most Protestants from most Catholics and transformed anti-Catholic nativism into a political movement. In the decades before the Civil War, the country experienced a burst of political and social reform aimed at eliminating property requirements for voting and holding public office, abolishing slavery, prohibiting the consumption of alcohol, improving mental hospitals, rehabilitating criminals, and providing a free education to every citizen. Beginning in New England in the 1820s, public education became, along with temperance and antislavery, one of the great reform movements of the antebellum period. By the early 1800s, most Americans had accepted the Jeffersonian ideology—that property-owning small farmers were the backbone of democracy and the protectors of freedom. By the 1830s, the Jeffersonian "yeoman farmer" had become the "common man" in Jacksonian political culture, and education had become the new panacea for democracy. The argument that every child, regardless of economic circumstances, had the right to an education became a part of national dogma. The public schools would guarantee American survival by solving the "immigration problem." Instead of the society breaking up under the centrifugal forces of race, religion, national origin, and class, it would grow stronger as people assimilated into a common culture. There, in the free schools, American children and the children of immigrants would learn to work hard, obey the law, love their country, worship their God, speak English, and govern themselves. Put bluntly, the public schools were "culture factories" where Anglo-American values would be perpetuated, immigrants assimilated, and democracy preserved.[10]

Combined with the prevailing image of the famine immigrants, the question of parochial schools became an explosive public issue. The spread of "nondenominational" public schools in Ireland, with their blatantly sectarian, Protestant bias, had left the Irish-Catholic hierarchy exceedingly suspicious of the common school movement, and Irish immigrants brought those fears across the Atlantic. For them, public schools in the United States were "Protestant schools"— complete with Protestant ministers on school boards, required reading of the King James Bible, and avowedly anti-Catholic curricula. Educational assimilation was synonymous with religious assimilation, which was exactly what most Protestant educators had in mind during the nineteenth century.[11] Yankee and French Catholics had similar fears about the ultimate intentions of the public school movement, and in 1843 had urged on all Catholic parents the obligation to "let the previous inheritance descend without diminution. You must, therefore, use all diligence that your child be instructed at an early age in the saving truths of religion, and be preserved from the contagion of error."[12] But Yankee Catholics did not feel as strongly about the threat of the public schools, nor were they as compelled to cultural separation as the Irish. Their hope was to work with public school leaders to make the common schools culturally acceptable to Catholic children.

The Irish too could have accepted the public schools if they had allowed each religious group to sponsor its own devotions and study periods, or even if they had been religion-neutral. In some areas, such as New York City's Sixth Ward, where Irish immigrants were by far the largest population group, even the public schools reflected Irish values because all the children and many of the teachers were Irish. Those schools did not threaten the spiritual lives of Catholic children. But in other areas, where the Irish population was scattered and the expense of building parochial schools prohibitive, the immigrants often had to choose between keeping their children out of school altogether or enrolling them in "Protestant schools." Many parents often chose to keep children out. During the 1870s, for example, as many as 25 percent of Boston children, most of them Irish Catholic, were not attending any school. The only alternative was to find some way of constructing parochial schools where religious values could be preserved and Catholic culture transmitted to the young. Establishing parochial schools became a major ecclesiastical effort of the nineteenth century, especially after 1884, when the Third Plenary Council of Baltimore made the whole issue an act of faith, a spiritual requirement that each parish have its own parochial school. In those parochial schools, religious training took precedence over academic discipline. Priests, nuns, and brothers constituted the teaching staffs; religious devotions and doctrinal instruction consumed a good deal of class time each day; and teachers regularly urged children to consider vocational careers as priests or nuns. In their own way, the parochial schools were "culture factories" as well, no less committed to a way of life than the public schools. Irish Catholics dominated the administrative and teaching staffs, and the schools passed on to students the Irish emphasis on sexual puritanism, intense religiosity, public devotion, and strict loyalty to church authorities.[13]

But to Anglo Protestants, the parochial schools were a slap in the face, a bald, callous admission that Irish Catholics had no intention of accepting American values and assimilating into the society. Through the public schools, native Americans had hoped to "smooth the rough edges" of the famine immigrants, transforming what they saw as lazy, defective criminals into law-abiding, hard-working, Protestant citizens. The appearance of the parochial schools undermined those hopes and enraged many American Protestants who had not accepted Roman Catholicism as a permanent fixture of life in the United States. For Yankee Catholics, the concern was not so much the parochial school as the Irish way of handling it. On several occasions the controversy erupted into violence. In 1844, when Bishop Francis Patrick Kenrick of Philadelphia wrote the local school board asking that Catholic children be exempted from reading the King James Bible at school, a storm of protest broke out in Kensington, a suburban community composed largely of Catholic-hating Protestant immigrants from Northern Ireland. Protest meetings bitterly denounced Kenrick, and the hostility quickly escalated into rioting. Before peace was restored three days later, more than forty people were dead, sixty had been injured, and a number of Catholic buildings had been razed.[14] Although Yankee Catholics were angry about Protestant expectations, they were also sorry that the Irish had brought Old World disputes to America and were quite convinced that political compromise rather than public demands would secure necessary changes in public schools.

The question of using tax funds to support public schools also was an issue throughout the nineteenth century, especially after 1841, when Bishop John Hughes of New York asked public school officials to divert funds to Catholic parochial schools. After weeks of intense debate, the New York legislature specifically prohibited the use of any public funds in private schools. During the 1850s a good deal of Know-Nothing violence, the kind of nativism Yankee Catholics had so long feared, was aimed at parochial schools. After the Civil War, several states—Illinois in 1870, Pennsylvania in 1873, and Colorado in 1875—followed New York's earlier lead in outlawing the use of state funds for religious institutions. The school controversies of the 1840s, 1850s, and 1860s, as well as hostile Protestant reaction, left people like Bishop Hughes convinced that there was no middle ground between public and parochial education in the United States. Yankee Catholics despaired that the isolationism and ethnocentrism of the incoming Irish immigrants would ever be tempered.[15]

By requesting tax support, increasing the number of parochial schools, and criticizing the sectarian nature of the public schools,

Irish-Catholic leaders seemed critical of America's most prized institution—the common school. Along with the prevailing view of Irish-American culture and the hostility of Yankee Catholics, the parochial school issue had increasingly isolated Irish Catholics from mainstream society. The common school movement with its promotion of universal, compulsory, tax-supported education, was the most cherished of Anglo-Protestant reforms, Yankee society's way of preserving its own dominance and preventing the cultural Balkanization that mass immigration threatened to create. Catholics' opposition to the common school movement, and especially their requests for public financing of parochial education, seemed to undermine American political culture.[16] Yankee opposition only made the need for parochial schools more imperative, at least in the eyes of Irish Catholics. Under the influence of the Third Plenary Council, the number of parochial schools increased by 1900 to nearly four thousand with 854,000 students and by 1910 to nearly five thousand with 1,237,000 students.[17]

Finally, the Irish alienation from Anglo Protestants and Yankee Catholics revolved around the pan-Irish nationalism so powerful in Great Britain, Canada, and the United States. Ironically, the nationalism of the Irish intensified after they came to the United States. In prefamine Ireland, the peasants' primary affiliation had been to town, parish, or county. One's origin in Mayo or Galway or Cork was a primary means of ethnic identification. But thrown together in American slums and victims of a common prejudice, the immigrants acquired a sense of Irish identity that transcended older loyalties to parishes or counties. The intense bitterness of the Great Famine, combined with the constant flow of new immigrants between 1845 and 1880, sustained and nurtured an unprecedented loyalty to Ireland. In his poem "The Irish-American," T. D. Sullivan crystallized those feelings:

> Columbia the free is the land of my birth
> And my paths have been all on American earth
> But my blood is as Irish as any can be,
> and my heart is with Erin afar o'er the sea.[18]

To peasant workers suffering from discrimination in the United States, such nationalism was an expression of identity; a manifestation of vengeance toward an England responsible for centuries of suffering; and a search for respectability and acceptance. In their pro-Irish organizations, their mythologizing of the Celtic past, their immigrant societies and schools dedicated to preserving the Gaelic language, and their love of Irish literature the immigrants sought to prove to themselves their worth and value despite prevailing stereotypes. In achieving Irish liberation they expected to gain Anglo-American respect and to be considered no longer a conquered people.[19]

Many Americans, especially Anglo Protestants and Yankee Catholics, resented the love the Irish retained for the Old World. To Anglo Protestants, Irish-American nationalism was like the parochial school movement—a rejection of America and an affirmation that the Old World was more important than the New. They also feared the implications of Irish-American nationalism. The Irish-nationalist endeavors ranged from harmless political rhetoric and fund raising to outright violence. Immigrant-aid societies, like the Irish Emigrant Aid Society or the Ancient Order of Hibernians, regularly sponsored Irish speakers and dinners, bazaars, and raffles to raise money for Irish independence. More radical Irish-American nationalists sometimes resorted to political insurgency. During the Civil War, the Fenian Brotherhood became active in Irish ghettoes and the Union Army. The "Fenian Marseillaise," which frightened many Anglo Americans, became a political hymn for the Fenians:

> Away with speech, and brother, reach me down that rifle gun.
> By her sweet voice, and hers alone, the rights of man are won.
> Fling down the pen; when heroic men pine sad in dungeons alone,
> 'Tis bayonets bright with good red blood, should plead before the throne.[20]

During the 1860s, Fenians held conventions and raised money for Irish independence. In 1866 a radical Fenian group known as the Irish Republican Brotherhood actually sent an invasion force into Canada. By seizing Canada and holding it hostage, the Brotherhood hoped to convince England to free Ireland. The scheme failed and the Fenian Brotherhood gradually declined, only to be replaced in the 1870s by the Clan na Gael as the premier Irish-American nationalist group. To many Anglo Protestants, the extreme loyalties of the Fenians and the Clansmen were as anti-American as they were pro-Irish. For many Yankee Catholics, Irish-American nationalism threatened to encourage the equating of all Catholicism with Gaelic extremism, a sure-fire way of bringing on a nativist crusade.[21]

Even more disturbing was the pattern of Irish-American crime and violence. As happened with many urban immigrant groups, the Irish-American crime rate was higher than the national average, but Anglo Americans treated it in the simplest of terms. Many of them considered the Irish an unruly, violent people. In 1870 a riot broke out when Anglo-Irish "Orangemen" paraded through New York City celebrating the 1690 Protestant victory at the Battle of the Boyne. When Irish Catholics openly attacked another such march in 1871, the subsequent riot left thirty-seven people dead. In the late 1860s and early 1870s, the Molly Maguires, a radical group of Irish Catholic miners, waged a terrorist campaign against Welsh and English mine bosses and operators who kept wages low and working days long. In 1874 and 1875 the Molly Maguires allegedly assassinated nine people, and the subsequent campaign against them, journalistic as well as judicial, aggravated anti-Irish sentiments among Anglo Protestants and Yankee Catholics. Most Americans rejoiced when nineteen Molly Maguires were executed in 1876, since they were "typical" of all the Irish.[22]

Finally, a number of Irish immigrants and second-generation Irish Americans became prominent in labor unions and left wing politics in the United States. The rapid pace of nineteenth-century industrialization and the rise of powerful corporations had transformed the American political economy, destroying subsistence farming and cottage industry and rendering laissez faire values irrelevant. The many lower-class Irish who were working took on a particularly critical view of economic activity, rejecting the notion that benign, impartial laws governed the economy. They came to favor new forms of interest-group activity and government intervention in the economy. The Irish poet John Boyle O'Reilly condemned poverty and class differences in his writings; journalist Patrick Ford bitterly described urban poverty in the pages of the *Irish World*; and Henry George, author of *Progress and Poverty* (1879), proposed a "single tax" on all profits from the sale or rental of land. Terence Powderly became a leader of the Knights of Labor in the 1880s and Ignatius Donnelly became a crusader for the Populist movement in the 1890s. Irish criticism of American society and "radical" solutions for social problems became another source of resentment among Anglo Protestants and Yankee Catholics.[23]

Radical Irish nationalism, Irish social criticism, labor violence, and the characteristics of the famine immigrants all split the Catholic community in the United States, threatening the image of the church and the desire of leading clerics, especially Yankee Catholics and second-generation Irish priests, to prove that Roman Catholicism and American democracy were compatible. The last thing many church leaders wanted in the 1870s was that the stereotype of the famine Irish be reinforced by any new stereotype of the radical Irish. Church leaders like Archbishop Joseph S. Alemany of San Francisco, Bishop Richard J. Gilmour of Cleveland, and Archbishop Michael Corrigan of New York denounced socialism, labor violence, and radical Irish nationalism. They worked to create great distance between the Roman Catholic church and the radical voices, but in the process isolated the church for a time from a significant segment of the Irish community interested in both reform and Irish liberation.[24]

Church leaders also campaigned to take the edge off some of the most visible and socially bothersome characteristics of Irish culture. The Irish wake was particularly troubling to the church hierarchy because it occurred independently of the church and because Anglo Protestants found it so strange. The tradition of mourning the dead through singing, dancing, drinking, eating, and then marching in procession to the cemetery had been condemned for years in Ireland by Catholic bishops. The condemnation continued in the United States through the 1860s until the church finally compromised with the Irish peasants. Thereafter a funeral Mass became part of the ceremony of death and the parish priest began attending the wake. As it did when it transformed Celtic rites centuries earlier, the church had incorporated a social custom into the formal religious process.[25]

To deal with the poor image of the first Irish immigrants, church leaders in the nineteenth century also promoted the temperance movement. The Catholic temperance crusade gathered momentum in the late 1840s and early 1850s with the tour of Father Theobald Mathew of Ireland. Mathew and others traveled throughout Catholic communities in the United States, organizing parish temperance societies and urging people to "take the pledge" of total abstinence. Other Catholics who were more moderate on the issue did not demand total abstinence but only wise and judicious use of alcohol. Like moderate Irish nationalism, the Catholic temperance movement was actually a drive for middle-class respectability, with white-collar Catholics far more likely to participate than blue-collar Catholics. Many church leaders wanted the temperance society to replace the working class local saloon as a social and political center.[26] But despite the efforts of the church hierarchy, the temperance movement never caught on among the Catholic immigrants as it did among Anglo Protestants in the United States.

By the 1870s changes in Irish immigration were precipitating changes in the debate between Yankee and Irish Catholics. The famine immigrants, with their poverty, alcoholism, violence, and illiteracy, had frightened most Yankee Catholics, but the post-1865 immigrants were fundamentally different. They came from a culture of poverty that remained unbroken until late in the nineteenth century, but by then the devotional revolution had transformed most Irish into devout, practicing Catholics. The British school system had reduced Irish illiteracy to only 16 percent by 1900, and constant emigration had relieved pressures on the economy. Not only were the immigrants changing, but Irish Americans had become quite different from their predecessors. By the 1880s, more upwardly mobile second-generation Irish Americans were assuming increasingly important positions in the church, displacing older Yankee Catholics. Born in the United States and beneficiaries of church educations, they too were more prosperous, literate, and politically comfortable, not at all like the famine immigrants. Indeed, they had come so far from the famine years that they shared many of the fears of the Yankee Catholic prelates who had preceded them.[27] Although they were replacing the Yankee Catholics in positions of power in the church, they too now worried about the image of Catholicism.

One group, led by Bishop John Ireland of St. Paul and James Cardinal Gibbons of Baltimore, was so preoccupied with the isolation of the Irish and the perceived separateness of the Catholic church that it went beyond condemnation of radicalism, the wake, and alcoholism. As long as large numbers of American Protestants saw the church as an Irish "fifth column," the threat of anti-Catholic violence would never disappear. So the group sought acceptance in the United States, not unlike Yankee Catholics who had earlier worked to function successfully among Anglo-Protestant elites. Its members praised America, lauded the public schools as the bastion of democracy and at the same time defended parochial schools, supported the separation of church and state, urged participation in the ecumenical movement as a way of reaching an accommodation with Protestants, and called on all Catholics to work hard, obey the law, and defend their country. They promoted a middle-class, nonviolent form of Irish nationalism, and in such groups as the Knights of Columbus, founded in 1882, they even imitated the Masonic society of American Protestants. Known as "liberals" or "Americanizers," they hoped to make Roman Catholicism an accepted institution in American society.[28]

But other Irish-American clerics, with little faith in Protestant largesse, opposed the work of the "liberals." Indeed, they were afraid of the secular enticements as well as of Protestant pressures in American society. It was one thing to reform the Irish immigrants and quite another to praise "Protestant virtues" and mimic Protestant values. For years church leaders had worried about the loss of Catholic immigrants who upon arrival in the United States failed to attend church, accept the sacraments, or marry endogamously. These conservatives—people like Archbishop Michael Corrigan of New York and Bishop Bernard McQuaid of Rochester—wanted Catholics to remain separate and distinct and to limit their contacts with Protestants to the workplace. They did not want Catholic immigrants to stand out as impoverished, crime-prone people, but neither did they want to deal with that image by acquiescing to Protestant values. Years of criticism and persecution by Protestants had left them pessimistic about really achieving public acceptance. They had no use for the ecumenical movement, no love for public schools, and no intention of "Americanizing" or "liberalizing" the church.[29]

Between 1845 and 1900 more than 4 million Irish Catholics immigrated to the United States, thus triggering a struggle with Yankee Catholics for control of the church. With their intense nationalism, anti-Protestantism, and aggressively visible religious faith, the Irish had upset the comfortable minority status of Anglo-American Catholics. For those Anglo Catholics conditioned to compromise, accommodation, and acquiescence as the terms of cultural survival, the Irish immigrants, especially during the famine years, were a nightmare guaranteed to bring down the wrath of American Protestants. Not until later in the nineteenth century did the struggle between Yankee and Irish Catholics subside. By then the second-generation Irish Americans were somewhat more prosperous, and literate. Disciplined immigrants had replaced their famine predecessors. Not only were these new Irish less threatening to Anglo Protestants than the famine immigrants, they had overwhelmed by sheer numbers the older Yankee and French Catholics in the United States. American Catholicism was becoming almost synonymous with Irish Catholicism, and the first ethnic succession in the church was coming to an end.

4

The Great Debate: Language and Nationality in Roman Catholicism

Just as the new Irish immigrants and their second-generation Irish-American cousins were becoming less objectionable to Anglo Protestants, changing immigration patterns made the question of assimilation even more urgent, injecting the ethnic question into church politics for two generations. Although the struggle for power between Yankee and Irish Catholics during the middle decades of the nineteenth century had involved problems of nationalism, political style, and liturgical values, it had not involved language, because English had already replaced Gaelic among the Irish populations on both sides of the Atlantic. Although the two peoples argued and competed religiously and politically, they understood one another linguistically. With the mass migration from central and eastern Europe, however, questions of nationality became mixed with questions of language, creating an ethnic struggle that raged within the church for two generations. Not until the 1940s, nearly a generation after the National Origins Act of 1924 had severely limited immigration and imposed rigid quotas on European immigrants, did the problems of nationality and language become less intense. On a small scale, the language issue appeared first among the French-Canadian immigrants and then exploded with the mass arrival of millions of German Catholics. Their struggle for ethnic identity within Roman Catholicism would serve as a model for subsequent waves of Slavic, Italian, Iberian, Magyar, Lithuanian, and Hispanic immigrants.

In Quebec, French-Canadian Catholics were a close-knit people united by language, religion, and national pride. Since 1763, when

England won control of Canada after the French and Indian War, they had lived as an ethnic minority, suffering culturally from Anglo-Protestant ethnocentrism. They did not experience the utter devastation that the Irish had. On a cultural level, the French Canadians had gained official recognition of their Roman Catholicism in 1774 with the Quebec Act, and the church had enjoyed political establishment since then. And although the Quebec economy was plagued by serious problems, it was nevertheless in better shape than rural Ireland. Still, the presence of English rule greatly intensified the French-Canadian sense of religious and ethnic pride. With the English language and Protestant religion the backbone of larger Canada, the French Canadians transformed their own faith and tongue into cultural symbols, almost ideological icons. Charles F. St. Laurent wrote in 1896 that

> despotic governments invariably begin their tyrannical work of assimilation by religious persecutions. They sap-dry the fountain head of faith, by abolishing language. When these two national ingredients, these vital factors, are destroyed, death is at hand. The language of the oppressor is imposed, and the oppressed have to mourn over the loss of ancestral inheritance.[1]

When nineteenth-century English revivalism spread throughout Canada as it had through Ireland, searching for converts and promoting Protestant values, the French Canadians made their religion a badge of faith, loyalty, and ethnic identity. Conquered politically but liberated ethnically, they fused religion, language, and nationality. It became next to impossible for French Canadians, in their own minds, to distinguish between love for the church, devotion to the French language, and a desire for ethnic liberation. Indeed, they were convinced that the erosion of their language would lead inevitably to the loss of their religion, leaving them vulnerable to Anglo-Protestant cultural imperialism but also to eternal damnation. The three ingredients of French-Canadian culture—religion, language, and nationality—had melted together into an intense preoccupation with *survivance*, the constant struggle since 1763 to preserve their identity amidst the pressures of Anglo acculturation. Though not as malignantly hostile to English Protestantism as the Irish, the French Canadians were nonetheless imbued with an ethnic identity possessed only by the victims of imperialism.[2]

The lives of French Canadians revolved around French-speaking Roman Catholic parishes and parochial schools where they could safely insulate themselves from the Anglo world of Protestantism and secular industrialism. French-Canadian Catholicism was among the most devout in the world because it had been an ideological refuge for French Canadians for more than a century. Religion was central to their lives. Because Jesuit missionaries in seventeenth-century Canada had possessed diplomatic credentials and served as financial agents of the French Crown, church and state had formed a close association that never really separated, even after the English took over. The church played a dominant and expected role in politics, assumed widespread social welfare responsibilities, and enjoyed a position of endowed power in Quebec. It was an establishment institution despite the hostility of the English. Religious culture in French Quebec was also conservative, traditionalist, and tied inseparably to the past. Among French Canadians virtually all forms of change were suspect because they threatened to undermine accepted patterns of behavior and thought. What people wanted more than anything else was to preserve their village existence and its twin foundations of church and language. Finally, French-Canadian Catholicism possessed a strong strain of Jansenism, with its sexual puritanism, emphasis on moral propriety, and belief in the salvation of only the elect. French Canadians shared much with the Irish, not only historically but theologically, but it was the issue of language and culture that gave the *habitants* of Quebec a sense of spiritual isolation and exclusivity.[3]

At the parish level, religion and tradition imbued the lives of the *habitants*. Spiritual survival and salvation depended on stability and the preservation of traditional customs. Any alteration in social custom or religious practice might well spell the death of the old order, a possibility the French Canadians considered only with great fear. In between the major rites of human existence—baptism, confirmation, marriage, and extreme unction—the French Canadians were likely to attend Mass and confession weekly. Most were unable to distinguish between the secular and sacred worlds, accepting easily a holistic unity between all observed phenomena and unexplainable mysteries. They possessed a simple, confident faith in their power to manipulate their environment through the medium of the Roman Catholic saints. St. Joseph, the patron saint of Canada, and St. Anne were especially helpful with sickness, while St. Antoine helped people find lost objects. St. Mark's celebration brought rain for crops and the Corpus Christi procession in June blessed crops. The use of burning candles and spruce branches; placing holy medals on endangered animals, people, or buildings; drinking holy water; and having the priest bless houses, seeds, and fishing poles were all accepted methods of asserting control over the secular world. Formal religion and the peasant world of magic had come together in Quebec, but the faith of French Canadians was so intense that belief in the devil and evil spirits had all but disappeared. The power of God, the saints, and the church were so overwhelming that evil had been essentially obliterated. Priests stood at the center of the peasant world, the mediators between man and God and life and death. When England began its crusade against their culture after 1763, the French Canadians had looked to their priests also as the protectors of both language and faith. Extreme loyalty to the institutional church, sexual puritanism, ethnocentrism, and political and social conservatism all came with the ***habitants*** when they began emigrating in the mid-nineteenth century. Quebec's location permitted frequent visits home, and the contact repeatedly strengthened their religion, language, and nationality.[4]

The French Canadians encountered the same hostility from Know-Nothing activists that the Irish Catholics had at midcentury. But although the fears of Anglo Protestants eased somewhat by the late 1860s, French-Canadian workers in New England mill towns found themselves competing with the Irish for factory jobs, much to the resentment of the Irish. Beyond economic rivalry, the two groups also fought over language and religion. Convinced that language guaranteed the faith and that faith guaranteed eternity, the French Canadians wanted to worship in their own language. Except for the Latin rite, nothing in the Irish-Catholic parishes seemed familiar—not the sermons, confessionals, devotions, festivals, personal relationships, or climate of opinion. The French missed the Gregorian chants and high church solemnity traditional to Quebec and found the simplicity of Irish Catholicism and the timidity of Yankee Catholicism to be spiritually empty. They resented Irish domination of the church, felt trapped in America between the suspicions of Anglo Protestants and the anger of Irish Catholics, and desperately wanted French-Canadian nationality parishes complete with French-speaking priests and French parochial schools.[5]

Irish Catholics opposed French-Canadian demands for independence and feared the immigrant French-speaking priests as threats to their own episcopal power. Neither group really understood the other, even though they both worshiped Tridentine Catholicism and had experienced centuries of English oppression. While language symbolized the faith of the French Canadians, priests did so for the Irish. Having lost much of their Gaelic heritage, the Irish could not appreciate how intensely the French rallied behind language. While French Canadians looked to priests as guardians of the language and the faith, the Irish looked to them as the agents of resistance, the embodiment of national liberation. When French-Canadian immigrants demanded their own parishes and clergymen, the Irish viewed these demands as an affront to Irish ethnicity and Irish Catholicism. So they resisted French-Canadian demands for nationality parishes.[6]

French Canadians tried continuously to get local church authorities to recognize their need for separate nationality parishes. Irish Catholics resisted because of their resentment of French-Canadian isolationism, and Yankee Catholics opposed them because they feared the French would become too visible and upset the now-traditional religious equilibrium in New England. Eventually the French Canadians took their case to the Vatican, and in 1849, after considering the merits of the appeal, Roman authorities permitted the first French-Canadian nationality parish in the United States—Saint Joseph in Burlington, Vermont. Recognizing the potential for controversy and the need to administer to the spiritual needs of the French-Canadian immigrants, the Vatican in 1852 created the Diocese of Portland covering New England and named Breton-born Louis de Goesbriand as bishop. The French now had their own symbol of episcopal power. As hundreds of thousands of French Canadians immigrated in the 1850s, 1860s, and 1870s, more French parishes were established, and French-speaking priests and nuns arrived from Belgium, France, and Quebec. In each parish the immigrants built a parochial school for children to study French, Roman Catholicism, and the history of Quebec. By 1890 there were eighty-six French-Canadian parishes and fifty-three French-Canadian parochial schools, such as Notre-Dame des Canadiens, Saint Jean Baptiste, or Sacre-Coeur de Marie.[7]

But even with their own parishes, the French-Canadian religious rivalry with Yankee and Irish Catholics continued. In Canada the immigrants had elected lay parishioners as their own church directors. Known as *marguilliers,* these laymen controlled parish finances and administrative affairs. Local priests as well as bishops had to negotiate with them over use of church funds. It was a natural arrangement, as far as the French Canadians were concerned, and was not only good religious politics but also a fine example of American democratic values. The trustee issue had raised its head again, this time with Yankee and Irish Catholics defending episcopal power against an immigrant community initiative. An ethnic transition had occurred in the church. Since the French had used their own money to construct chapels and operate parochial schools, they expected to control them. But in the United States, bishops were the only custodians of ecclesiastical property. French-Canadian immigrants might have paid for the churches and schools with their own money, but Yankee and Irish-Catholic bishops controlled them, whether in English-speaking or French-speaking parishes. Such an arrangement was intolerable for most French Canadians, particularly since they were certain that Yankee and Irish Catholics were bent on obliterating their language and culture.

The best example of French-Canadian independence was the "Flint affair" of 1884-1886. Thousands of French Canadians had poured into Fall River, Massachusetts, in the 1870s looking for work in the textile mills, but their presence threatened the jobs of Irish workers. That the French Canadians were extremely conservative in their politics, intensely anti-union, economically subservient to employers, and willing to work as strikebreakers further enraged the Irish, who were trying to organize collectively and secure wage increases from mill owners. One French Canadian proudly observed in 1880 that "the Canadian French whenever a strike has taken place, wherever any of these public demonstrations against law and order in any place have been made, have never taken part in the movement, and have stood at home like good, law-abiding citizens".[8] The economic submissiveness of the French Canadians was matched only by their ethnic isolationism.

In 1870 a separate parish, St. Anne's, was opened for the French Canadians, and in 1874 they also organized Notre Dame des Lourdes with Father Pierre Bedard as pastor. The Irish minority in the parish left in 1879 and formed Immaculate Conception parish when Father Bedard helped recruit French-Canadian strikebreakers to replace Irish workers boycotting their jobs. When Father Bedard died in 1884, Bishop Thomas Hendricken of Providence, an Irish-born cleric with deep misgivings about separate language parishes, appointed Father Samuel Patrick McGee as the new pastor at Notre Dame. Outraged French-Canadian parishioners protested the appointment to no avail, forced McGee to move from the rectory, and physically and verbally abused him, as well as his successor, Father Owen Clarke. Bishop Hendricken then interdicted the parish, denying all spiritual services and sacraments there. The parishioners held their ground until 1886 when Bishop Hendricken, under instruction from Rome, named Father Joseph M. Laflamme as the rector of Notre Dame. All penalties were lifted and the principle of ethnic churches in Fall River was secured.[9] The struggle between Yankee and Irish Catholics on the one hand and French-Canadian Catholics on the other in the 1850s, 1860s, and 1870s was a rehearsal for the larger, more intense nationality controversies of the 1890s and early 1900s.

Despite its intensity, the controversy over French-nationality parishes soon became a minor regional issue; nationality was transformed into a national dispute within the church in the 1880s when large numbers of German Catholics began arriving. The language problem had erupted among German Catholics as early as the 1780s in Philadelphia when immigrants demanded German-speaking priests. But it became a national Catholic issue only after the arrival of large numbers of German-Catholic immigrants. Between 1870 and 1900, more than 3 million German-speaking people immigrated to the United States, and approximately 40 percent of them were Roman Catholics. Although a German settlement belt existed already from northern Massachusetts to Maryland and through the Ohio River valley to the Great Lakes, most of the German Catholics settled in the "German triangle" bounded by Milwaukee, Cincinnati, and St. Louis.[10]

Most German Catholics came from southern and southwestern Germany. Generally isolated from the major currents of European commerce and intellectual life and locked into traditional rural folkways, the German-Catholic world was one of *Gemeinschaft,* where personal and family values greatly outweighed commercial and political ones. Their High German dialect and geographic isolation gave them a certain insularity from the outside world, a desire to be left alone. Although German Catholicism had long been sharpened by cycles of competition and violent confrontation with Prussian Lutheranism, its intensity varied from region to region.

Where it was a minority religion or bordered a Protestant region, German Catholicism was likely to be intense and well defined as a measure of personal identity. In each province, church and state had fused, coming under the control of a local sovereign. With the Napoleonic Wars and final collapse of the Holy Roman Empire, the church lost its position of privilege in many provinces of what would later become Germany, surrendering a good deal of ecclesiastical property and becoming subject to state control. But despite the political difficulties in the nineteenth century, German Catholicism underwent a spiritual renaissance not unlike the devotional revolution in Ireland. Attendance at Mass rose substantially as did membership in religious confraternities and the number of young men and women entering vocations. Many religious and political associations, such as the Federation of Christian Trade Unions and the Society of St. Boniface, appeared early in the nineteenth century and promoted Roman Catholicism in Germany. The church had retained its position as a major fixture in German culture.[11]

Despite the religious renaissance they both shared, German and Irish Catholicism were quite different. The Irish were devoted to ascetic simplicity in worship and emphasized internal, individual devotions, the contemplative tradition of ancient Celtic monasticism. They were suspicious of the ornate and ceremonial, at least within a Roman Catholic perspective, and their religion emphasized legalism, authority, individual piety, puritanical restraint, and liturgical clarity. German Catholics, on the other hand, had a profound love of pageantry, ceremony, and ritual. Their spirituality expressed itself in elaborate processions, choirs, orchestras, bands, parades, vocalists, and passion plays, devotions requiring widespread communal participation rather than private, individual worship. To the Irish, such displays were at best peripheral to "true religion" and at worst sacrilegious, but to the Germans they were an integral part of religious culture and spiritual well-being. That commitment to communal rather than individual piety reflected itself as well in differences in church administration. While the Irish were often perfectly willing to leave administrative affairs to the priest, as long as he was Irish, the Germans preferred to have elected boards of laymen work closely with the priest, much like the French Canadians expected the *marguilliers* to control parish finances.[12]

Nor did the Germans share the nationalism of the Irish. In the 1870s Otto von Bismarck instituted *Kulturkampf*—a "culture battle" between Prussian Lutheranism and German Catholicism to annul papal authority, parochial schools, and the vocational orders in the name of German nationalism. It was, in short, aimed at giving the state control over educational policy and ecclesiastical appointments as a way of promoting national unity and political centralization. The May Laws of 1873 gave Prussia control over the Roman Catholic clergy. Bismarck's crusade helped give German Catholics a sense of spiritual renaissance and religious solidarity, but it also linked nationalism with Protestantism. In Ireland, nationalism and Catholicism had fused, just the opposite of what was happening in Germany. For centuries German Catholics had lived a communal existence in their village parishes, their loyalties focusing directly on home and family rather than on distant ideas or centers. German Catholics had little appreciation for the details of Irish-American nationalism, and they had a difficult time even relating to the premises of political nationalism at all. For a time in the mid- to late nineteenth century, some German-Catholic nationalists, afraid the church would become alienated from German unification by the anticlerical and anti-Catholic attitudes of many German Protestants, toyed with the idea of creating a German National Catholic Church. But their goal of linking Catholicism and German nationalism never really succeeded. Not until they came to America did a sense of political nationalism begin to emerge in the German-Catholic community. In the Old World they had defined themselves only as Catholics, since the real ethnic separation divided them from Lutherans, Reformed, and Pietists. But in the United States, they became German Catholics, separate not only from Protestants but from other Catholics as well. Nationalism was a vehicle for liberation in Catholic Ireland, but this was not so in Germany, where many Catholics in the 1870s and 1880s saw it as a tool of oppression.[13]

But if German Catholics had little sense of political nationalism, they possessed an intense sense of cultural nationalism. Like the French Canadians, they were convinced that language and faith in America were inextricably connected. The Reverend Anton H. Walburg of Cincinnati expressed the sentiments of German Catholics and German Protestants when he said that a "foreigner who loses his nationality is in danger of losing his faith and character. When the German immigrant . . . seeks to throw aside his nationality . . the first word he learns is generally a curse, and . . . like as the Indians . . . he adopts the vices rather than the virtues."[14]

The German Catholics' greatest fear was that of losing their religion in the United States, and the first step toward such a tragedy would be losing their language. Irish-Catholic parishes where English was spoken, therefore, were almost as dangerous as Protestant churches because they threatened to undermine language and culture. Father Peter Abbelen best summarized the differences in Irish and German Catholicism in his "Memorial" essay in 1886 to the Congregation of the Propaganda:

> The only means by which Catholic Germans ... shall be able to preserve their Catholic faith and morals is that they shall have their own priests, who shall instruct them in the language and in the traditions of their fatherland. Wherever ... Bishops have fallen into ... refusing them ... permission to build a school or church, committing them to the pastoral care of a priest ignorant of their language ... there has prevailed ... a truly deplorable falling away from the Church .... Besides a difference of language, we must not by any means make light of the difference and discrepancy of Catholic customs ... among Germans and Irish. The Irish, on account of oppression and persecution which they suffered for religion's sake in their own land, love simplicity in divine service, and in all practice of religion, and do not care much for pomp and splendor. But the Germans, from the liberty which as a rule they have enjoyed ... from earliest times ... love the beauty of the church edifice and the pomp of ceremonies, belfries and bells, organs and sacred music, processions, feast days, sodalities, and the most solemn celebration of First Communion and weddings. These and other like things, although not essential to Catholic faith and life, foster piety and are so dear and sacred to the faithful that not without great danger could they be taken away from them.[15]

German-Catholic clerics worried constantly about the spiritual implications of emigration, whether parishioners leaving the villages of southern Germany would remain faithful in the New World. To protect themselves, they became committed to nationality parishes, German-speaking priests, and German-language parochial schools. There was, of course, no love lost between German Catholics and German Protestants, so German Catholics essentially seceded from pan-German ethnicity, segregating themselves into a carefully isolated religious community. In their drive for autonomy, they ran directly into the fears and expectations of Irish Americans.

German Catholics began establishing separate parishes soon after their arrival. Holy Trinity parish, St. Peter's parish, and St. Alphonsus parish were serving German Catholics in Philadelphia by 1853, and in northern Ohio there were St. Stephen's and St. Vincent de Paul parishes in Cleveland, St. Bernard parish in Akron, and St. Joseph parish in Lorain. By the 1850s there were eight German-nationality parishes in the Archdiocese of New York. At Most Holy Redeemer Church in New York, a German-nationality parish established in 1844 on East Third Street, German Catholics tried to rebuild and preserve the religious faith of the fatherland. Their devotion to Roman Catholicism and German culture was strong, and the only way of maintaining their identity in Anglo-Protestant and Yankee and Irish-Catholic society was through the establishment of nationality parishes. Father Abbelen's claim that "scarcely ever will you find German and Irish united in matrimony" was true at Most Holy Redeemer as well.[16] German Catholics confined themselves socially to protect the faith. At Most Holy Redeemer, they were also less likely to change residences than their Irish neighbors. It was easy for an Irish family to move and find an English-speaking parish, but this was not so for the Germans. So rather than take the risk, they usually stayed close to Most Holy Redeemer. As well as providing them with the German language and German priests, the parish also ensured them of a familiar devotional style. Typical of nineteenth-century piety, Jesus and Marian devotions were popular, along with parish societies like the archconfraternities of the Immaculate Heart of Mary and of the Holy Rosary. Saints Joseph, Teresa, Joachim, Anne, and Alphonsus were especially popular. Organs, choirs, bands, and processions were always visible; the *Jager-compagnie,* a parish militia society, was active; all Masses were enriched by music; and the *Unterstutzung-Verein* provided health, death, and welfare benefits to the immigrant community.[17]

Roman Catholic dioceses spread throughout the "German triangle" as German immigrants arrived. In 1844 John Martin Henni became bishop of Milwaukee, giving German Catholics an episcopal representative, though just as unofficial as Louis de Goesbriand was for the French Canadians. Since most midwestern Catholics were German, Bishop Henni insisted on appointing German-speaking priests in his diocese. He took the same approach later as archbishop of Milwaukee. More than 95 percent of his German-speaking parishes had their own parochial schools, where German was taught or served as the language of instruction. In 1855 all of the parish social organizations and clubs in German-speaking parishes across the country united into a federation known as the *Central-verein;* German-Catholic priests formed the German-American Priests Society in 1887; and German-Catholic newspapers and magazines became part of a national *Pressverein* that same year. But when Archbishop Henni, anticipating his own death in the 1880s, began petitioning the Vatican to appoint a German-speaking coadjutor bishop with the right to succeed him, the German-Catholic drive for autonomy collided directly with the Irish-Catholic need to assimilate the immigrants, both administratively and pietistically.[18]

For Catholic liberals worried about the image of the church, the German and French-Canadian migrations threatened to do just what the coming of the famine Irish had done—stimulate new rounds of Anglo-Protestant nativism. Although the appearance of second-generation Irish Americans as well as the migration of the postfamine Irish had done much to dispel Protestant fears, the arrival of the French Canadians and Germans did not. Not coincidentally, anti-Catholic nativism was on the rise again. In 1887, Henry F. Bowers organized the American Protective Association, a Protestant association dedicated to limiting or even outlawing Roman-Catholic immigration and to transforming those Catholics already in the country. To ease fears, Catholic liberals, usually descendents of Yankee Catholics or upwardly mobile Irish Americans, sought to transform the immigrants. So to their campaign for education, obedience, self-control, and temperance, the liberals added ethnic assimilation. Bishop John Ireland of St. Paul wanted all Catholic immigrants to acculturate as quickly as possible. To German Catholics, Ireland urged

> that your children learn well, and speak well, the English language .... Your children are Americans ... their hopes ... are bound up in the folds of the flag. They would be neither loyal to her, nor to themselves, did they not seek to know her language; and if one language is to be known by them better than another, give to the English the first and honored place.[19]

Cardinal James Gibbons of Baltimore, during an 1891 visit to Henni's back yard in Milwaukee, preached:

> Woe to him who would breed dissension among the leaders of Israel by introducing the spirit of nationalism into the camps of

> the Lord. Brothers we are, whatever may be our nationality, and brothers we shall remain . . . . Let us glory in the title of American citizen. We owe all our allegiance to one country, and that country is America.[20]

Not all Catholic leaders, of course, reflected the same desire to assimilate the immigrants. Just as "conservatives" like Archbishop Michael Corrigan and Bishop Bernard McQuaid had resented Ireland's and Gibbons's willingness to accommodate themselves to Protestant culture and public schools, they were also suspicious of any high-pressure campaign to assimilate the immigrants. Both Corrigan and McQuaid recognized that the German and French-Canadian Catholics were among the most devout in the church, strong and faithful in their institutional loyalties and sincere in their individual pieties. If language and culture were intimately involved in that loyalty, so be it. Perhaps the immigrants were right to fear that loss of the language would lead to loss of the religion. Irish Catholics, of course, argued that although they had recently lost the use of the Gaelic language, it had not retarded their commitment to the Kingdom of God. Still, the conservatives were not impressed and preferred letting the immigrants have their way and letting the natural forces of time and acculturation, rather than any forced campaigns, change ethnic patterns. Heaven forbid that the church become as obnoxious to the immigrants as Anglo Protestants had been.[21]

A full-scale war of words erupted between German and Irish Catholics in the 1880s when Irish-American priests in Wisconsin began complaining to Bishop John Ireland and Cardinal James Gibbons that Bishop John Henni was "Germanizing" the diocese of Milwaukee. In St. Louis, on the other hand, Archbishop Peter Richard Kenrick was countering Henni by establishing German parishes that enjoyed a second-class status because their priests had no juridical authority as pastors. They were resident priests without power. More than eighty-one non-Irish priests in St. Louis appealed to the Vatican in 1884 demanding an end to their second-class status through the upgrading of their parishes and the granting of full pastoral authority to them. German priests in Milwaukee openly supported their St. Louis colleagues. Many Irish-American priests, particularly liberals like Ireland and Gibbons, saw a German conspiracy in the making. Their fears were magnified in 1886 when Father Peter Abbelen, Vicar General of the Archdiocese of Milwaukee, personally visited Rome, with the blessing of the new archbishop, Michael Heiss of Milwaukee, and complained that German parishes in the United States were discriminated against by the "Irish church" authorities. Not only did he want the German parishes to enjoy full status; he also wanted the Vatican to instruct American bishops to end the "Americanization" process.[22]

The visit triggered a storm of protest from the Irish-American and Yankee-Catholic clergy, who resented the German appeals to Rome, vehemently denied that they were guilty of discrimination, and feared for the future of the church. For a time, Abbelen's visit even united the "liberals" and "conservatives" in the hierarchy. Conservative Bishop Bernard McQuaid, who already had spoken out against Ireland's and Gibbons's plans to rapidly acculturate the immigrants, worried that it would "be a dangerous precedent to set, to let nationalities legislate through Rome, in an underhand way, without the knowledge of other bishops of the country."[23] Bishops John Ireland and John Keane of Richmond, known for their "liberal" goals of assimilating the immigrants, were even more critical, accusing the Germans of manipulating the facts, planning to establish a separate church within a church, and weakening any hope of converting Protestants.[24]

The dispute became more bitter in the 1890s with the "Cahensly controversy." Peter Cahensly, a wealthy German businessman concerned about the welfare of German-Catholic immigrants, visited the United States in 1883 to establish the St. Raphael Society, an emigrant-aid association for German Catholics. A member of the Prussian Parliament and a well-known philanthropist, Cahensly had a great deal of influence, and upon his return from America he voiced concern about the future of German Catholicism in the United States. During the 1880s he established St. Raphael societies throughout Europe, and at an 1890 convention of those associations in Lucerne, Switzerland, he argued that large numbers of German Catholics were abandoning the church in America because the Irish-Catholic hierarchy was unresponsive to their needs. The convention then issued the Lucerne Memorial, a document calling for the establishment of separate nationality parishes in America with priests of the same nationality as the parishioners; foreign-language parochial schools in each of the nationality parishes; and sodalities and confraternities in which membership was based on nationality. Finally, the memorial demanded that the American-Catholic episcopate formally reflect the nationality percentages of its Catholic members rather than having the Irish in so dominant a position. Cahensly then carried the memorial to the Vatican for papal review.[25]

Not surprisingly, the Lucerne Memorial enraged the Irish-American hierarchy. Since the number of German Catholics by 1890 was second only to the number of Irish Catholics in the United States, the memorial was actually a call for the wholesale appointment of German-speaking bishops until their number approximated that of the Irish. Catholic liberals like Ireland, Keane, and Kenrick bitterly condemned the memorial, and Gibbons, in milder terms, called it inappropriate for the United States. Even Catholic conservatives like Bishops Michael Corrigan and Bernard McQuaid, who had long defended the right of immigrants to preserve their language and culture, resented "foreign" intervention in American ecclesiastical affairs. Only the German-Catholic press and German-Catholic clerics in Wisconsin and Ohio defended the Lucerne Memorial. Conscious of Gibbons' point of view, the Vatican decided not to intervene but offered a spirit of compromise by appointing James Schwebach and Sebastian Messmer, both German-speaking priests, as bishops of La Crosse and Green Bay, Wisconsin. By 1910 there were more than two thousand parishes using German language services, more than twenty-six hundred German-speaking priests, and twenty dioceses with more than fifty German-speaking priests each. More than 95 percent of German-Catholic parishes had parochial schools where German was taught. But Cahensly's comprehensive plan for reformation of the power structure of the church in America was stillborn.[26]

No sooner had the Cahensly controversy subsided than a new dispute over foreign languages again divided Irish and German Catholics. Anti-Catholic nativism in the 1880s and 1890s was creating new concerns about the use and abuse of foreign language instruction in public schools. Since early in the nineteenth century, German immigrants in some states had enjoyed enough political influence to legislate German as the language of instruction in public schools. By the 1880s, however, many native Americans and liberal Catholics were concerned about the status of English in those schools. It was not uncommon for all subjects to be taught in German without English even presented as a second language. Those concerns led to new education laws in several states, including the Edwards Law in Illinois (1889) and the Bennett Law in

Wisconsin (1889), requiring English instruction in all the schools of the state, parochial as well as public. German Protestants and German Catholics showed a rare display of unity in opposing the legislation, not only as an antiethnic and anti-immigrant measure but as violation of freedom of religion.

The controversy became a religious question when Archbishop Ireland endorsed the Bennett Law to force German Catholics to accept reality and learn the English language. Archbishop Michael Heiss of Milwaukee protested Ireland's support and became even more upset when Ireland addressed a convention of the National Education Association praising public schools as the glory of America. According to Ireland, parochial schools would be unnecessary if public schools allowed religious instruction. The Catholic press in general but particularly the German-Catholic press condemned Ireland's remarks, seeing them as a thinly veiled attack on the German-language parochial schools. Ireland raised even more wrath in 1891 when he tried an experiment with public schools in Faribault, Minnesota. He rented the parish parochial school there during regular school hours to the public school system. Only Roman Catholic children attended, and they were taught by religious and lay teachers. But religion classes were offered only before and after regular school hours when the property reverted back to the parish. For Ireland, the arrangement was the best of both worlds, securing funds from the public school system while seeing to the religious needs of Catholic children. But to all conservative Catholics, German Catholics, and some liberal Catholics the experiment was dangerous, capable of undermining parochial education by provoking the ire of Protestant authorities. The Bennett Law, under pressure from outraged German-Americans in Wisconsin, was quickly repealed, but the issue had driven another wedge between Irish and German Catholics and between Catholic conservatives and liberals.[27]

The controversy over "liberalism" and "Americanization" peaked in the mid-1890s when a number of European clerics condemned the "liberal" views of the American church. Familiar with Cahenslyism and worried about the loss of large numbers of immigrant Catholics, they claimed that American Catholicism was too cooperative and accommodating, almost acquiescing to the spirit of Protestantism. More specifically, they charged that "Americanism" was synonymous with a rejection of pastoral authority and of the influence of the Holy Ghost alone in directing church affairs; the preference for public over parochial schools; the desire to revise Catholic beliefs and make them more acceptable to Protestants; the rejection of religious vows as anachronistic in the modern world and of supernatural over natural instincts; and the acceptance of active over passive virtues.

In 1899 the Vatican officially condemned the "American" heresy. Conservative archbishops like Michael Corrigan of New York and Frederick Katzer of Milwaukee praised the pope for trying to stamp out Catholic liberalism, and liberal archbishops like John Ireland, James Cardinal Gibbons, and Patrick Riordan of San Francisco denied they had ever adhered to such a point of view. But the pope's active intervention gave the liberals cause for reflection, and after 1900 they were much more cautious in their requests for "Americanization" of the immigrants.[28] Yankee Catholicism had given way to Irish Catholicism, but German and French-Canadian Catholics had managed to carve out an episcopal place for themselves in the church. By that time, the immigration question was becoming even more complicated because of mass migrations from Poland, Lithuania, Italy, Spain, Portugal, Austria-Hungary, and Mexico. American Catholicism now had to worry about absorbing and nurturing millions of new foreigners. After more than two hundred fifty years in America, Roman Catholics were still trying to define their collective identity.

5

The East-European Catholics

Between 1890 and 1930 the cities of the Northeast and Midwest filled with East-European immigrants—Poles, Lithuanians, Czechs, Slovaks, Rusins, Ukrainians, Magyars, Slovenes, and Croatians. At the same time those cities were also absorbing large numbers of Italians, Jews, southern blacks, and rural whites, becoming diverse collections of ethnic communities. Although American nativists looked with suspicion and disgust on the rising ethnic ghettoes and tried desperately to confine the immigrants behind the boundaries of the ghettoes, the new urban communities were not pathological expressions of frightened, morally disabled people. The immigrants did not hide inside the ghettoes just because of external prejudice. To people living in a strange land, the ethnic churches, fraternal halls, saloons, and parochial schools offered familiarity and security, havens where people could confront American society on their own terms.

Within the large immigrant communities, there were even more distinctions. Except for a few areas like the Irish Sixth Ward in New York City or the Italian Lower East Side of Manhattan, the ethnic ghettoes were not residential enclaves for particular groups. Instead, the more common pattern was residentially mixed neighborhoods with separate churches and social institutions. Cultural differences divided the East-European Catholics, even though they often lived in the same residential areas and shared the Tridentine piety of sixteenth-century Roman Catholicism. Separate national histories, traditional political rivalries, distinct languages, and great varieties of folk values set them apart from one another despite the forces of assimilation. In the United States, East Europeans insisted at first on maintaining unique identities. But although their group identities were unique, East-European Catholics generally turned to similar institutions, based on certain shared experiences, to maintain cultural continuity. During the first decades of the twentieth century, their ethnic lives revolved around older visions of land, family, church, and nation.

The central cultural experience in the lives of East Europeans, especially those immigrating to the United States, was the peasant heritage. By the end of the nineteenth century, the years of serfdom were over, but the network of roles and values associated with peasantry survived. For centuries economic, political, and social roles had been rigidly determined by class and status. Peasants used their master's fish, game, timber, and water, but in return they had to work his land and loyally serve him in peace and war. The scheme of life seemed perfectly ordered, with masters destined by God to rule and peasants to serve. Since the gap between the two classes was so enormous and so rarely breached, each group had a clear sense of identity and expectations. Indeed, those two roles were so rigidly defined in many areas of eastern Europe that no middle class of merchants and craftsmen appeared until migrating Jews began filling those roles in the sixteenth century. The peasants viewed themselves as a working people obligated by fate to labor for a living all their lives. Once in America, that identity survived as they assumed their places in the blue-collar economy of the Midwest, generally preferring work to education for several generations.[1]

Peasant identity also revolved around the sense of community. Until nineteenth-century economic changes created the new class of migrant laborers, the peasants had powerful attachments to place and home. During the feudal past, serfs had been considered basically a capital item, a fixed asset inseparable from a particular piece of land. In many instances, generation after generation of family life had passed in a single place, and the peasants had developed an emotional attachment to their home. The life of migratory labor proved quite disorienting to many of them, and they yearned for stability again, for the diurnal routine of life and work in the company of family and neighbors. Although they supported themselves by farming, they were not a rural people. They lived instead in clustered villages where nobility, peasants, Jews, priests, and foreign workers, all serving to define even further one another's special place in society, were common. That Old World love of community and place became a love of and loyalty to their American neighborhood once they set up their "urban villages" in the United States.[2]

A special attachment to land and property also defined East-European values. Land was the essence of peasant life—a cultural, social, and economic constant that rigidly determined status in the world. In every peasant village, land translated into status, the place one's family occupied in the community. From the nobleman with thousands of acres down to the lowliest landless peasant, property was the measure of existence. Land was life and fertility, and far more than an economic asset; peasants worked it not just to make a living but to stake out their destiny in the universe. Ownership of land brought recognition, status, and prestige in the rural villages. Thomas and Znaniecki, in describing that relationship in the life of Polish peasants, wrote:

> Land property is . . . the main condition of the social standing of the family. Without land, the family can still keep its internal solidarity, but it cannot act as a unit with regard to the rest of the community; it ceases to count as a social power. Its members become socially and economically dependent on strangers, and often scatter about the country or abroad. . . . The greater the amount of land, the greater the possibility of social expression.[3]

When changes in the Atlantic economy threatened that relationship to the land, the peasants began a migratory search for the work and cash they needed to redeem, save, expand, or acquire land. Eventually that quest brought them to America.[4]

The purpose of land and eventually of emigration was to protect, nourish, and sustain the peasant family. Land predetermined family status; so peasants were extremely reluctant to sell it or divide it up in inheritance proceedings because the reduction or loss of the property undermined family well-being, emotionally as well as economically. In the Old World the cement of peasant society was the family, and individual identity was inextricably connected to the family. A complex series of obligations governed family relationships. According to the religious principle of *paterfamilias,* accepted by the vast majority of East European peasants, fathers ruled their homes with absolute authority, subject only to the control and teachings of God and the church. Marriage was an institution of respect and of economic solidarity, not romance; husbands owed their wives loyalty, fidelity, and financial support, while wives in turn owed fidelity and obedience. Children owed their parents emotional and financial support before and after marriage. Since marriage usually brought two pieces of property together, married people were more highly esteemed in the community than single people. Status and reputation were village questions, tied completely to family and land; so individual independence was quite impossible. Daily life was public, society highly personal, and family reputations the standard gauges of respectability. Among East-European Catholics, the family was the magnet attracting the loyalty of generation after generation of children to the village.[5]

For centuries the peasant family, particularly the landed family, had been emotionally and economically independent. A wide variety of social, economic, and political institutions supported it. Church rituals of baptism, confirmation, marriage, name day, last rites, and burial, along with ritual community occasions like Holy Week, Christmas, and village saints' days, created bonds between family and village. The social order was highly ceremonial, symbolic, communal, and predictable, with every villager part of the larger whole. Certain about the outline of the future because of the consistency of the past, the peasant family enjoyed a peculiar sense of security and freedom unknown to later generations. It was not, of course, any feeling of political liberty or guaranteed prosperity; peasant life hardly brought either of these. But peasants did enjoy a warm confidence about the meaning of life, a profound sense of comfort within the network of existing family and village ties.[6]

Nineteenth-century economic changes, by integrating peasant families into the larger Atlantic economy and undermining land tenure, destroyed the sense of security and threatened the family. The consolidation of small estates, loss of land, and decline of cottage industries destroyed the economic independence so central to the peasant family. When family members began moving to cities in search of work, the cycle of family and village religious holidays was broken, since the celebration of communal bonds required widespread participation. Instead of the collective, predictable cycles of the past, family and village life became governed by impersonal forces in the Atlantic economy. Class and interest-group relationships began to replace the old communal order. Insecure and economically vulnerable, peasants had to build a new set of institutions outside the nuclear family to guarantee survival.[7]

They responded to change in many ways. The economic decline of the nuclear family forced peasants to extend the reach of kinship ties beyond the household. Marriage, apprenticeships, dowries, foster parents, godparents, and family donations linked several families together, increasing the number of people prepared to support distressed households. Peasants also turned to voluntary associations to support schools, organize trades, supply loans, promote political activity, and provide health, life, and burial insurance. Between 1870 and 1900, the twelve hundred residents of the village of Huslenky in Moravia formed more than fifteen such associations, including a mutual benefit society for masons and an agricultural society for tenant farmers. In a community world where traditional relationships were disintegrating, the extended family ties and voluntary associations provided order and stability. Since nineteenth-century Catholic revivalism was spreading throughout Europe and actively promoting the importance of parish life and of religious confraternities and sodalities, the changes in the Atlantic economy, by encouraging associational life, reinforced religious change. In parish after parish throughout nineteenth-century eastern Europe, peasants joined religious associations, confraternities, and sodalities to augment social life and preserve the faith amidst unprecedented economic change. When they began moving by the hundreds of thousands to the New World, these voluntary associations provided them with some measure of collective support as well as with strong leadership systems.[8]

In addition to work, community, property, and family, East-European Catholics also used language and nationality to define themselves. Because of the complicated political history of central and eastern Europe, as well as the limited education and social isolation of most peasants, the degree of political nationalism varied from place to place. In the Old World, however, the combination of history and language had generated, if not political nationalism, at least a strong sense of ethnic identity. Between 1386 and 1572 Poland and Lithuania were joined together in a close political alliance. Both had strong national traditions based on long periods of political independence and a powerful Roman Catholic faith. In the 1790s both lost that independence, with Lithuania falling into the Russian orbit and Poland being divided up between Prussia, Austria-Hungary, and Russia. After 1860 the Russian government began suppressing the Lithuanian language and prohibiting use of the Latin alphabet. It imposed similar restrictions on eastern Poles by outlawing the Polish language, closing many parochial schools, and seizing land from Polish nobles. Polish nationalists rebelled several times against Russian authority in the nineteenth century. Political domination and cultural imperialism at the hands of Germans, Austrians, and Russians sharpened Lithuanian and Polish ethnic consciousness.[9]

The Austro-Hungarian Empire, home for millions of German, Czech, Slovak, Polish, Croatian, Slovenian, Magyar, Rusin, and Ukrainian Catholics, was an unstable coalition of diverse nationalities. The Hapsburgs had long governed central Europe, and Hungarian Magyars had chafed under Austrian rule. Magyar nationalism erupted in an unsuccessful revolt against Austria in 1848-1849, but in 1867 Franz Joseph, emperor of Austria and king of Hungary, gave Hungary a separate constitution and parliament, with shared ministries of war, finance, and foreign affairs. Long before the great migration, Magyar Catholics became separated from German-speaking Austrians and the other nationalities of the empire.[10]

The rest of the empire resented Austrian and Magyar oppression. Until late in the ninth century, the Czechs and Slovaks had been united under the Great Moravian Empire, but in 896 Magyar armies invaded and conquered Slovakia, separating it from Czech Bohemia and Moravia. In Bohemia and Moravia, the Czechs struggled to maintain their independence from the Germans on the west, Prussians on the north, and Austrians on the south. But in 1620 the Hapsburgs brought Bohemia and Moravia into the empire, reducing the Czechs to second-class status. At the same time, the Slovaks suffered under Magyar domination. For Czechs and Slovaks, power and prestige were in Vienna and Budapest, not Prague or Bratislava, and the elites in those cities were Austrian Germans and Hungarian Magyars. Czech ethnicity emerged against the background of German authority, while Slovak identity was cut by the edge of Magyar oppression.[11]

Slovenes and Croatians came from the southern reaches of the empire, along the Adriatic coast. The Slovenes lived in and around the city of Trieste and throughout Styria, Carinthia, Carniola, Istria, Gorizia, Gradisca, and in parts of Croatia, Hungary, and Italy. Slovenia came under German rule in the eighth century, and like Bohemia enjoyed a highly educated civilization. Between 1809 and 1814, France seized Slovenia and incorporated it into the colony of Illyria. During those years, the Slovenes developed an incipient liberal nationalism that yearned for liberation from German control in Austria. Major cities like Trieste had large German-speaking populations while rural areas were overwhelmingly Slovenian. With German landlords in the countryside and German commercial and industrial elites in the cities, Slovenian nationalism developed in the presence of German control.[12] Croatia had similar problems with Hungary. Croatia had been independent until 1002, but political unrest had inspired Magyar conquest. From 1102 to 1849 Croatia was an autonomous kingdom under Hungarian supervision, with the exception of the Illyrian colony status during the Napoleonic Wars. Like the Slovenes, the Croatians then developed a flowering nationalism in the absence of Magyar rule. When Magyar authority returned in 1814 and imperial officials tried to discourage the Croatian language, Croatian culture managed to thrive, with ethnic newspapers, reading rooms, literature, and schools appearing throughout the country.[13] Like that of the Slovaks, Croatian nationalism was partly a product of Magyar domination.

Finally, the Ruthenian people lived in the eastern regions of Austria-Hungary, from Galicia and Bukovina in Austria to Transcarpathia in Hungary, as well as in western Russia. They were divided into two groups: slightly more than half of them were Rusins (Carpatho-Ruthenians) and the others were Ukrainians (Galician-Ruthenians). Related linguistically, they had quite different political histories. Magyars had dominated Rusins for a thousand years; so the Rusins, without a tradition of national independence, had a comparatively weak political nationalism. Their loyalties were generally divided between the Magyars, Russians, and Ukrainians. The Ukrainians, on the other hand, were much more nationalistic. During the Middle Ages, Kiev and the Ukraine had been independent, and since the eighteenth century Ukrainians had maintained a distinct vernacular and literature. Dominated by Russia and Austria-Hungary, and overrun periodically by Lithuanians and Poles in the Middle Ages, Ukrainians had developed a nationalism that was a powerful force in their ethnic identity.[14]

If work, land, family, language, and nationality had contributed to East-European ethnicity, they all functioned within the larger context of Roman Catholicism. Religion was the marrow of East-European ethnicity, the philosophical cement holding society together. Caught for centuries between the Eastern Orthodoxy of Russia, the Islamic fundamentalism of the Turks, and the various

Protestant faiths of the West, East-European Catholicism became well defined and intimately associated with peasant life. Religion explained the mysteries and tragedies of human existence, provided peasants with a reassuring knowledge of the cosmos, directed the pace and substance of social life, and often helped supply the makings of a patriotic nationalism. For most East-European Catholics, the church was a revered institution bringing meaning into their lives. In celebrating festivals, honoring patron saints, joining sodalities and confraternities, attending parish schools, and partaking of the sacraments of the church, peasants came to terms with life and death.

Peasant religion in East Europe was a mixture of folk tradition and formal Catholicism, with organized religion providing supernatural intervention when folk values seemed inadequate. Peasants viewed the natural world from a unique perspective quite independent of Catholicism, uniting all nature into a cosmic whole. Animals, plants, minerals, sun, moon, stars, and the earth were alive, imbued with a measure of knowledge, individual consciousness, and awareness of the things around them. Peasants gave a name to every animal, tree, river, stream, meadow, mountain, hill, and valley, as well as to days, weeks, months, and seasons. All of creation had a spiritual essence, and there was a balance and solidarity to nature that man had to carefully respect. In thought and deed, people had to honor nature, taking and killing only what was necessary for survival. When coming upon a poisonous snake, for example, the peasant would much prefer to avoid the reptile or scare it off than to kill it. Disobedience and disrespect toward nature could easily ignite vengeance and retaliation. On the other hand, careful observation of the behavior of plants, animals, and the elements helped peasants predict the future, avoid danger and tragedy, and control the fear, decay, sickness, and misery leading to death. What another generation would call superstition was actually a highly complicated, integrated spiritual network linking all natural activities into a holistic unity. The sacred and profane, the spiritual and temporal, were one and the same.

Beyond the world of animals, objects, and natural phenomena, peasant religion functioned in the world of spirits. The existence of such mythological beings as devils, witches, dwarfs, water spirits, house ghosts, goblins, cloud-beings, vampires, nightmares, and generalized spiritual entities was taken for granted. All these beings functioned actively in the world according to supernatural laws, and when the events of the natural world appeared disruptive or illogical, the peasants blamed those spirits and appealed to magic for understanding and control. The ultimate source of magical power was the heavenly magic of God, Jesus, the Virgin Mary, and the pantheon of saints and angels. For most peasants, the activities of God and Jesus were detached and distant, rarely interrupting the usual flow of the natural world. They turned instead to the Virgin for their magic—to heal the sick, ward off evil, and avert danger. Saints and angels were used to fight devils, praise God, and perform highly specialized duties, like putting out fires, the special function of St. Agatha. Although heavenly magic and its concourse of living, benevolent spirits were overpowering, the evil magic of satanic spirits was very real, a force to be reckoned with through the power of heavenly magic. By seeing life in terms of magical causality, peasants learned to deal with their environment, avoiding the fatalistic surrender to outside forces that political oppression and economic poverty often spawn.

Finally, peasant religion existed on the formal level of ceremonial Catholicism. Parish activities bound peasants into a moral, communal whole. In the chapel and its surrounding cemetery occurred the most important events of life. Peasants sacrificed to build a beautiful church and then treated it with reverential awe and adoration. Villages of poverty-stricken families living in huts but attending lovely churches were not uncommon. Unlike the ascetic simplicity, private devotions, individual worship, and dominance of the priest in the Irish Mass, the tradition of the East Europeans was more communal, involving the singing of Mass responses and a preference for a rich ceremonialism like that of the Germans. At weekly or daily Mass, peasants sensed a community of interest as they expressed faith through songs, gestures, communion, prayers, standing, sitting, and kneeling at the same time. Special services during Lent and on Easter, Christmas, and patron saints' days reinforced the moral consensus, as did the family ceremonies of baptism, confirmation, marriage, ordination, and burial. To all these were added the meetings of parish societies, visits by the bishop, priests' jubilees, missionary revivals, and group pilgrimages. On private, individual levels peasants had ritualized behaviors for attending confession, saying prayers, and dealing with the priest. They understood and used the same prayer books, consecrated objects, medals, pictures, missals, and family ceremonials. They lived in a world of religious and social consensus, circumscribed by the church and supervised by the priest, making up a system of values revolving around an intimacy of language, culture, and tradition.[15]

Although most East-European Catholics shared the same natural, supernatural, and formal religion, there were still differences among ethnic groups, particularly in the intensity of institutional commitment. Among Polish and Lithuanian Catholics, the church complemented their devotion to the land, helping to explain the mysterious, overcome uncertainty, and secure the future. Their venerated saints, particularly St. Stanislaus for the Poles and St. Casimir for the Lithuanians, intervened with God on behalf of peasant welfare. Specific saints performed lesser miracles. Lithuanians, for example, appealed regularly to St. George as the protector of animals. Poles and Lithuanians both had a special reverence for the Virgin Mary, a devotion intense enough to elevate her almost to a deity in a nineteenth-century Mariolatry. For Poles the most hallowed shrine in the country was that of the Black Madonna in Czestochowa; for Lithuanians it was the shrine of Our Lady of Siluva. During pilgrimages to those holy places, both Poles and Lithuanians appealed for divine protection, redemption, and blessings. In both societies, local parish priests played critical roles in interpreting the sacred world and guiding the peasant relationship with God.[16]

Polish and Lithuanian Catholicism was also highly ethnocentric, with religious identity and political nationalism closely connected. During the seventeenth and eighteenth centuries, Russian and Prussian governments bordering Poland and Lithuania viewed Roman Catholicism as a form of political treason and a cultural intrusion. Throughout the nineteenth century, after taking Poland and Lithuania, Russian authorities tried in vain to restrict the church and suppress both languages. In 1864 and 1865 the tsar ordered that all teaching of religion in public schools be conducted in Russian and shortly thereafter ordered that Russian be used as the language of instruction in public and parochial schools. Russian authorities injected their language into Catholic liturgies. They outlawed crosses on Catholic churches, devotional processions, and parish temperance associations; demanded prior approval of all clerical appointments; eliminated clerical visitations with parishioners; forbade new construction of chapels or repair of old ones; and censored all sermons. But instead of transforming Polish and Lithuanian Catholicism into Russian Orthodoxy, the Russian assault only intensified local nationalism and Catholic identity. The struggle against Russian domination often seemed to go hand in hand with defense of the church and promotion of the faith.[17]

But if the Poles and Lithuanians connected religion and nationality, they were not as intense about it as the Irish and French Canadians. They had, of course, strong loyalties to the institutional church, which were reflected in all forms of commitment. Beyond regular attendance at Mass and parish activities, the Polish and Lithuanian peasants were quite willing, even under economic duress, to contribute financially to the local parish. During prosperity they were especially generous, making sure that local priests lived in comfort and security. Polish and Lithuanian families always took great pride whenever a son entered the priesthood. Unlike that of the Irish priests, however, the influence of Polish and Lithuanian priests did not extend far beyond religious questions. In both Poland and Lithuania, although most people were Roman Catholics, there were large numbers of Jews, Protestants, Eastern Rite Catholics, and Russian Orthodox, creating a social heterogeneity that prevented the total fusion of religion and nationality. Nor was Lithuanian religious nationalism as strong as its Polish counterpart. Lithuanians had been converted to Roman Catholicism quite late in the Middle Ages, and their historical identity with the church was not quite as powerful as that of the Poles. Until well into the nineteenth century, Lithuanian nationalism and Lithuanian Catholicism were subcultures of Polish nationalism and Polish Catholicism. Not until the great Russian assault on Lithuanian culture in the nineteenth century did Lithuanian nationalism emerge from the Polish shadow. Polish and Lithuanian ethnicity had evolved against the dual backdrop of Prussian Lutheranism and Russian Orthodoxy, requiring a tentative political posture from the church as boundaries shifted and domination changed. For centuries, on the other hand, the overwhelmingly Roman Catholic society of Ireland had resisted Anglo Protestantism with unparalleled passion, and priests had served as religious as well as political leaders. The church and national identity in Ireland, and to a lesser extent in Quebec, had become virtually synonymous. Although the political dimensions of Polish and Lithuanian ethnoreligion did not rival those of the Irish or French Canadian, they were more powerful among the Poles and Lithuanians than among most other East Europeans.[18]

Religious life among Czech Catholic peasants was quite different. Like other peasants, Czechs pursued religion on a number of levels—the natural, supernatural, and formal, mixing ancient traditions with more modern forms of Catholicism. They too believed in supernatural spirits such as water spirits (*vodnik*) or forest ghosts (*bejka love*). Snakes living beneath their houses supposedly were household spirits. The Easter season was especially filled with folk customs. Peasants colored Easter eggs in a modern version of ancient fertility customs. On Good Friday the peasants refused to plow the fields, believing the earth was the repository of the dead Christ. They got up before dawn to bathe in a creek or pond and to wash their animals to guarantee good health. To celebrate the feast of Corpus Christi, priests blessed catkins and pussy willows, which were then placed behind picture frames and between boards in stables to prevent sickness and tragedy.

The peasants were also devoted to national and local saints, arranging their agricultural season around the Roman Catholic calendar. First plowing was reserved for St. Gregory's Day (March 12). Turnips and cabbage were sown on St. Mark the Evangelist Day (April 25) and then transplanted on St. Vitus Day (June 15). Flax was sown on St. Adalbert's Day (April 23), and potatoes were hoed before St. John the Baptist Day (June 24). Throughout Bohemia peasants paid homage to St. Wenceslaus, the tenth-century duke of Bohemia, and his mother, St. Ludmila, for planting the church in their homeland. The Blessed Agnes of Bohemia rivaled St. Ludmila for their devotions. On May 16 each year, the feast of St. John Nepomuk was celebrated with bonfires and votive lamps in memory of his martyrdom. A cult devotion to Saints Cyril and Methodius was slowly developing in the nineteenth century. Tens of thousands of peasants also made annual pilgrimages to the shrines of the Virgin Mary—at Hostyn in Moravia and at Pribram in Bohemia.[19]

But Czech Catholicism parted company with its Polish and Lithuanian counterparts on the question of institutional commitment. Religious conflict had characterized Czech history since the fifteenth century, preventing Czech nationalism and Roman Catholicism from ever achieving the unity they reached in Poland and Lithuania, let alone Ireland and Quebec. The old Bohemian kingdom became the first Protestant country in Europe when Jan Hus led his revolt against the church. A priest who greatly resented German influence in Bohemia and praised Czech ethnicity, Hus preached all of his sermons in the native tongue, personally helped transform the Czech alphabet, and through his writings created a literary language out of a peasant idiom. His execution for heresy in 1415 gave Czech nationalists a martyr, and Czech nationalism became intricately entwined with a Protestant, rather than a Roman Catholic, spirit. When the German-Catholic Hapsburgs took over Bohemia after the Battle of White Mountain in 1620, Roman Catholicism was reimposed on every peasant village. But most peasants, even though they superficially accepted "recatholicization," saw their local priest as an agent of Hapsburg as well as Roman authority. In parts of southern Bohemia, the church owned vast amounts of property and acted as landlord for many peasants. Those Czechs often became as alienated from the church as later generations of Sicilian peasants would be. So although it was carefully concealed, a deep hostility toward the institutional church permeated much of Bohemia.[20]

A strong tradition of liberal "freethought" also permeated Bohemia in the nineteenth century. Ranging from a tolerant indifference toward religious concerns to militant agnosticism and anticlericalism, Czech "freethinkers" wanted nothing to do with organized religion, especially with the Roman Catholicism they associated with German oppression. Committed to separation of church and state, freedom of thought, and scientific rationalism, they helped undermine the Roman Catholic emphasis on authoritarian control, conservatism, and corporate society. By the late nineteenth century, the Roman Catholicism professed by most Czechs had become compromised by nationalism, liberalism, and rationalism.[21]

Many Czech nationalists had hoped that their religious skepticism would spread to Slovakia, but the Slovaks remained devout and highly committed. Slovakia accepted Christianity under the missionary endeavors of Sts. Cyril and Methodius, who came from Byzantium in the ninth century, converted the population, and then declared their loyalty to Rome, leaving Roman Catholicism as the spiritual heritage of the Slovaks. A mountainous country lying between the plains of Hungary and Poland, Slovakia generally had been able to avoid the cyclical warfare between Tartars, Turks, Swedes, Russians, Germans, Poles, and Lithuanians and enjoyed the stability and conservatism of people tied to the same isolated region for generations. Not unlike the Roman Catholics of southern Germany, the Slovaks were a highly traditional people, devoted to their families, parishes, and villages. The liberalism and rationalism of Czech culture, with its devotion to humanism, individual liberty, and moral autonomy, had no place in Slovak culture. During and after the Catholic Reformation, Jesuit scholars adopted the Slovak vernacular to teach the peasants and wean them away from their temporary loyalty to German Lutheranism. Slovaks thereafter identified Roman Catholicism with their national aspirations. When Magyars in Hungary tried to eradicate the Slovak tongue in the nineteenth century, the language took refuge in Catholic churches where people openly used it in their songs, prayers, and confessions. Finally, Magyars worked to isolate Slovaks from the liberal nationalism of pan-Slavic culture and to preserve their traditionalism. Not surprisingly, the Slovak Catholic peasants paralleled Polish Catholics in the intensity of their devotions.[22]

Magyar Catholicism was unique as well, especially in its natural and supernatural convictions and political identity. Like other peasants, Magyars believed in a world where good spirits competed for power with evil spirits. Evil spirits or devils or witches, known as *taltos*, performed all sorts of wizardry. Peasants worried about the "evil eye" looking upon them and bringing misfortune. Parents anxiously had their baby baptized as soon as possible to prevent the devil spirits from stealing it and substituting a devil's baby. To protect themselves through divine intervention, Magyar peasants also appealed to a pantheon of saints, particularly St. Stephen, the patron saint of Hungary; St. Elizabeth of Hungary, who guaranteed bountiful harvests at the Whitsun festivals; St. Gregory and St. Blaise, the patrons of children and teaching; St. Mark, on whose patron day in April the wheat crop was blessed; St. Ivan, the patron of marriage and fertility; and St. Lucia, whose powers could thwart the evil designs of witches.[23]

But like the Czechs, the Magyars did not easily make the jump from informal peasant religion to a universal devotion to formal, institutional religion. In the tenth century, the largest Magyar clan accepted Christianity, and in return Pope Sylvester II, in the year 1000, named Stephen the First as king of Hungary. But the Reformation divided Hungary into Catholic and Protestant camps. Calvinist ideas came into Hungary in 1520 and flourished in the German mining and trading centers of the north, in Transylvania, and finally in Hapsburg Hungary. Lutheranism was especially influential in the cities, Calvinism in Transylvania and the Plains, and Unitarianism in remote Magyar villages of the eastern Carpathians. By the mid-nineteenth century only half of Magyars were Roman Catholics. Perhaps one-sixth of the population was Calvinist and Greek Orthodox. Eastern-Rite Catholics and Lutherans each claimed one-tenth of the population. Approximately 2 percent were Hungarian Jews. National identity and Roman Catholicism, so closely connected in Ireland, Quebec, Poland, Lithuania, and Slovakia, did not come together in Hungary, because religious loyalties were divided. Magyar Catholicism was also compromised by a liberal nationalism similar to that of the Czechs. Mid-nineteenth-century rebellions against the Hapsburg regime by liberal nationalists like Louis Kossuth identified German oppression in Vienna with Roman Catholic conservatism. As in Bohemia and Moravia, Magyar nationalism, liberalism, and industrialism had a decidedly Protestant flavor. Without the ideological fervor of political nationalism, Magyar Catholicism never developed the overwhelming mass loyalty and commitment to the institutional church that were characteristic of the Catholicism of the Irish, French Canadians, Poles, Lithuanians, and Slovaks.

The Catholicism of the peasant Slovenes and Croatians rested between that of the Poles and Lithuanians on the one hand and the Czechs and Magyars on the other. Slovenes and Croatians too believed in mythological shepherds, nymphs, satyrs, ghosts, spirits, and witches capable of influencing human life. They maintained the traditional values of the nineteenth-century peasant village—social solidarity, strong kinship ties, and a subsistence, family economy. A suspicion that good things like respect, status, health, prosperity, and security all existed in finite quantities was strong, implying the necessity of balance. Whenever "things" were out of balance, those finite assets were denied to someone in the village. To maintain that balance, the peasants turned to the church. Each Slovenian or Croatian village had at least one church, usually sitting on high ground for all to see. Parish priests kept vital statistics and received maintenance support from local taxes, which most people willingly paid. The religious calendar was full of local saints' days, and roads were marked by numerous wayside shrines. Five regional Masses were held at the mountain church of Sveta Ana (St. Ann) on Krizna Gora in Slovenia, and villagers from forty miles around participated in all-night singing and prayer vigils. In 1800 a German observer wrote of Slovenia:

> However poor a village may be, its churches are usually clean, well-found and strongly built, especially the steeple. One church does not suffice for the village; many parishes have as many as seven or nine such temples, standing on mile-high mountains and dedicated to various saints. Yet as a rule such churches are visited only once a year. As there is usually no priest's house at the temple, all the vestments for the church ceremonies are carried up. On the feast day the innkeepers set up in huts or branches or tents; there is a sermon and a feast, and then since there is no shelter other than the temple of the Lord, all the faithful crowd into it to spend the night.[25]

But in both Slovenia and Croatia, the political and ethnic quagmire of nineteenth-century Austria-Hungary prevented any fusion of faith and nationality. In Slovenia, liberal nationalists directed their wrath against the Hapsburgs in Austria, who had long allied themselves with Roman Catholicism. The Protestant Reformation, by giving rise to a native Slovenian literature, had spawned a local national consciousness, but the masses of peasants remained loyal to the Catholic church and its local peasant monks and priests. Local priests, despite the church's close ties with the Hapsburgs, resisted Germanization. The breach between Slovenian nationalists and Hapsburg Catholicism widened late in the nineteenth century when church leaders in Slovenia began calling for a "Christian nationalism." Afraid that incipient Slovenian nationalism would break up the Empire and undermine church influence, these leaders campaigned for "Roman Catholic unity" rather than ethnic independence and for the prudent demise of the Slovenian language and assimilation into a Croatian or even "German-Slavic" cultural order based on religious unity. For Slovenian liberals, that was not much different from what they already had. They treated the church as a reactionary force in the empire, and although peasants remained devoutly Roman Catholic, they did not identify closely with the institutional church hierarchy. Nationalism and faith did not really blend.[26]

Nor did religion and nationality melt in Croatia. Both Slovenia and Croatia possessed strong loyalties to Western Europe, but among Croatians that identity was sharpened by centuries of conflict with Byzantine Orthodoxy and Turkish Islam. Byzantine culture and Eastern Orthodoxy had moved far up the Adriatic in the Middle Ages, converting the Serbs to the Cyrillic alphabet and the Orthodox tradition. Croatians resisted both and remained loyal to Latin and Roman Catholicism. The expansion of Islamic Turks into southern and central-eastern Europe in the fifteenth and sixteenth centuries further sharpened Croatian identity. But despite a sharp religious identity, Croatian nationalism was directed against both the Hapsburgs in Vienna and the Magyars in Budapest. Croatian liberals often resented the church's close association with the established powers of the Empire. In Croatia devout Roman Catholicism did not acquire a nationalistic dimension comparable to that of Ireland or Poland, and the institutional commitments of the peasants were consequently not as intense.[27]

While the religious differences among Poles, Lithuanians, Czechs, Slovaks, Magyars, Slovenians, and Croatians revolved around questions of language, local tradition, and political nationalism, the Rusins and Ukrainians were even further separated by Eastern Rite or Uniate Catholicism. Christianity had first come to the Ukraine from Constantinople and the Byzantine Empire and was adopted as the state religion by Vladimir the Great in 988. With the great schism between Roman and Eastern Christianity, the Ukrainians recognized the patriarch of Constantinople, not the pope, as their spiritual leader. They remained Eastern Orthodox until the fourteenth century, when Poland acquired control of Galicia in the western Ukraine and began to catholicize the population. More than two centuries later, in 1596, the Act of Union brought the Rusins and Ukrainians back into the Roman Catholic fold. The pope left the Orthodox rite with its Old Slavonic liturgy and ceremonies in place, allowed communicants to receive both the wine and bread during the celebration of the Eucharist, and permitted priests to marry before their ordination. The Eastern Rite also had some followers in Poland, Slovakia, and Hungary, but these were a minority. Because of the tradition of the Eastern Rite, they were also among the most loyal to the church, not only because they had consciously left Eastern Orthodoxy but also because they often had had to struggle to maintain the Eastern Rite against demands to assimilate from such Latin Catholics as the Poles and Magyars. In Transcarpathia and the Ukraine, the Eastern Rite was the tradition of the majority, which set them apart from all other East-European Catholics.[28]

As they passed through Castle Garden and later Ellis Island, the East-European Catholics already possessed a strong sense of ethnicity based on shared perceptions of village, land, work, family, history, nationality, and religion. Like every other immigrant group, they tried to reconstruct Old World institutions as a means of coping with their new environment. In the great urban centers of the Northeast and upper Midwest, a series of Polish, Lithuanian, Czech, Slovak, Magyar, Slovene, Croatian, Rusin, and Ukrainian communities appeared, not as separate and enclosed residential villages but as organizational communities revolving around the Catholic parish, religious associations, and parochial schools. These immigrants could not, of course, recreate American life in an Old World mold, but their ethnic communities, particularly the church, played a critical role in their acculturation and assimilation.

6

The Mediterranean Catholics

Along with several million East Europeans came millions of Mediterranean Catholics to the New World. The migrations were quite similar. Overpopulation, industrialization, urbanization, and the appearance of a migrant work force in the expanding Atlantic economy had undermined traditional village life for both peoples. Just as similar forces were "pushing" both groups from Europe, job opportunities in America and political and religious freedom were "pulling" them across the Atlantic. Both groups had also come from the integrated world of village, land, and family and had mixed older folk elements with formal Roman Catholicism. They also came in chain migrations in which large portions of whole villages moved to new communities in the United States. The migrations of the Portuguese, Spaniards, Basques, Southern Italians, Melkites, and Maronites were not much different from the journeys of the Poles, Lithuanians, Czechs, Slovaks, Magyars, Slovenians, Croatians, Rusins, and Ukrainians.[1]

But the groups were also very different. Race and skin color became a problem in the United States. Most southern Italians and Syrians, for example, had darker complexions than Irish, German, and East-European Catholics, and their place in American society was at least partially determined by skin color. Language also separated them from East-European immigrants as well as from the general society. Complicated national histories did the same. Large numbers of Basque immigrants, for example, had chafed for years under French and Spanish control and considered themselves quite distinct. Southern Italians, after years of foreign occupation and exploitation at the hands of northern Italians, did not even consider themselves inhabitants of Italy. Finally, Mediterranean Catholics, from the devoted Syrian-Lebanese Maronites to the anticlerical southern Italians, had unique perspectives on religion and the church. Religion set them apart from Protestants as well as from other Catholics.

Between 1860 and 1924 approximately 2.2 million Italians settled in the United States. Most of them came from an area known as the Mezzogiorno (the six provinces of Abruzzi, Campania, Apulia, Basilicata, Calabria, and Sicily in southern Italy). By 1870 perhaps 80,000 people had emigrated from northern Italy. Relatively prosperous, cosmopolitan, industrialized, and fair skinned, they considered themselves superior to southern Italians, and especially superior to Sicilians. Like other ethnic groups, they established an associational network in the United States, forming such mutual aid groups as the Society of Italian Unions and Fraternity and establishing newspapers like *L'Eco d'Italia*. Their arrival raised the eyebrows of many Protestants and caused some resentment among Irish and Yankee Catholics, but the new immigrants were few in number and quickly merged into mainstream America. Indeed, they were swamped and generally disappeared in the mass immigration from the Mezzogiorno in the 1890s and early 1900s.[2]

Unlike many East Europeans, southern Italians had little sense of patriotic nationalism when they left for the United States. Until the 1860s Italy had been divided into many small principalities and city-states. The country enjoyed considerable renown during the Renaissance, but by the nineteenth century it had gone the way of Spain, declining in prominence as France, England, and Germany had risen to power. By 1850 Sardinia, the Papal States, and Sicily were independent, but Austria controlled Lombardy and Venetia, and the Hapsburgs ruled Parma, Tuscany, and Modena. Some Italian nationalists nostalgically yearned for the glory of the years when Italian culture and Western civilization had been synonymous. Beginning in the 1850s, patriotic idealists like Camillo di Cavour and Giuseppe Garibaldi inaugurated the campaign for Italian unification. Allied with France against Austria, Sardinian armies conquered Parma, Lombardy, Tuscany, and Modena. Garibaldi's troops defeated Naples and Sicily in 1861. Garibaldi then ceded Sicily to Sardinia, and Victor Emmanuel became king of Italy. Austria ceded Venetia to Italy in 1866, and the Papal States joined the new country in 1870.[3]

Most southern Italians, however, hardly shared the patriotic nationalism; Italian unification had done nothing to improve their lot or soften their alienation. Everything south of Rome was terribly neglected. The Italian government sponsored land development and public education programs, but only in the north. Periodic promises of land reform, especially confiscation and redistribution of the great *latifundia* estates, were repeatedly ignored and forgotten. The government taxed everything the *contadini* (peasants) raised—wheat, cows, citrus, olives, mules, pigs, sheep, and poultry. The peasants often rebelled against the government, and at Naples in 1862 and Sicily in 1863, Sardinian armies crushed the insurrections. *Contadini* alienation was so deep than an extended guerrilla war plagued Italy throughout the last decades of the nineteenth century.[4]

Oppression at the hands of the northern Italians seemed only the latest episode in a long history of invasion and occupation. During the previous three thousand years, succeeding invasions of Etruscans, Greeks, Carthaginians, Romans, Moslems, Normans, Spaniards, French, and Austrians had overrun southern Italy. Southern Italians had grown suspicious of outsiders, and a powerful strain of isolationism permeated Mezzogiorno culture. For the *contadini,* the watchwords of survival in the alien political world were suspicion and caution. Real justice and law were not one and the same; indeed, they were usually contradictory. Instead of guaranteeing justice, the law—whether Greek, Roman, Moslem, Norman, Austrian, or French—had been an instrument of oppression, crushing local sovereignty and enslaving peasant masses.[5] Disrespect for law, authority, and government became ingrained in Sicilian culture, with peasants taking for granted the hostility of their political environment and automatically assuming that personal security and liberty were family responsibilities. An extended clan of relatives, *la famiglia* was the purpose of Italian existence. All other political, economic, social, and religious institutions paled in comparison. Patriotism did not exist beyond the family, and obedience to law simply meant obedience to the family. When the *contadini* managed to transcend the family, their horizons did not extend much beyond the village. If an immigrant was the first of his family to settle in the United States, he would usually seek out the fellowship of people from his own village in Italy. This was the spirit of *campanilismo*—localism. In Chicago, for example, western Sicilians generally lived together, with the immigrants from Altavilla on Larrabee Street, those from Alimena and Shiusa Scalfani on Cambridge Street, and those from Bagheria on Townsend Street. In the absence of *la famiglia,* they turned for security to friends and neighbors—*paisanos*—in the spirit of *campanilismo.*[6]

Southern-Italian Catholicism was quite different from the faith of Irish, German, East-European, or French-Canadian immigrants. Centuries of invasions, discrimination by northern Italians, and exploitation at the hands of rich landlords had left southern Italians intensely suspicious of the upper classes—the *signori.* A major landowner interested in protecting its property, the church had worked to accommodate each succeeding generation of foreign rulers, usually becoming part of or at least allied with them and, as far as the *contadini* were concerned, also becoming part of their problems. As a prominent landlord regularly collecting tithes and rents, the church alienated many peasant tenants. The *contadini* often saw the church as just another branch of the *signori.*[7] They had little respect for the church or its representatives. While the Irish and French Canadians placed great spiritual importance on regular attendance at Mass and on confession and Holy Communion, *contadini* men usually confined church attendance to Easter Sunday and their patron saints' days. Compared with the Irish or the Poles, the southern Italians sent few young men into the priesthood. Unlike the Irish, who revered priests and looked to them as spiritual and temporal leaders, the southern Italians often disdained the clergy. Celibate and cassocked, the priests appeared effeminate to the *contadini,* an especially severe handicap in a culture prizing virility. And as collectors of rents and tithes, the priests seemed to serve as agents for the *signori.*[8]

But like the religion of East Europeans, the faith of the *contadini* was a syncretic mixture of the natural and supernatural. In the capricious, often cruel world of the Mezzogiorno, where death and poverty constantly stalked the *contadini,* there were no random events, at least in the peasant mind. Virtually nothing was a matter of chance. Every level of human experience, including love, hate, sickness, natural calamities, and death, as well as all the phenomena of nature, were highly integrated and tied directly to the benign or malignant forces of the unseen world. Roman Catholicism fused with the magical power of the "other side." What someone might have called pagan magic was simply the traditional rites of older Greek, Roman, Norman, Moslem, Sicilian, and Byzantine civilizations upon which Roman Catholicism had been superimposed. Italian folk religion included an assortment of rituals, oaths, charms, spells, incantations, potions, amulets, and behavior codes aimed at propitiating the spirits, thwarting danger, controlling devils, and averting death. The source of danger and pain was always *mal'occhio* or the evil eye, and the *contadini* possessed a variety of magical spells to bring success to every endeavor—from bathing or baking bread to planting crops or going to sleep at night. For especially worrisome problems or imminent dangers, the *contadini* sought out the services of magicians or supposed witches whose especially powerful spells could overcome the most deep-seated curses. In that context of magic, the peasants enjoyed power and control over their environment and were neither passive nor fatalistic. Magic was a daily, sometimes hourly, expression of faith in and vulnerability to the supernatural world.[9]

In its orientation to magic and folk tradition, *contadini* religion was closely linked to the local village in the spirit of *campanilismo.* Each village had its own shrines, patron saints, madonnas, and apocryphal histories. Although the church played an indispensable role in such rites of passage as baptism, confirmation, marriage, and burial, intricacies of theology were of little interest to Mezzogiorno peasants. They were much more concerned with the present, immediate problems of everyday life. Even God was a distant force preoccupied with the complex affairs of the universe and too busy to worry about the petty needs of poor peasants. Instead of directing their prayers to that distant authority, from whom they felt quite separate, the *contadini* created an intermediate body of powerful advocates functioning between them and God. These were the saints, whom all Catholics revered but whom southern Italians elevated to the level of cult worship in the spirit of *clientismo.* Instead of appealing to a distant, abstract God who might not be listening, they turned to local patrons or specialized saints to serve as emissaries to God, pleading the case of *contadini* clients. Unlike most other Catholics, the southern Italians venerated a myriad of saints, like San Rocco, Santa Lucia, the Madonna del Carmen, Santa Rita, or San Biagio. The *contadini* relationship with the saints was almost a covenant theology. In return for devotion as well as gifts of money or lighted candles, the peasants expected positive treatment—illnesses to be healed, harvests to be abundant, unfaithful husbands to be restored, or strangers to be removed. When problems were not solved, the *contadini* had no qualms about blaming the saint and turning to others. Life for the *contadini* was capricious and unpredictable, and the saints as well as God were capable of responding just as irrationally or oppressively as any government. One simply had to find the saint willing and prepared to respond positively and rationally to peasant needs.[10]

In each Italian village, the central religious event was the annual feast day (*festa*) to celebrate the local patron saint. On that day the *contadini* released their spirituality in a great burst of holiday energy. Everyone attended High Mass after donating gifts to the parish. Picture cards or wax figures of the saint changed hands as vendors hawked their goods. In return for special contributions, a few faithful were able to carry the statue of the saint through the village in a *festa* procession. Marching brass bands accompanied the statue, as did colorfully dressed members of the sodalities and confraternities. Hundreds of people followed the procession, some making an atonement of their own by walking barefoot or on their knees; some carrying large, brightly lit candles; and others weeping or quietly meditating in trancelike states. Along the way, people pinned currency on or placed coins at the base of the statue. Fireworks, animal fairs, games of chance, songs, and dancing were all part of the *festa*. Blessed with enormous vitality, the folk Catholicism of the *contadini,* though quite different from other immigrant faiths, bound the ethnic community into a whole.[11]

From the western end of the Mediterranean, approximately 140,000 Spanish peasants came to America during the Great Migration. Most were ethnic Spaniards, and perhaps 20,000 were Basques. The church was the central fabric of Spanish culture, occupying a unique role in political nationalism as well as the worldview of most peasants. In 718 Moslem invaders from North Africa conquered Iberia and tried for centuries to convert Catholic Spain. They tried in vain. Between 718 and 1492, Catholic leaders directed the *Reconquista* of Spain, a seven-centuries-long crusade to purge the Moslem "infidels." In the process, Spanish Catholicism acquired a cultural militancy unmatched in the Western world. The final expulsion of Moslem invaders at Granada in 1492 coincided with the unification of Spain, which came when Queen Isabel of Castile married King Ferdinand of Aragon. National unity and militancy coexisted and inspired one another in a symbiotic relationship. Beginning in 1478, for three centuries the Inquisition or Holy Office tried to eliminate heresy, punishing even the slightest deviations from orthodoxy. Spanish identity and Roman Catholicism became inextricably entwined.[12]

Although religion and nationality were closely linked, the ethnopolitical loyalties of Spanish peasants by the nineteenth century were still not as intense as those of the Irish. The Irish-Catholic struggle for survival was a contemporary concern to the nineteenth century, not a distant historical phenomenon as it was for Spain. While Irish Catholics consciously exercised their faith as a religious and political statement, Spanish peasants, after so many centuries, were taking the political dimension of religion for granted. But like peasant religion in general, Spanish Catholicism was a complex concern of formal religion and informal spiritualism fusing the natural and supernatural. Most Spanish peasants had an elaborate set of instrumental devotions to various saints as a means of propitiating nature and God. Spain had three divine patrons—the Virgin of Pilar, St. Teresa, and St. James—and thousands of regional and local patrons and shrines, a kind of *clientismo* similar to that of the southern Italians. There were nearly four hundred shrines dedicated to the Virgin Mary throughout the country, for Mary was central to peasant devotions. In the Nansa Valley, for example, there were three shrines to the Virgin Mother: Our Lady of La Peña in Calis, Our Lady of Luz in Peña Sagra, and Our Lady of Mt. Carmel. The Virgin became a collective symbol of maternity in peasant life, the object of honor, reverence, and the familiar love and devotion extended to an elderly, earthly mother. Peasant love for the Virgin Mother was absolute because faith in her power and willingness to respond was so strong. Salvation was not a major preoccupation. Shrines, saints, chapel images, and devotions were more directly aimed at protection or prosperity in this life.[13]

The location of shrines was critical to peasant identity. Village and regional loyalties in Spain were strong, and over the years the geographical placement of shrines divided village from village and cultivated from uncultivated land. Peasants attached great significance to special geographical features, as if mountains or caves or rivers marked the boundary between the natural world they perceived and the supernatural world they tried to appease. Through donations, devotions, and individual promises at particular shrines, peasants confirmed the boundaries of their existence, reinforced the village identity, and exerted control over their environment.

Knowing they did not have the power to control their environment completely because there were certain "powers beyond," they placed their shrines at geographical points separating their temporal world from other peasant villages and their natural world from the supernatural. When problems seemed particularly bizarre or unexpected, they often attributed it to *mal ojo* (the evil eye) and turned to the occult, employing the services of local *divinas* (women with magical powers) to cast spells and hexes capable of neutralizing evil forces and accelerating the response of patron intermediaries.[14]

Peasant religion, both formal and informal, created a world within a world, a sense of belonging and of the imminence of the divine. Each village shrine and each devotion had begun as a revelatory act through the divine appearance of a heavenly being who guaranteed the value of individual piety and promises. In the sacred nature of certain animals like the swallow and the bee, plants like roses and juniper, and special geographic locations, the peasants walked the fine line between this world and the next, confident that the power and love of God, triggered by their own devotion and the intercession of the Virgin Mother and the saints, would order their lives and fulfill their destinies. To the Spanish peasants, nothing in their world was purely accidental or purely temporal; even the most apparently random events were all simply part of a much larger, meaningful whole.

The most separate and unique group of nineteenth-century Catholic immigrants—the Basques—also came from Spain. They were the most ethnically conspicuous. Referring to themselves as "Euskaldunak," or speakers of the Basque language, they were an enigma to non-Basque neighbors in southern France, northern Spain, Latin America, and the United States. For more than four thousand years the Basques have occupied their homeland in the Pyrenees and married endogamously, so much so that their collective blood types differ radically from those of the surrounding Spanish and French population. They consider themselves a separate people, even a separate race. Linguistic scholars generally agree that the Basque language is not part of the Indo-European group. Its syntax, morphology, and vocabulary are quite different. Beyond that, they have no idea about its origin. For the Basque people, the language was a secret code wherever they lived, insulating them from the outside world, culturally and physically. The Basques also viewed themselves as a physically strong people, able to endure hardship and survive because of physical and mental strength. Basque festivals in the Old World as well as in the New featured contests of physical strength and endurance. Finally, the Basques had a strong sense of unique identity, so much so that the language was replete with pejorative adjectives for non-Basques. Aloof, suspicious of strangers, and extraordinarily devoted to a sense of peoplehood, the Basques were an ethnic island in both Iberia and the United States.[15]

Basque immigrants first arrived on the American continent in the eighteenth century as Jesuit missionaries, sailors, ship captains, shipping agents, and merchants in the Spanish colonies. With the discovery of gold in California and the "gold rush" of 1849, hundreds of Basques emigrated from Spain, southern France, northern Mexico, and Latin America. Most of them were French and Navarrese Basques speaking French as well as Basque. When the gold boom began to dissipate in the early 1850s, Basques turned to work in the cattle and sheep industries, their traditional Old World pursuits, and began to spread throughout California and western Nevada. With the "new immigration" of the 1880s, thousands of Spanish and Vizcayan Basques began settling in the Great Basin area of eastern Oregon, southern Idaho, northern Nevada, and northwestern Utah. Despite common cultural origins, the French and Navarrese Basques of California and the Vizcayan and Spanish Basques of the Great Basin remained largely separate, with their own ethnic institutions and relatively little contact with one another.[16] Regardless of internal differences, their presence in California and the Great Basin inspired an always bemused and sometimes hostile reaction from surrounding Americans. A Canadian traveler in California in 1852 remarked that the

> Basques are a strange people, and we have large numbers of them amongst us. Generally speaking they are peaceable, hard working men, but when their passions are aroused they are very dangerous. They are probably the oldest people of Europe who have retained their customs and original language.... They are very powerful athletic men; their amusements after a hard days work being pitching quoits, and the iron bar, or heaving heavy stones.
>
> These fellows would make the finest soldiers in the world but they are too proud to enlist in any service. Their language is a

> mixture of barbarous old French and older Spanish, and not to be understood by the natives of either side of the Pyrenees. The Mexicans view them with a species of stupid wonder.[17]

Like many other new immigrant groups, the Basques came to the Great Basin in "chain migrations" of kinship and village associations. Although the Basques divided into French-Navarrese and Spanish-Vizcayan communities, they had little sense of political nationalism. They were loyal to language and the sense of "Euskaldunak," but beyond that their most powerful feelings of fidelity were confined to family, village, and at most to regional heritage. The consequence of regionalism and chain migration was much the same as it was for the Italians or the Slovaks. By transporting family and village loyalties to the New World, Basque ethnicity remained narrowly drawn and culturally confined.[18]

In addition to language, physical uniqueness, and sense of peoplehood, Basque ethnicity revolved around Roman Catholicism. Like Irish Catholicism, Basque Catholicism fell under the influence of French Jansenism when Basque clergymen trained in Jansenist seminaries. Their faith was one of *indarra,* or great devotion, to an authoritarian clergy, rigid acceptance of church discipline and dogma, and an ascetic, puritanical approach to morality. Unlike other Mediterranean Catholics, the Basques were devoted to the institutional church, willing to attend Mass and confession regularly, contribute financially to the maintenance of the chapel and rectory, and participate in fasting (*barurr*) and abstinence (*bijilia*). They were also known for the almost universal participation of men and women in the day-to-day affairs of the parish. In the tradition of the Basque patron saint, St. Ignatius, they were vigorous defenders of the church.[19]

Basque Catholicism was characterized as well by a rich liturgical calendar that bound the community close together and by a world of magic that the priest and church could control and manipulate. Processions of the entire community marked the feast days of St. Mark, St. Ignatius, and Corpus Christi; the Rogation Processions and the cemetery vigils held each Sunday between May and September also inspired universal attendance. On All Saints' Day children went to the community cemetery and set up a market to sell prayers for the dead. As for magic, the Basques believed in evil spirits known as *belhargile* and had faith in the ability of the priest to exorcise them. For that matter, the priest could also give an *eiharr meza,* a "desiccation Mass" to harm people. Basque Catholicism was unique in its devotion to the death theme. Funeral rites were the most vigorous expression of faith. Death was a central spiritual experience in Basque culture, setting in motion a series of sponsored Masses, funerary banquets, and special contributions for the salvation of the deceased. The rituals sometimes went on for years and involved family members, neighbors, and villagers. Anniversary Masses were celebrated for years after a death, and Basques felt a special obligation to attend the funerals of friends, relatives, employers, and employees. In Basque churches, each family possessed a rectangular space on the floor called a *sepulturie.* At Mass, Basque women arranged their chairs on their family *sepulturie.* Whenever a death occurred in the household, women covered the space with a black cloth and surrounded it with candles, symbolizing a burial place. The funeral process united the ethnic community, for Basques would meet, talk, share news, and revive old loyalties. They commonly held *gauelas,* or wakes, at the home of the deceased or at a nearby Basque hotel, and their *artu-emon* custom called for sponsoring a Mass for the dead, making a record of the donation, and expecting a similar donation when their own family needed it. Such Basque ethnic associations as the *Sociedad de Socorros Mutuos* in Boise, Idaho, sponsored burial crypts, cemeteries, and burial insurance for Basques in the Great Basin.[20]

The Portuguese constituted the other immigrant group from Iberia. Like its Spanish counterpart, Portuguese Catholicism had been sharpened to a crusading zeal by the eighth-century Moorish invasion from North Africa and the seven-hundred-year campaign by Iberian Christians to expel the Moslem "infidels." The subsequent years of the Inquisition, by trying to root out all heresy, had etched a powerful Catholic identity on Portuguese nationalism. For the Portuguese peasant, the village church was the focal point of life, the center of social as well as spiritual affairs. But as with other nineteenth-century peasants, another religious dimension—the supernatural—permeated the institutional Catholicism of the Portuguese. They attributed a wide range of ailments and misfortunes to the evil eye (*mau olhado*) or to evil air (*ar ruim*) and worried about the devil, evil spirits, and the influence of witches (*bruxas*) and sorcerers (*feiticeiros*). Like southern Italians, they turned to special healers (*curandeiras*), spells, and incantations, as well as to the powers of Roman Catholic saints and the Virgin Mother.[21] The most popular Portuguese saints were St. Anthony the Franciscan, whom peasants revered as the restorer of lost objects; St. John the Baptist, the peasant matchmaker; and St. Peter, the magnifier of romantic and sexual powers. All three saints' days were in June. Peasants had several devotions to the Virgin, but none could rival their dedication to Our Lady of Fatima, which developed during World War I after three children claimed to have seen the Virgin. A healing spring soon appeared at the site of the apparition. The Portuguese built a special shrine there, which quickly attracted tens of thousands of pilgrims each year. The Fatima devotion rapidly became the most important in Portugal.[22]

The mix of religion and magic was not the only dimension of Portuguese ethnoreligion that resembled its Sicilian counterpart. Like the southern Italians, Portuguese peasants had an extreme regionalism known as *bairrismo,* or loyalty to the local village. Most Portuguese peasants had little sense of nationalism because their political vision did not transcend the region and because the fusion of nationalism and religion was so distant in their past. *Bairrismo* was particularly important because most Portuguese immigrants were from the Azores and Cape Verde Islands, the former off the Portuguese coast and the latter far off the African coast. They identified hardly at all with continental Portuguese. Early in the nineteenth century, New England whalers began putting in at Azorean and Cape Verdean ports to take on supplies, fresh water, and Portuguese seamen. Many of those men eventually settled along the New England coast as whalers and fishermen while others moved to the textile-mill towns outside of Boston. Nearly 200,000 Portuguese settled in the United States between 1820 and 1924, and more than 80 percent were Azoreans and Capeverdeans.[23]

Bairrismo, particularly identification with an island, was quite strong among the Azoreans, and their Catholic faith reflected that localism. Like the southern Italians, the Portuguese celebrated a number of *festas* in honor of various patron saints, and like the Spanish they were devoted to *romarias,* or pilgrimages to remote shrines and sanctuaries, and made votive offerings at local shrines setting the boundaries of their village or region. One observer wrote that

> Every Sunday there is a festa in some church of the neighborhood. All the afternoon, rockets go up at intervals from the village, and crowds of people come from the neighboring hamlets, and even from the towns. . . . It is a huge picnic party, and when the pilgrimage is over they enjoy themselves thoroughly.[24]

Each locale had its special devotions distinguishing it from other areas. On the island of São Miguel in the Azores, peasants celebrated Lord Holy Christ of Miracles—Santo Cristo Day—venerating an image of Jesus brought to Portugal by two nuns in 1514. They also celebrated the *festa* of the Lord of the Stone. Madeirans made Christmas the special *festa* of the year. Pico Islanders were especially devoted to *Bom Jesus* (Good Jesus Day). Because of the intense localism, the Portuguese religious calendar was filled with patron saints' days; various regions emphasized one or several more heavily than others. In 1942 a New Englander described the Portuguese Christmas *festa* known as *Meninho Jesus:*

> The loveliest of all local customs was Menin Jesus, the little Jesus, brought by the Portuguese from the Western Islands. . . . Every window in their houses had a candle behind it. In the front room was a pyramid of graduated shelves. One candle on top, on the next shelf two saucers of sprouted wheat; on the next, two candles; on the next four saucers of sprouted wheat, and so on. These represented the Resurrection and the Light. At the bottom was a creche of little figures brought from the Western Islands. To everyone who came was given a tiny cordial glass of homemade wine . . . and a tiny cake.[25]

The bounties of the earth and the blessings of heaven symbolically came together in *Meninho Jesus.* Finally, the spirit of *bairrismo* often caused the resentment of continental Portuguese, not unlike the resentment southern Italians felt toward their northern countrymen. Continental Portuguese often looked down on the Azoreans and Capeverdeans as isolated, provincial people lacking sophistication and breeding. The islanders, of course, found continental Portuguese to be hopelessly conceited, and when church clerics came from Portugal to island parishes, the Azoreans and Capeverdeans often felt alienated and resentful, feelings that sometimes separated them from the institutional church.[26]

The major national *festa* among Portuguese peasants was the *Festa do Espirito Santo,* or Holy Ghost Festival, in honor of St. Isabel, the Holy Queen of Portugal, who built a church dedicated to the Holy Ghost during the fourteenth century. In the Azores, the *festa* was especially popular, with every village having a Holy Ghost Brotherhood responsible for the festivities. The festival included a lengthy procession through the village, the ceremonial crowning of the Queen of the Day, and the blessing and distribution of food to the poor. The crown was symbolic of the cultural union between the Portuguese empire and the Roman Catholic church. For Azoreans who were vulnerable to poverty, volcanos, and plagues, the Holy Ghost festival was a way of inviting divine protection. Azorean history was full of miraculous events confirming the power of the festival. When the Azoreans and Capeverdeans began coming to the United States, they carried their Roman Catholic faith, peasant supernaturalism, exaggerated *bairrismo,* and various *festas* and patron saints with them, contributing to the religious mosaic of American Catholicism.[27]

In addition to the Italians, Portuguese, Spaniards, and Basques, there were millions of Eastern-Rite or Uniate Catholics scattered throughout the Mediterranean area. Like the Uniate Rusins and Ukrainians in eastern Europe, they were loyal to the pope but remained faithful to their own liturgies, languages, customs, and canonical law. Instead of the Latin Rite, they followed one of five other rites: Byzantine, Alexandrian, Antiochan, Armenian, or Chaldean. Although their doctrine adhered to the Latin theology, Eastern-Rite Catholics received both the bread and wine during communion; crossed themselves from right to left rather than left to right; allowed priests to marry; and used the Julian instead of the Gregorian calendar. During the Great Schism of 1054, which divided Roman Catholicism from Eastern Orthodoxy, most of these groups had turned away from Rome in favor of the national Orthodox churches. Under different circumstances and at different times, they had returned to the Roman fold in terms of theological and sacramental loyalty but not in terms of style. The "keys of the kingdom" resided in Rome, but these Catholics preferred and retained their eastern traditions instead of Latin ones. The major Eastern-Rite groups in the Mediterranean, Asia Minor, and India were the Catholic Copts of Egypt, Ethiopian Catholics, Catholic Armenians, Malabar Catholics, Chaldeans, Syrian Melkites, and Lebanese Maronites.[28]

The most prominent Eastern-Rite groups emigrating to the United States in the nineteenth and twentieth centuries were the Melkites and Maronites. Melkites traced their origins back to the early Christian community at Antioch. When the Monophysite controversy developed in the fifth century, claiming that Christ could not have simultaneously been a man and God, the Melkites rejected the idea and gradually linked themselves to church leaders in Byzantium. Under Byzantine and later Moslem rule during the Middle Ages, Melkite patriarchs assumed civil as well as religious power in the Christian communities. Unlike the traditions of Western civilization, which stressed the separation of church and state, those of the Eastern Orthodox churches blended religion and nationality into a single political culture. The Western dualisms between church and state gave rise to the idea that not all power rested in the state and that other segments of the society could criticize and transcend the political establishment. Each country believed in religious sovereignty as well as political sovereignty, and the two were not one and the same. But in the East a more authoritarian tradition emerged. Since the patriarch was an agent of the state, the church could play no role in criticizing national politics. Under those circumstances, the Melkites came to see religion as nationality, and the goal of Syrian independence took on powerful religious tones. Not until 1725, after a century of Roman Catholic missionary endeavor under the sponsorship of French diplomats, did Melkite bishops break with the Eastern church at Constantinople. Their return to Rome made them an Eastern-Rite group.[29]

The ecclesiastical roots of the Lebanese Maronites were different, even though these people shared with the Melkites the Byzantine Rite, the Arabic language, and the same racial heritage. Maronite ties to Western Christianity were much stronger and deeper than those of the Melkites, which explains the later pro-West atmosphere of Lebanese society. In the fourth century, the Syrian monk Maron and a few followers established a monastery in the Orontes River valley and devoutly defended Roman Catholicism against Islam as well as against the Eastern-Orthodox schisms. With Maron as the abbot of the monastery and founder of the group, Maronite Catholicism had a strong contemplative tradition, preferring meditative to active piety. Canonized by grateful Roman Catholics for his vigorous defense of the faith, Maron became the patron saint of Lebanese Christians. In the 690s these Christians migrated to the Syrian mountains of contemporary Lebanon and converted most of the population. From the arrival of the first crusaders through the nineteenth century, the Maronites cultivated political and religious ties with the West and became the largest Christian denomination in Lebanon. As with other Eastern-Rite groups, their identification of religion with nationality was particularly strong, and Maronite spirituality became synonymous with Lebanese independence.[30] Perhaps sixty thousand Maronites along with fifty thousand Melkites migrated to the United States during the years of the "new immigration."

Contrary to what many American Protestants assumed, Roman Catholicism was hardly a monolithic culture, and the immigrants from the Mediterranean during the late nineteenth and early twentieth centuries complicated the diversity of the church. In Roman Catholicism, piety and religious commitment were dependent on local history, culture, and nationalism. Like the Irish and French-Canadian Catholics, the Maronites and Melkites more than most other immigrant groups blended religion and nationalism into a single organic whole, with the church playing a critical role in political as well as religious identity. At the same time, like the Rusin and Ukrainian Catholics, the Maronites and Melkites were a Uniate people, recognizing the legitimate, transcendent authority of the pope but retaining their local liturgies, language, and married clergy. At the other extreme of religious commitment were the southern Italians, for whom religion was a powerful emotional force quite independent of the church. While the Melkites and Maronites looked on the institutional church as a vehicle in their drive for freedom and independence as well as salvation, the southern Italians looked on the church as an oppressive force, one that had for centuries made life more, rather than less, difficult for the *contadini*.

In between were the community-centered values of Spanish and Portuguese Catholics, whose total loyalty to the institutional church had waned over the centuries or been compromised by the spirit of *bairrismo,* but whose identification with Roman Catholicism was still overpowering. Like the faith of the southern Italians, the faith of the Spanish and Portuguese operated less through the sacramental powers of the priesthood than through direct relationships with a pantheon of helpful saints ready to rescue the devoted and penitent from unexpected disasters. Finally, there was the unique society of Basque Catholicism, a puritanical piety that shared the Jansenist roots of Irish and French-Canadian Catholicism and the singular sense of ethnic isolation common to the Basque people. The arrival of all these groups into twentieth-century American society complicated the attempt to forge a Roman Catholic identity in the United States.

7

The Nationality Church

The mass immigration of nearly 9 million Roman Catholics between 1890 and 1925 transformed the church from a minority religion to the largest denomination in the United States. The associated growing pains were particularly difficult, not only for the country as a whole but for the church as well. A diverse people committed to their individual group lives, the Catholic immigrants from eastern and southern Europe frightened large numbers of native Americans and triggered another round of anti-Catholicism, led by the American Protective Association in the 1890s and the Ku Klux Klan after World War I. Roman Catholicism was rapidly becoming the nation's most visible faith, but many Americans were not ready for it. Nor were large numbers of native Roman Catholics, particularly those of Irish and English extraction.

The "new immigrants" seemed a strange lot. Their peasant backgrounds and peasant traditions appeared unsuited for an industrial society, just as their pantheon of saints, natural and supernatural spirits, magical notions, and intense Mariolotry were contrary to the ascetic legalism of the Irish and the discreet conservatism of the English. The peasant Catholics were also quite different from one another, and their varying levels of ethnoreligious commitment and political nationalism seemed confusing and sometimes sacrilegious to what had become an Irish church where faith and politics had fused. Finally, the languages, foods, costumes, holidays, and crowded, poverty-stricken ghettoes in the cities of the Northeast and Midwest unsettled many American Catholics, especially Irish Catholics, who already felt vulnerable in the Anglo-Protestant culture of the United States.

Catholic concern about the "new immigrants," however, was not nearly as intense as it had been in the 1880s and 1890s, at least in terms of the internal stresses it caused the hierarchy. The early disputes between the Irish on the one hand and the Germans and French Canadians on the other, the Cahensly debates of the early 1890s, and the "Americanist" heresy of the late 1890s had effectively suppressed any overt drives to transform immigrant culture. Still, Irish and English Catholics were afraid of being victimized by a resurgent nativism aimed at the new immigrants, of having to mix socially with them, and of the possibility that they might fall away from the church. To blunt anti-Catholicism without forcibly "Americanizing" the new immigrants, church leaders urged American Catholics to reach out in Christian charity, and to separate the new immigrants from other Catholics but to keep them in the fold of the church. They agreed, sometimes reluctantly, to establish nationality parishes.[1]

The nationality parish had already been forged by mid-nineteenth-century German and French-Canadian immigrants. It served several purposes. Most new immigrants believed that language and faith were inextricably linked, that in losing the language they risked losing their spiritual bearings, as if English and Protestantism and secularism were ideological companions. In English-speaking "Irish" parishes, immigrants felt out of place, unable to appreciate the rigid authoritarianism of Irish Catholicism or the saints, missals, and devotions peculiar to Ireland. When possible, they tried to attend parishes more familiar to them. Many Polish and Czech Catholics, especially early in the migration, settled near German-Catholic churches, just as Lithuanians attended Polish churches a few years later. Slovenes in New York, for example, worshiped in the basement of St. Nicholas, a German parish on Second Street, until 1916 when they dedicated their own ethnic parish, St. Cyril. In Pittsburgh, Slovaks first attended St. Wenceslaus Church, a Czech parish in the Troy Hill section, until they established St. Elizabeth's in 1895. But even then, religion in an alien tongue hardly seemed religion to them. The village church and priest, the festivals, and local saints were the institutions through which peasants came to terms with life and death. In America, they needed, for a time, to celebrate the same festivals, exalt the same patron saints, join the same confraternities and sodalities, and listen to the same ethnic priests they had in the Old World. Only Slovak or Polish or Rusin parishes with Slovak or Polish or Rusin priests provided ceremonial links with the past and spiritual continuity in the present.[2]

Beyond satisfying immigrant cultural and spiritual needs and fending off Protestant evangelism, the nationality parish saved the church from ethnic schism. By the 1880s Irish clerics and Irish parishioners dominated most territorial parishes, except in the Mexican areas of the Southwest and the German settlements of the upper Midwest. Irish influence was so great that most territorial parishes were little more than Irish-nationality parishes, a fact most immigrants tacitly accepted when they referred to territorial units as "Irish parishes."[3] Since Irish Catholicism was so passionately committed to ascetic legalism and puritanical authoritarianism, commitments that most eastern and southern Europeans did not share, internal conflict was certain. Separating the new immigrants into nationality parishes minimized those conflicts. For Irish parishioners, the nationality parish also satisfied their own nativist fears. By 1900, large numbers of Irish Americans were second- and third-generation workers who resented large-scale immigration and frequently battled over jobs and wages with Slavic, Italian, Portuguese, Syrian, and French-Canadian laborers. More acculturated to Anglo-American society than ever before, they had lost touch with their own immigrant roots and had little or no sympathy for the plight of the immigrant. Most first-generation Irish immigrants arriving in the 1880s and 1890s were products of the devotional revolution and the English school system. They wanted nothing to do with the strange languages and ways of the eastern and southern Europeans, and especially feared the possibility that their children might marry them. So nationality parishes insulated Irish immigrants and Irish-American Catholics from the new immigrants. In their own churches, schools, and parish societies, the Irish usually encountered only other English-speaking Irish Catholics. The nationality parish proved a segregationist blessing for both the Irish Americans and the new immigrants.[4]

The establishment of nationality parishes followed a consistent pattern. As immigrants began settling within the boundaries of a territorial parish, the bishop assigned a foreign priest as assistant pastor to minister to them. Once their membership was large enough, the immigrants would be given part-time use of the parish chapel. An Italian living in East Harlem recalled:

> In 1886 the Italians in East Harlem lived within a radius of a quarter of a mile. There was one church to go to and that was

> what we used to call the "American Church" at East 115th Street. . . . In those days we Italians were allowed to worship only in the basement part of the church, a fact which was not altogether to our liking.[5]

That was a typical experience unless the immigrants were the first to settle an area. In New Waverly, Texas, for example, Polish immigrants from Silesia first settled the area and established St. Joseph's parish in 1870. Although the priests and parishioners were overwhelmingly Polish, the parish was territorial rather than national because the immigrants had been there first and built the church. The same was true of the Infant of Prague parish in Buffalo, New York, because Czech immigrants dominated the neighborhood. But when the immigrants moved into a settled neighborhood with an existing territorial parish, they went through the same process as those Italians in East Harlem, using an existing parish on a part-time basis. These "annex" congregations were usually popular with local priests because attendance at Mass increased, as did financial contributions.[6]

Eventually, the immigrants asked the bishop for their own nationality parish, often after a lay committee of some kind had already purchased property and erected a chapel. Just as church authorities appreciated the "annex" congregations because they increased attendance and contributions, they often opposed separate nationality parishes. In Minneapolis, for example, a group of Slovak laymen, tired of attending a Polish national parish, decided in 1891 to build a Slovak church. They purchased a site, got permission from Bishop John Ireland to build the church, and then incorporated as a parish. They wanted to name the church SS Cyril and Methodius, the same name as their fraternal association, but Ireland refused, telling them that the name of one saint was sufficient. They agreed, but went ahead and had all parish stationery printed with SS Cyril and Methodius. As well as fearing competition for membership, local priests also feared a decline in attendance and contributions because of the new nationality parishes. Resources, they argued, were already spread too thin. Some Irish Catholics also worried that the nationality parishes would retard acculturation and inspire new suspicions that the Catholic church was a "foreign" element in the United States. Ultimately, however, local priests had to acquiesce or face the possibility of the new immigrants organizing independent Catholic congregations.[7]

As a compromise, bishops often tried to create mixed nationality parishes, such as St. Alphonsus in New York in 1900, which was English and German. Some bishops were more committed to mixed parishes than others. In the diocese of Green Bay, Wisconsin, for example, mixed parishes abounded, primarily because there was an ethnic mix in rural areas where the total population needed separate churches but was insufficient to support individual congregations. Between 1875 and 1900, bishops Francis Krautbauer, Frederick Katzer, and Sebastian Messmer created an extraordinary number of mixed nationality parishes:

- English and German: 17
- English and French: 9
- English, French, and German: 8
- Dutch, English, and German: 4
- German, Bohemian, and English: 3
- French, Dutch, German, and English: 2
- Dutch and German: 2
- German and Bohemian: 2
- Walloon and French: 2
- German and French: 2
- Dutch and Flemish: 1
- Polish and Bohemian: 1
- Polish and German: 1
- English and Polish: 1
- German, Polish, and English: 1
- English and Bohemian: 1
- English, Dutch, German, and Bohemian: 1

All too often, the mixed parishes did not prove to be successful compromises, because the same problems of language, custom, institutional commitment, and separate devotions plagued the parish. A mixed French-Canadian and German parish, for example, might be no more meaningful to the German parishioners than a territorial parish dominated by the Irish. More often than not, the mixed parishes separated into one territorial and one nationality parish as both groups insisted on their own language and traditions.[8]

Each of the new immigrant groups went through the transition of worshiping in an alien church, forming an "annex" congregation or being part of a mixed parish, and finally establishing its own nationality congregation. Nationality parishes composed of Polish immigrants began appearing in the 1870s. (St. Stanislaus, the largest Polish parish in the country, was founded in Chicago in 1893.) Bohemian immigrants constructed the first Czech Catholic church in 1854 in St. Louis and dedicated it to St. John Nepomuk. Sixty years later there were 270 Czech-speaking priests serving in 320 parishes and missions, and 55 of those parishes used the Czech language. Father Karoly Boehn established a Magyar parish in Cleveland in 1890. Parish organization in Chicago grew spectacularly between 1840 and 1900. Bishop William J. Quarter started establishing nationality parishes for German Catholics in the 1840s, and by 1870 there were 9 nationality and 16 territorial parishes in Chicago. Bishop Thomas Foley (1870-1879) and Archbishop Patrick Feehan (1880-1902) continued that trend, jointly establishing 47 territorial and 63 nationality parishes during those thirty years.[9] In diocese after diocese throughout the immigrant communities, nationality parishes flourished in the late nineteenth and twentieth centuries:

Cleveland

Polish

St. Stanislaus parish, Cleveland (1873)
Sacred Heart of Jesus parish, Cleveland (1888)
Assumption parish, Grafton (1894)

Polish

Immaculate Heart of Mary parish, Cleveland (1894)
Nativity of the Blessed Virgin parish, Cleveland (1898)
St. John Cantius parish, Cleveland (1898)
St. Barbara parish, Cleveland (1905)
St. Hedwig parish, Cleveland (1905)
St. Stanislaus parish, Lorain (1908)
St. Hedwig parish, Akron (1912)
SS Peter and Paul parish, Cleveland (1927)

Slovak

SS Cyril and Methodius parish, Cleveland (1902)
Nativity of the Blessed Virgin parish, Cleveland (1903)
St. Wendelin parish, Cleveland (1903)
Holy Trinity parish, Lorain (1906)
St. Andrew parish, Cleveland (1906)
St. John the Baptist parish, Akron (1907)
Our Lady of Mercy parish, Cleveland (1922)
St. Benedict parish, Cleveland (1928)

Magyar

St. Ladislaus parish, Lorain (1890)
St. Michael parish, Lorain (1903)
St. Emeric parish, Cleveland (1904)
Sacred Heart of Jesus parish, Akron (1915)
St. Margaret parish, Cleveland (1921)
St. Michael parish, Cleveland (1925)

Ukrainian

SS Peter and Paul parish, Cleveland (1910)
St. John the Baptist parish, Lorain (1914)
Holy Ghost parish, Akron (1915)
St. Mary parish, Cleveland (1952)

Italian

Holy Rosary parish, Cleveland (1892)
St. Rocco parish, Cleveland (1922)
Holy Redeemer parish, Cleveland (1924)
Our Lady of Mt. Carmel parish (West Side), Cleveland (1926)
St. Anthony parish, Akron (1933)
Our Lady of Mt. Carmel parish (East Side), Cleveland (1936)

Lithuanian

St. George parish, Cleveland (1901)
Our Lady of Perpetual Help parish, Cleveland (1920)

Bohemian

St. Procopius parish, Cleveland (1872)
St. John Nepomucene parish, Cleveland (1902)
Holy Family parish, Cleveland (1911)

German

St. Stephen parish, Cleveland (1869)
St. Joseph parish, Cleveland (1896)

Slovenian

St. Vitus parish, Cleveland (1893)
St. Lawrence parish, Cleveland (1901)
SS Cyril and Methodius parish, Lorain (1905)

Croatian

St. Paul parish, Cleveland (1902)
St. Nicholas parish, Cleveland (1902)
St. Vitus parish, Lorain (1922)

Syrian Melkite

St. Joseph's parish, Akron

Lebanese Maronite

Our Lady of the Cedars of Mt. Lebanon parish, Akron
St. Maron parish, Cleveland

Ukrainian

Holy Ghost parish, Akron
SS Peter and Paul parish, Cleveland
St. John parish, Lorain
St. Josephat parish, Parma

Hartford, Connecticut

Italian

Our Lady of Mt. Carmel parish, Meriden (1894)
St. Michael parish, New Haven (1895)
St. Anthony parish, Hartford (1898)
Our Lady of Lourdes parish, Waterbury (1898)
Our Lady of Pompeii (Holy Rosary) parish, Bridgeport (1903)
St. Anthony parish, New Haven (1903)
St. Peter parish, Torrington (1907)
Holy Rosary parish, Ansonia (1909)
St. Donato parish, New Haven (1915)
St. Anthony parish, Bristol (1920)
Sacred Heart parish, Stamford (1920)

St. Ann parish, Hamden (1920)
Our Lady of Pompeii parish, East Haven (1921)
Our Lady of Mt. Carmel parish, Waterbury (1926)
St. Lucy parish, Waterbury (1926)
St. Raphael parish, Bridgeport (1925)
St. Sebastian parish, Middletown (1930)

Polish

St. Stanislaus parish, Meriden
St. Casimir (Sacred Heart) parish, New Britain (1894)
St. Michael the Archangel parish, Bridgeport (1899)
St. Stanislaus parish, New Haven (1902)
SS Cyril and Methodius Parish, Hartford (1902)
St. Mary parish, Middletown (1903)
St. Joseph parish, Norwich (1904)
Holy Name parish, Stamford (1904)
St. Joseph parish, Rockville (1905)
St. Michael parish, Derby (1905)
St. Hedwig parish, Union City (1906)
St. Casimir parish, Terryville (1906)
St. Stanislaus parish, Waterbury (1912)
St. Adalbert parish, Thompsonville (1915)
Our Lady of Perpetual Help parish, New London (1915)
Immaculate Conception parish, Southing (1915)
St. Joseph parish, Suffiend (1916)
St. Stanislaus parish, Bristol (1919)
St. Mary parish, Torrington (1919)
Sacred Heart parish, Danbury (1924)
SS Peter and Paul parish, Wallingford (1925)
St. Joseph parish, Ansonia (1925)
St. Anthony parish, Fairfield (1927)
Holy Cross parish, New Britain (1927)

Lithuanian

St. Joseph parish, Waterbury (1894)
St. Andrew parish, New Britain (1895)
Holy Trinity parish, Hartford (1903)
St. George parish, Bridgeport (1907)
Holy Trinity parish, Hartford (1912)
St. Anthony parish, Ansonia (1915)

Slovak

St. John Nepomucene parish, Bridgeport
Sacred Heart parish, Torrington (1905)
SS Cyril and Methodius parish, Bridgeport (1907)
All Saints parish, New Britain (1918)
Holy Name parish, Stratford (1923)

Magyar

St. Stephen parish, Bridgeport (1899)
St. Ladislaus parish, South Norwalk (1907)

German

Church of the Sacred Heart parish, Hartford
St. Boniface parish, New Haven
St. Joseph parish, Bridgeport
St. Mary parish, Meriden
St. Cecilia parish, Waterbury
St. Peter parish, New Britain

French

St. Anne parish, Hartford
St. Louis parish, New Haven
St. Anthony parish, Bridgeport
St. Laurent parish, Meriden
St. Anne parish, Waterbury
St. Mary parish, Willimantic (1905)
St. Ann parish, Bristol (1907)

Syrian Melkite

St. Ann parish, Danbury
St. Ann parish, Waterford

Lebanese Maronite

St. Anthony parish, Danbury
St. Maron parish, Torrington
Our Lady of Lebanon parish, Waterbury

Ukrainian

St. Vladimir parish, Stamford
SS Peter and Paul parish, Ansonia
Protection of the Blessed Virgin Mary parish, Bridgeport
St. Mary parish, Colchester

St. John the Baptist parish, Glastonbury
St. Michael parish, Hartford
St. Josephat parish, New Britain
St. Michael parish, New Haven
St. Michael parish, Terryville
Protection of the Blessed Virgin Mary parish, Williamantic

Boston, Massachusetts

Italian

St. Mary parish, Salem
St. Anthony parish, Somerville
St. Leonard of Port Maurice parish, Boston (1873)
Sacred Heart parish, Boston (1888)
St. Lazarus parish, Boston (1892)
Holy Rosary parish, Lawrence (1904)
Our Lady of Mt. Carmel parish, Boston (1905)
St. Anthony parish, Revere (1906)
St. Tarcisius parish, Framingham (1907)
St. Francis of Assisi parish, Cambridge (1917)
St. Ann parish, Marlboro (1921)
Holy Family parish, Lynn (1922)
St. Anthony parish, Everett (1927)
St. Peter parish, Malden (1972)

Polish

St. John the Baptist parish, Salem
Our Lady of Czestochowa parish, Boston (1893)

Polish

Holy Trinity parish, Lowell (1904)
Holy Trinity parish, Lawrence (1905)
St. Michael parish, Lynn (1906)
St. Hedwig parish, Cambridge (1907)
Sacred Heart parish, Ipswich (1908)
St. Michael parish, Haverhill (1910)
St. Casimir parish, Maynard (1912)
St. Adalbert parish, Boston (1913)
Our Lady of Ostrobrama parish, Brockton (1914)
St. Peter parish, Norwood (1918)

Lithuanian

St. Casimir parish, Brockton (1898)
St. Francis parish, Lawrence (1903)
St. Peter parish, Boston (1904)
St. Joseph parish, Lowell (1908)
Immaculate Conception parish, Cambridge (1910)
St. George parish, Norwood (1912)

German

Holy Trinity parish, Boston (1844)

Armenian

Holy Cross parish, Cambridge (1920)

Portuguese

Our Lady of Good Voyage parish, Gloucester (1889)
St. Anthony parish, Lowell (1901)
St. Anthony parish, Cambridge (1902)
SS Peter and Paul parish, Lawrence (1907)

French

St. Joseph parish, Salem
St. Jean Baptiste parish, Lowell (1868)
St. Mary parish, Marlboro (1870)
St. Anne parish, Lawrence (1871)
St. Joseph parish, Haverhill (1876)
Our Lady of Victories parish, Boston (1880)
St. Jean Baptiste parish, Lynn (1886)
Sacred Heart parish, Brockton (1891)
Our Lady of Pity parish, Cambridge (1892)
St. Joseph parish, Waltham (1894)
St. Anne parish, Salem (1900)
St. Louis de Gonsague parish, Newburyport (1902)
St. Louis de France parish, Lowell (1904)
Sacred Heart parish, Lawrence (1905)
Our Lady of the Assumption parish, Chelsea (1907)
Notre Dame de Lourdes parish, Lowell (1908)
St. Stanislaus parish, Ipswich (1910)
St. Theresa parish, Dracut (1927)
St. Marie parish, Lowell (1931)

Syrian Melkite

Our Lady of the Annunciation parish, Boston
St. Joseph parish, Lawrence

Lebanese Maronite

St. Theresa parish, Brockton
St. Anthony parish, Lawrence
Our Lady of Mercy parish, Worcester

Ukrainian

Christ the King parish, Boston
St. John the Baptist parish, Salem.

In dozens of parishes throughout the Northeast and Midwest, the pattern of nationality parishes was the same as in Cleveland, Hartford, and Boston.[10]

For large numbers of these immigrant Catholics, the nationality parish played a central role in their adjustment to American society. Like an earlier generation of Irish, German, and French-Canadian Catholics living in an Anglo-Protestant culture, the southern and eastern Europeans at first felt vulnerable and sought isolation in the nationality parish. When the peasant economy of the Old World had disintegrated in the nineteenth century, threatening the nuclear family with economic destruction, peasants developed an associational life based on extended kinship ties, occupation, health and burial needs, politics, and religion. An organizational community life filled the void left by the collapse of the communal village. The proliferation of these Old World associations was an effective transition to life in the New World because the immigrants brought their associations with them to the United States. With the nationality parish and parochial school at the center of this associational network, the immigrants emotionally survived the stress of migration.[11]

The ethnoreligious associations reflected the Roman Catholic village and protected peasants from the Protestant world. Church newspapers, parish sodalities and confraternities, parochial schools, emigrant aid and mutual benefit societies, and religious associations dedicated to particular shrines and patron saints reconstructed the community that had died in the economic changes of the Old

World. More than 80 percent of East-European immigrant children attended parish schools using or teaching Old World languages. Although the immigrants often moved within the city or from city to city, the need for ethnic churches, parish schools, and Catholic societies remained strong. Between 1870 and 1880, for example, the Czech immigrants in Chicago established forty-nine mutual benefit societies, most originating in the villages of Bohemia and Moravia. The societies connected family members not only to other family members but also to others sharing mutual economic, social, or religious interests, horizontally integrating the ethnic community. Some societies were based on occupation, joining bakers or meatcutters or painters into individual groups. Societies like choirs, theater groups, and literary clubs had educational or cultural themes. Others were dedicated to patron saints like St. Procopius, St. John Nepomucene, St. Wenceslaus, St. Ludmila, and St. Agnes. Larger national associations of the immigrant parish and religious societies also appeared. The Polish Roman Catholic Union, Lithuanian Roman Catholic Alliance, Czech Roman Catholic Central Union, Slovak Catholic Federation, Croatian Catholic Union, Grand Carniolan Slovenian Catholic Union, Greek Catholic Union (Rusin), Ruthenian National Association (Ukrainian), and the American Hungarian Catholic Society supported parish societies in providing life insurance, sponsoring social events, and helping finance parochial schools. Parish newspapers—like the *Narod Polski* (Polish), *The New World* (Lithuanian), *Greek Catholic Messenger* (Rusin), *Svoboda* (Ukrainian), and the *Napredak* (Croatian)—kept immigrants in touch with neighbors, friends, and the Old World. The church, the parochial school, and parish societies provided cultural continuity for eastern and southern Europeans in America.[12]

The parish became the social and emotional center of the neighborhood, a concept the immigrants held dear. Few peasants, except for some Poles in south Texas, Slovenes in Minnesota, or Czechs in Nebraska, were able to acquire the land they yearned for so desperately. Soon after immigrating most of them realized how difficult it would be to acquire a decent farm. Yet their peasant need to define status in terms of property persisted; so the immigrants transformed it into a passion for home ownership. Even while sending large sums of money back to Europe, contributing to the construction of the parish church, and struggling in low-paying jobs, they managed to save money and accumulate the equity necessary for a down payment on a house. To finance home construction and provide mortgages, the former peasants established ethnic building and loan associations, like the Pulaski Building and Loan Association of Chicago. In 1904 an Illinois state official marveled at the dozens of Czech and Polish associations:

> The industry, thrift, and ambition to own a home prevalent to such a marked degree . . . is responsible for the standing and splendid record of these institutions. The people, believing and trusting in them, deposit their savings and hundreds of homes have been and will continue to be acquired through the popular agency.[13]

The small lot, comfortable home, and secure neighborhood became the New World equivalent of that Old World farm and peasant village. In their social values, the immigrants were traditional and conservative, preoccupied with the need to preserve what they had almost lost in the Old World.

Inside the nationality parish, the immigrants and their children constructed a new community. In Detroit, for example, the Poles started their own church in 1870 after spending years at St. Joseph's and St. Mary's, both German-Catholic parishes. They approached Bishop Caspar Borgess of Detroit, a German Catholic, about the need for a Polish national parish in 1870, and although somewhat reluctant because of financial pressures, he gave them permission in 1872, when St. Albertus was dedicated. Sitting on the corner of St. Aubin and East Canfield at the edge of the original Polish neighborhood, St. Albertus attracted large numbers of Polish families to the east side of Detroit. St. Casimir's served the Polish residents of west Detroit.[14]

As the Detroit population expanded north in the early 1900s, Polish immigrants found themselves worshiping again in a non-Polish parish, so they approached the diocese about the need for another nationality parish. In 1925 they received permission to establish St. Thaddeus parish. Father Sylvester Kaminski was assigned as the first pastor, and he served the parish for more than forty years, becoming a beloved institution to three generations of parishioners. Father Kaminski supervised construction of a wooden church in 1925 and soon opened a parochial school. By 1926 a brick building was serving as church, school, and convent; thirteen teaching nuns operated the school. Eventually, the parish covered two city blocks with its church, school, convent, rectory, and activities center. Father Kaminski also erected a grotto shrine to Our Lady of Czestochowa, with rows of votive lights and kneelers for worshipers, and placed it between the church and convent. As St. Albertus had a half-century earlier, St. Thaddeus became a magnet for Polish Catholics in northeast Detroit. The resident population of the parish grew from 200 families in 1925 to 450 in 1940, 800 in 1948, and 1,250 in 1954.

Poles there identified closely with St. Thaddeus parish, so much so that they could not distinguish between it and the neighborhood. When asked where they lived, parishioners routinely replied "St. Thaddeus," as if it were a political or housing subdivision. Located halfway between downtown Detroit and the northern suburb of Warren, the St. Thaddeus community was bounded on the east by Italians and on the west by blacks. Within the neighborhood were restaurants, bakeries, and ethnic markets serving fresh dark bread, Polish pastries and sausages, and dishes like kielbasa, pierogi, and golabki. Homes were well-kept wood-frame dwellings characterized by neat yards, flower beds, and small statues of the Virgin. The local funeral parlor fulfilled the needs of Polish-Catholic families and seemed almost an adjunct of St. Thaddeus church. Suspicious of their Italian and black neighbors, the people of St. Thaddeus were inner-directed, focusing their social energies on the parish.

It was the center of community life. Inside the church, and from the lips of Father Kaminski, they heard a familiar liturgy, listened to familiar sermons, and received absolution in their own language. In the parish parochial school, especially in the 1930s, 1940s, and 1950s, children received an education within the larger contexts of Roman Catholic values, Polish culture, the Polish language, and firm discipline. Most people in the parish viewed it as a mortal sin to let their children attend a public school, even if they could hardly afford the tuition at the parish school. Parish organizations dominated social life at St. Thaddeus, including the Dad's Club and Usher's Club for men and the Madonna Guild and Altar Society for women. On dozens of evenings each year, one or another of the parish societies sponsored a social event as part of the religious calendar. Polish and American holidays were celebrated, and various musical, athletic, or entertainment projects were undertaken. The parish was the vehicle for Polish ethnoreligion. At St. Thaddeus, they built a replica of Christ's tomb on Good Friday and filled Easter baskets with food blessed on Holy Saturday. On Christmas Eve they celebrated "Wigilja" supper, sang "koledy" Polish carols, and distributed "Oplatki" wafers to friends and relatives. Following funerals they held a "Stypa" feast and celebrated a "Poprawiny" the day after a wedding. The parish and neighborhood had melted together, at least in the consciousness of most residents. Art Krogulecki, a member of St. Thaddeus, remarked in 1971:

> I was born in this house forty-one years ago and right here I'm gonna stay. In the last three years I put four thousand dollars into fixing up the place. Did all the work myself. And now, after all these years, the place is just what we wanted. We're close to the church, school, bus lines, and it ain't too far from work. So why should we move? The suburbs don't offer us nothing we can't get here.[15]

The Polish immigrants and their children and grandchildren had created a new village in the northeastern reaches of Detroit.

St. Thaddeus was hardly unique. In hundreds of nationality parishes throughout the country, the church met the needs of immigrant Catholics in similar ways. In New York, for example, the number of nationality parishes mushroomed when hundreds of thousands of southern Italians arrived in the 1880s, 1890s, and early 1900s. Like so many others, the Italians desperately needed to create a community in the New World, one that fulfilled the demands of *famiglia* and *campanilismo* so central to Old World culture. In the English-speaking, Irish-Catholic parishes of New York they found none of that, and yearned for a more familiar setting. In 1908, for example, Angelo Ressano complained that in the West Farm area,

> there exists an Italian colony numbering almost 2,000 that lives completely forgetful of its Christian obligations. . . . The cause is the lack of Italian churches or chapels in this part of the city where a priest of the same nationality, preaching the word of God, may keep alive . . . the sentiments of true Catholics. The people, eager to satisfy their religious duty, but ignorant of the English language, are forced to walk five or six miles to go to an Italian church. . . . It is for this reason that the Italians of this area would be happy to have their own chapel with a good Italian priest.[16]

The disciplined authoritarianism, ascetic puritanism, English language, and ethnic Irish characteristics of so many Catholic parishes in the city did not meet the needs of southern Italians. They needed their own parishes.

Because of poverty, a tradition of anticlericalism, suspicion of institutions outside the family, and a constant flow of new immigrants into the city, southern Italians had a difficult time establishing churches. Beginning as missions in the basements of Irish or German parishes, or even in storefronts, saloons, private homes, and rag shops, they created the institutions of community religious life. Often they resented their situation. Father Nicholas Odone complained about a ten-year sojourn in the cathedral basement in St. Paul, Minnesota: "What a humiliation for us, here, numerous as we are . . . to have to come here in this low and humid hall, placed under the feet of a dissimilar people who sometimes look down on us, in more than one case depending on the humor of others."[17] For a time, church officials in New York City experimented with mixing the Italian immigrants with Irish or German parishioners in the same church. In the spring of 1866, for example, Archbishop John McCloskey established St. Anthony of Padua to serve the Italian and Irish settlements on the Lower East Side. But usually such experiments did not work. At Transfiguration parish on Mott Street in Manhattan in the 1890s, an Italian priest said Mass to more than a thousand people each week in the church basement. The Irish priest heading the parish "did his best to make the two races coalesce, by compelling the Italians to attend services in the upper church, but found that far better results could be obtained by having the two people worshiping separately."[18] The nationality parish seemed the only alternative if the Italian immigrants were to remain in the church.

Between 1866 and 1900, fourteen Italian parishes were established in New York City, including the Hamilton Ferry colony in Brooklyn in 1882; Our Lady of Mt. Carmel and Holy Rosary in East Harlem in 1884; St. Raphael's on Forty-first Street in Manhattan in 1886; Our Lady of Mt. Carmel in Brooklyn in 1887; St. Joachim in the Lower East Side in 1888; and St. Philip Neri in the Bronx in 1891. Between 1900 and 1930, when Italian immigration to the United States totaled more than 2 million people, another forty-four Italian ethnic parishes appeared in New York City. Eventually, there were seventy-four of them in Manhattan, Brooklyn, Queens, the Bronx, and Staten Island.[19]

In that parish atmosphere, the peasants tried to reconstruct the village life they had left behind in the Mezzogiorno. Their loyalty to "local sanctities" was powerful, and they readily continued devotions to such village patrons as San Rocco, Santa Lucia, and La Madonna del Carmine. They spent large sums of money helping to finance the local *festa* back home as well as in New York, named their mutual aid societies after the village patrons, and insisted on having statues and altars exactly like those back home. Although usually reluctant to contribute to Catholic charities and building funds, they were more than generous with their time and money in recreating the Old World village *festa.* Because of the crowding of southern Italians in New York City, there were *festas* for one village saint or another every week in the late spring, summer, and early winter, filling the streets with celebrating *contadini.* During the *festa,* the immigrants decorated streets and buildings with banners, posters, statues, votive lamps, and lanterns and set up booths and shrines. A carnival atmosphere of religious devotion and exuberance for life permeated the neighborhood, confirming the village identity and spirit of *campanilismo.* In 1892 an Irish priest described the *festa* of St. Donatus in New York City:

> The procession . . . was held on last Monday with all the noise of brass band and fireworks in the streets of the 6th and 14th wards of the city. This procession passed the Church of the Transfiguration about ten o'clock. A priest (in cassock and surplice) and four altar boys came after the brass band. Then came the statue of St. Donatus carried on the shoulders of four men. Women and small girls followed with large and small candles and the men of the society brought up the rear. . . . The whole church was decorated with tinsel.[20]

The *festa* reached its emotional peak after Sunday Mass when the priest explained the virtues of the patron saint and invoked him or her to protect celebrants from pain, tragedy, and evil. A huge processional, led by brass bands and a statue of the patron saint carried by several parishioners, wound through the streets. Hundreds, sometimes thousands, of people followed the statue, bearing small and large candles or wax sculptures shaped like afflicted parts of the body. Along the way they pinned money and other valuables to the statue and prayed for deliverance from personal problems. The gestures, postures, and devotions of the *festa* also had a great significance for *la famiglia*, turning the *festa* into a participatory family ritual. In the processional, for example, Italian families purchased large wax candles and carried them behind the patron statue. The height and weight of the candle reflected the size of an individual or family problem. In hope of curing a sick, twenty-three pound child, for example, a mother might carry a twenty-three pound candle in the procession. A severe family emergency might require a huge candle that several members of the family would have to carry, signifying unity in facing the crisis. Family members, particularly the elderly, would repeat past vows and promises to the patron saint in the presence of children and grandchildren, insisting that the young make the same promise and transfer it across generational lines. During the *festa*, parishioners would exchange domestic disaster stories, showing how the family was threatened by unemployment, sickness, and death and how the divine intervention of the patron had redeemed them from the threats. The annual Italian *festa* not only reminded the peasants of Old World identities, it also recommitted individuals to families as the primary loyalty in life, underlining the central theme of Mezzogiorno ethnoreligion. The *festa* was a critical link between the Old World and the New.[21]

The number of nationality parishes established in the nineteenth and early twentieth centuries reflected immigrant commitments and religious values. The complex interrelationships between faith, nationalism, history, church, and individual piety separating ethnic Catholics in the Old World became even more pronounced in the United States because of the new immigrants' proximity to one another. Statistics are not absolutely reliable because territorial parishes often served exclusively ethnic communities. In Wisconsin and Ohio, for example, there were dozens of territorial parishes for communities composed almost exclusively of German immigrants and their descendants. Those churches were just as ethnic as the Irish territorial parishes in New York City. Many territorial parishes in New England were French in composition, as were hundreds of territorial parishes serving Mexican immigrants and Mexican Americans in south Texas. But despite those territorial parishes, which had overwhelmingly ethnic flavors, the inclination to form a nationality parish and support a nationality parochial school was a strong indication of immigrant commitments to the institutional church. The establishment of nationality parishes was most frequent among Polish, German, Lithuanian, Rusin, Ukrainian, Slovakian, French-Canadian, Syrian, and Lebanese immigrants and least frequent among Italian, Spanish, Portuguese, Magyar, Czech, Slovenian, and Croatian immigrants. Although table 7.1, based on the 1860-1982 editions of the *Official Directory of the Roman Catholic Church,* does not indicate the numbers of territorial ethnic parishes, it does include all of the nationality parishes in the United States between 1860 and 1982.

The number of parish parochial schools also revealed levels of commitment to the institutional church, as shown in table 7.2.

The tendency to establish the nationality parishes and their associated parochial schools reflected the immigrants' commitment to the church as the major social and cultural focus of their lives. Groups with large numbers of parishes compared to their total population as well as large numbers of parochial schools compared to the number of nationality parishes had powerful institutional loyalties to the church. The total number of parishes and parochial schools, however, is meaningful only in the context of the number of immigrants coming to the United States between 1880 and 1940. With nearly 3 million permanent immigrants settling here, the Germans were second only to the Irish as the largest Catholic group in the country. There were also 2.2 million Italians, 1.3 million Poles, 1.5 million Mexicans, 1 million French Canadians, 450,000 Magyars, 450,000 Slovaks, 300,000 Czechs, 270,000 Croatians, 240,000 Rusins, 180,000 Slovenes, 180,000 Portuguese, 160,000 Ukrainians, 200,000 Lithuanians, 110,000 Spaniards, 70,000 Maronites, 60,000 Melkites, and 30,000 Basques.[23] Although the Italians had a total of 308 nationality parishes in 1940, they were one of the largest Catholic immigrant groups, having an average of 7,100 people for each nationality parish. The Poles, on the other hand, had 449 nationality parishes in 1940 and an immigrant total of 1.3 million permanent settlers, which meant approximately 2,900 immigrants for each parish. For Czechs and Slovaks, the numbers are even clearer. With 33 nationality parishes in a population of 300,000 permanent Catholic immigrants, the Czechs had approximately

Table 7.1
Nationality Parishes, 1860–1982[22]

Ethnic Group	*1860*	*1880*	*1900*	*1920*	*1940*	*1960*	*1982*
Poles	—	25	144	404	449	412	339
Italians	2	6	52	257	308	297	235
Germans	87	222	336	280	237	153	73
Rusins*	—	—	(19)	(189)	159	174	242
Slovaks	—	—	12	107	155	138	127
Ukrainians*	—	—	(19)	(189)	128	180	196
French Canadians	8	40	86	93	111	92	72
Lithuanians	—	—	17	95	105	90	84
Magyars	—	—	6	51	71	62	36
Mexicans	—	—	—	13	57	22	19
Maronites	—	—	3	22	34	44	48
Czechs	1	18	29	34	33	24	7
Croatians	—	—	1	19	33	28	25
Melkites	—	—	—	13	27	24	31
Slovenians	—	—	10	31	26	20	13
Portuguese	—	—	5	16	21	22	27
Romanians	—	—	—	9	14	15	12
Spanish	—	—	—	9	7	18	—
Belgian	—	4	4	5	5	2	1
English	1	12	11	6	4	—	—
Dutch	1	2	1	1	3	1	—
Armenian	—	—	—	—	2	6	4
Maltese	—	—	—	1	2	2	—
Tyrolese	—	—	—	1	1	1	1
Japanese	—	—	—	—	1	1	1
Albanian	—	—	—	1	1	—	1
Chaldean	—	—	—	1	1	2	4
Russian	—	—	—	—	1	3	5
Scandinavian	—	—	1	1	—	—	—
Chinese	—	—	—	—	—	2	2
Filipino	—	—	—	—	—	1	—
Algerian	—	—	—	—	—	1	—
Capeverdean	—	—	—	—	—	1	1
Korean	—	—	—	—	—	—	4
Total	100	329	737	1,759	2,006	1,848	1,608

*The totals for Rusins and Ukrainians are combined until after 1920, when they were recorded separately in the *Directory.*

Table 7.2
Nationality Parishes and Parochial Schools, 1940

*Ethnic Group**	*Nationality Parishes*	*Parochial Schools*
Polish	449	360
Italian	308	133
German	237	210
Rusin	159	100
Slovak	155	99
Ukrainian	128	92
French	111	98
Lithuanian	105	43
Magyar (Latin Rite)	58	21
Magyar (Byzantine Rite)	13	8
Mexican	57	28
Maronite	34	2
Czech	33	24
Croatian (Latin Rite)	31	16
Croatian (Byzantine Rite)	2	——
Melkite	27	1
Slovenian	26	11
Portuguese	21	3
Romanian	14	——
Spanish	7	——
Belgian	5	2
English	4	——
Dutch	3	——
Armenian	2	——
Maltese	2	——
Tyrolese	1	——
Japanese	1	——
Albanian	1	——
Chaldean	1	——
Russian	1	——
Total	2,006	1,253

*There was also a total of 153 parishes in 1940 designated as "For colored only."

10,000 for each parish, while the Slovaks, with 155 parishes serving an immigrant total of 450,000, had only 1,900 people for each parish.

These comparisons show that the Poles, Germans, French Canadians, Rusins, Ukrainians, Lithuanians, Maronites, and Melkites had the most powerful need to establish nationality parishes and parochial schools. Among Poles, Lithuanians, Slovaks, and French Canadians, the fusion of faith and nationality had over the centuries made religion a central dimension of ethnic identity. The fact of historical oppression had only added to those cultural loyalties. Among the Rusins, Ukrainians, Melkites, and Maronites, religion and nationalism had also functioned closely together, but it was their Uniate values that especially set them apart. For them, religion, language, liturgy, and nationality had all melted together, and in the United States they felt quite distinct from American Protestants as well as from Latin Rite Catholics. Among German Catholics, centuries of conflict with Lutheranism on the one hand and Russian Orthodoxy on the other had sharply defined religious loyalties. These Catholics too carried that faith to the New World.

For Italians, Mexicans, Czechs, Slovenes, Portuguese, Spaniards, and Magyars, the ethnic need to establish nationality parishes and parochial schools was not nearly as intense. Resentment of the political ramifications of Hapsburg Catholicism had helped compromise the ethnoreligious commitments of many Slovenes, Croatians, and Magyars, and they had a difficult time attracting their own priests to the United States. There were, for example, more than 150,000 Croatians living in America before the first Croatian priests arrived.[24] Among Italian and Mexican Catholics, centuries of resentment and alienation from the institutional church as well as powerful regional loyalties left many of the immigrants with only a modest need for the nationality parish. Only slightly more than a third of the Italian parishes had parochial schools attached to them, while 90 percent of the French-Canadian parishes had them. And while there was one ethnic parochial school for every 2,400 Rusin immigrants in 1940, Italians had one school for every 17,000 immigrants. In 1908 more than 85 percent of the children of Polish, French, Rusin, Slovak, and Ukrainian immigrants attended parochial schools, but only 12 percent of Italian children in New York City were enrolled in church schools.

Like the Croatians, Mexicans had a difficult time attracting Spanish-speaking let alone Mexican priests to their parishes because Mexican young men were so unlikely to ever take vows. In the Diocese of Corpus Christi in south Texas, for example, there were 147,000 Mexicans and only 14,000 Anglo Catholics in 1940, but only 22 of 115 priests in the diocese had Hispanic surnames. Spanish and Portuguese communities, except for the Basques, also had a difficult time attracting Iberian priests to the United States, and because so many centuries had passed since their own periods of intense nationalism, they did not have the same level of ethnoreligious commitment that many other European Catholics had. Finally, church loyalty of Czech immigrants had been weakened by the influence of freethought liberalism, by resentment of Hapsburg domination, and by the competing rivalries of faith and nationality.[25]

For millions of Roman Catholic immigrants, the nationality parish played a key role in easing the adjustment to urban society in the United States. Instead of finding themselves in an alien world full of strange nationality groups and a church dominated by the ascetic rationalism of the Irish, these immigrants were able to create a familiar world of traditional holidays, ceremonies, and saints in their churches; preserve the language and traditional values in their parochial schools; control social life in their parish societies; and confront God and mortality with the assistance of a priest who spoke their language and shared their past. For all the stress and misgivings the nationality parish imposed on the church in the late 1800s and early 1900s, it became a mainstay of Roman Catholic survival in the United States, the single most important institution in deflecting the proselytizing campaigns of evangelical Protestants and containing the centrifugal forces of nationalism and language. In the nationality parishes, despite their cultural diversity, the church maintained its Catholicity in the United States.

8

Conflict and Consolidation in the Immigrant Church

Nationality parishes helped the Catholic church absorb the new immigrants, serving their spiritual and cultural needs and protecting them from the proselyting campaigns of evangelical Protestants, while at the same time insulating native American Catholics from the newcomers' strange ways and preventing large-scale ethnic conflict between the various immigrant groups. With the nationality parishes, the church avoided the ugly possibilities of a malignant, anti-Catholic nativism since the immigrants quickly found a home in the new society and began acculturating. In the process, the Roman Catholic church became the largest, most visible religious institution in the United States. That success, however, was not achieved without a great deal of stress, conflict, and compromise. If the nationality parish proved to be an effective vehicle for ethnic accommodation, the road it followed was nevertheless strewn with obstacles. Years of conflict within and between various ethnic groups over liturgies, language, lay control, institutional commitment, individual piety, and political nationalism periodically threatened the stability of the church in the late nineteenth and early twentieth centuries. By 1945, however, two decades after the National Origins Act had stemmed the immigrant tide, the church was larger and stronger than ever.

No ethnic or religious organization can guarantee internal harmony, and the Catholic immigrant affiliations were no exception. The stress of migration and settlement combined with preexisting religious, regional, linguistic, racial, ideological, and political loyalties to create intense ethnic rivalries in the United States. Among the Portuguese, for example, a split developed between the Azoreans and Capeverdeans. The Azoreans descended from continental Portuguese. The Capeverdeans were of mixed European and African stock. In the color-conscious atmosphere of American society, the Azoreans considered themselves white and the Capeverdeans black. Recognizing the prevailing level of anti-black racism in the United States, Capeverdeans at first tried to associate closely with the Azoreans in social clubs and Catholic parishes. The center of Portuguese culture was Fall River, Massachusetts, where several nationality parishes served the immigrants: Espirito Santo, Our Lady of the Angels, St. Anthony of Padua, St. Elizabeth, St. Michael, Santo Christo, Our Lady of the Immaculate Conception, Our Lady of Mt. Carmel, St. John the Baptist, Our Lady of Lourdes, and St. Anthony's. But the Azoreans and Capeverdeans never came together in the Portuguese-nationality parishes. Finding themselves in job competition with the Capeverdeans and afraid of indirectly being victimized by anti-Capeverdean racism, the Azoreans kept to themselves. They excluded Capeverdeans from their social organizations and tried to segregate them in the local Portuguese parishes. To resolve the problem, the bishop of Fall River established a Capeverdean nationality parish—Our Lady of the Assumption—in 1905. Our Lady of the Assumption became the spiritual home for the "black Portuguese."[1]

While skin color divided the Portuguese, cultural and linguistic rivalries eventually separated the Rusins and Ukrainians. In the industrial centers of the Northeast, Rusins and Ukrainians shared a "Ruthenian" heritage as Roman Catholic Uniates with similar linguistic traditions. At first they worshiped with the Poles, Slovaks, and Magyars because no Byzantine Rite parishes existed and no priests had come from Galicia or Transcarpathia. Later they asked the Ukrainian metropolitan of Galicia to send a Uniate priest, and in 1884 Reverend John Volansky arrived in Pennsylvania and established the Ruthenian Uniate Church. Two years later, he dedicated St. Michael the Archangel Church in Shenandoah, Pennsylvania. By 1895 there were thirty Uniate priests in the United States, most of them Rusin because the Ukrainian migration did not become significant until after 1910. Indeed, by 1910 there were 140 Ruthenian parishes in the United States, with most of them still Rusin in composition.

Rusins and Ukrainians shared a great deal culturally, but internal differences gradually asserted themselves. When the Ruthenian church received its first bishop in 1907, he was a Ukrainian from Galacia, the Reverend Stephen Ortynsky. Rusins could never adjust to his being a Ukrainian, because Rusins constituted most of the

Ruthenian population in the United States. They criticized Bishop Ortynsky until his death in 1916. The controversy over ethnic leadership continued until 1924 when Rome appointed two Uniate bishops in America. The Ukrainian bishop was a Galician, the Reverend Constantine Bohachersky, and he headed the diocesan see at Philadelphia. The Rusin bishop was the Reverend Basil Takich, a Transcarpathian, who headed an episcopal see near Pittsburgh. Only after the arrival of these two bishops did the competitive rivalry between Rusins and Ukrainians subside.[2]

Basques divided along similar lines. By the late nineteenth century, two distinct Basque communities had appeared in the Far West: French Basques and Spanish Navarrese Basques lived in California, western Nevada, Arizona, New Mexico, Colorado, Wyoming, and Montana, while Spanish Vizcayan Basques were spread out through northern Nevada, eastern Oregon, and southern Idaho. The two groups were quite different, maintaining separate social organizations and insisting on having their own priests, usually frontier itinerants, minister to their spiritual needs. As long as most Basques were rural herders and farmers, there was little conflict between the two groups, but as large numbers of Basques began settling in western cities early in the 1900s, ethnic conflict developed over religion. In transitional areas where French, Navarrese, and Vizcayan Basques lived together, they argued continually about the ethnic roots of the priests visiting them. At the annual Basque festivals, each group insisted on selecting a priest who shared its particular Basque roots. The dispute became an annual event as all groups competed for the "right" priest to say Mass and hear confessions.[3]

Among Czech immigrants, ideological disputes repeatedly divided the community, usually over religious issues. An Austrian observer traveling in the United States early in the 1900s described the typical Czech immigrant as "apt to be quarrelsome, suspicious, jealous, clannish yet factious; he hates quickly and long, and is unreasoning in his prejudices."[4] His own prejudices were obvious, but the reality of Czech in-fighting was clear. Most Czech immigrants were nominally Catholic, but the liberal "freethought" movement throughout Bohemia in the nineteenth century had left many of them with religious feelings ranging from mild indifference to militant agnosticism. Liberal "freethinkers" organized their own fraternal groups, including the Czech-Slavic Benevolent Society, the

Western Bohemian Fraternal Association, and the American Sokol Organization. Czech Catholics, afraid of anticlericalism and liberal nationalism, developed religious fraternalism in organizations like the Catholic Central Union and the National Alliance of Czech Catholics. Where Czech freethinkers and Catholics lived together as neighbors, the only alternative to conflict was to avoid political and religious issues. In many of the Czech benevolent societies in Chicago, people concentrated on social, linguistic, and educational activities because of the certainty that religious or political discussions would quickly break down into bitter debate and division. In the Czech farming village of Milligan, Nebraska, in the 1920s, for example, only one-third of the people even claimed a Catholic loyalty, and "freethought" was widespread. When a Belgian priest began attacking liberal attitudes and urging Catholics to avoid contact with Protestants and freethinkers, parishioners demanded and secured his removal.[5] The alternative would have been bitter debate in the community.

Old World ethnic and political rivalries frequently asserted themselves in the immigrant communities. Among Slovaks, for example, competing attitudes about Magyar and Slovakian independence often split the community. Older Slovak priests were usually conservative and pro-Magyar, usually to the dismay of younger, pro-Slovak priests and parishioners, who resented Hungary's nine-hundred-year domination of Slovakia. Father Jozef Kossalko offered one of the first Slovak Masses at St. Stephen's in Streator, Pennsylvania, in 1885. A pro-Magyar opponent of Slovakian nationalism, Kossalko openly resisted pan-Slavism, ethnic nationalism, national confederations of Slovak societies, and parochial schools dedicated to the Slovak language. In 1907, while serving as pastor of St. John Nepomucene parish in Bridgeport, Connecticut, Kossalko repeatedly denied requests from some parishioners to build a parochial school where children could study Slovak. The dispute became so intense that Bishop Michael Tierney of Hartford agreed to establish another Slovak nationality parish—SS Cyril and Methodius—and assigned Father Matus Jankola as the new pastor. Parishioners soon had their parochial school. Old World resentments and loyalties were a continuing source of controversy in Slovak-American communities.[6]

Political ideologies provided another source of conflict among Roman Catholic immigrants. The Irish immigrants had already set the stage for ethnic debate and division over questions of politics and nationalism. For a time during the 1870s, especially after the emergence of such groups as the Fenians and Clan na Gael, Irish Catholics had divided over the tactics to be used in pursuing Irish freedom.[7] Similar battles erupted in other immigrant communities. Throughout the nineteenth century, differences surfaced between the liberal, intellectual refugees of the 1830s and 1840s and the peasant migrants of the "new immigration." Among Czechs, Poles, Germans, and Italians, refugee intellectuals had some success in raising the political consciousness of the peasants, but the whole process often created ethnic divisions as well as ethnic unity. In April 1914, for example, Count Michael Károlyi, leader of the Hungarian Independence party, came to the United States to secure political support in the American Magyar communities for independence from Austria and the creation of a democratic state in Hungary. Upon arriving in New York City, Károlyi was greeted with extraordinary dissension among Magyar Americans. New York Magyars had long been divided into two camps, one led by Géza Berkó, owner of the newspaper *Amerikai Magyar Nepszava,* and the other led by Louis Tarcai, editor of the socialist paper *Elore.* Tarcai accused Berkó of being a conservative aristocrat out of touch with peasant needs; that statement received great opposition from older Magyar clerics and great support from Magyar workers' benevolent societies. Berkó refused to work at all with Tarcai. When Károlyi arrived, he encountered two separate committees and two separate schedules of meetings. Eventually, New York Magyars rallied behind Tarcai, but the incident disrupted the community and made Károlyi's visit a political nightmare.[8]

Among Italian-American Catholics, the spirit of *campanilismo* was a source of continuing conflict. Of all the new immigrants coming to the United States, the southern Italians had the least-developed national or organizational perspective. Except for their loyalty to *la famiglia,* nothing compared with their loyalty for the *paese* or village. Southern Italian ethnic identity consisted of two concentric circles, the inner one dominated by the family and the outer one by the village. Nothing else transcended those values. Each village had its own patron saint and each annual *festa* celebrated those narrow loyalties.[9] In the Italian ghettoes of the United States, those parochial values frequently collided when immigrants competed to prove their loyalty to their own patron. The rivalries created ethnic parishes and benevolent societies dedicated to dozens of village saints. Most Czech parishes were dedicated to St. Wenceslaus, St. John Nepomucene, St. Ludmila, St. Procopius, or SS Cyril and Methodius. Poles usually dedicated their parishes to St. Stanislaus, St. Hedwig, St. Adalbert, St. Hyacinth, St. John Cantius, or Our Lady of Czestochowa. Although Italians frequently named their parishes after Our Lady of Mt. Carmel., their spirit of *campanilismo* and *clientismo* resulted in parishes honoring all kinds of village patron saints: St. Catherine of Genoa, Our Lady of Loretto, St. Blaise, St. Mary, St. Rita, St. Sebastian, St. Joachim, St. Rocco, St. Anthony, St. Joseph, the Madonna of Grazie, St. Roch, St. Francisco, St. Francis of Paolo, St. Vito, St. Clare, St. Lucy, St. Ann, St. Raphael, St. Michael, Our Lady of Sorrows, the Madonna of Libera, and St. Donatus. By 1920 every major American city had hundreds of Italian mutual-aid societies, each governed by one or a few families from a village group and dedicated to the village patron. Italians rarely established community-wide or national organizations.

Beyond competing to stage the most elaborate *festa* to commemorate their village patron, the southern Italians struggled to build parishes in the patron's name. Feelings ran high when the time came to name a new Italian-nationality church. In Newark, New Jersey, for example, a major rift appeared in 1926 when the Society of San Gerardo was helping to build a new parish church. Since loyalty to the *paese* was best demonstrated by having the patron saint named titular head of the local church, the immigrants fought over the dedication. The Society's leadership, facing demands from supporters of St. Gerardo Maiella as well as St. Lucy, decided that the church should be

> given the title of our glorious St. Gerardo Maiella. Out of sentiment of our dutiful respect for the pious and miraculous St. Lucy and not wanting to unjustly exclude this present titular of the Church, we thought of combining the two names by having the parish under the name of St. Lucy and also make the Church a shrine under the second name of St. Gerardo Maiella.[10]

In most Italian-nationality parishes, it was not uncommon to see a variety of patron statues amid great displays of burning candles arranged near the main altar. The variety of patron statues was the only way of satisfying *contadini* whose saint had not become titular head of the parish. The alternative would have been constant bickering and alienation from the church.

One issue inspiring frequent controversy in the immigrant parishes was local control and sovereignty, that is, whether church property, parish finances, and clerical decisions would be controlled by lay committees or clerical authorities. Early in the nineteenth century, Irish immigrants had fought the "trustee question" with the existing Anglo- and French-Catholic hierarchy, as had the Germans and French Canadians a few decades later. By that time, of course, the church hierarchy was fast becoming Irish in composition. The new Catholic immigrants from southern and eastern Europe faced the same problem. In the 1850s, for example, Czech immigrants settled New Prague in southern Minnesota. They set aside forty acres to support a parish church, and in 1858 built St. Wenceslaus, a log-cabin chapel. A parish committee then recruited Father Peter Maly as resident pastor. The church burned down in 1862, and in 1867 another chapel was built. But in 1875, diocesan officials asked the lay parishioners of St. Wenceslaus to hand over the deed to the church property to the bishop of St. Paul. Incensed and afraid that loss of the property would automatically lead to loss of lay control of St. Wenceslaus, the parishioners refused. After two years of debate, the bishop placed St. Wenceslaus under interdict, terminating administration of the sacraments there. Not until the end of the year was the deed finally transferred and the interdict lifted.[11]

Among Italian immigrants, the question of lay control revolved around celebration of the *festa*. In Italy, a lay committee in each village had sponsored the annual *festa*—making the preparations, collecting necessary funds, arranging facilities, and conducting the event itself. Those same committees functioned in the nationality parishes of the United States, but American Protestants as well as Irish-American Catholics had formed powerful stereotypes about southern Italians and crime and suspected those lay *festa* committees of graft. Priests frequently tried to take over the *festa* and its finances, but they usually encountered a storm of protest from parishioners who had little respect for priests in the first place. In 1908, for example, Father Mariano of Our Lady of Mt. Carmel parish in White Plains, New York, decided to abolish the annual *festa* as well as the procession of St. Rocco, intending to use the collection instead to construct a new church. The congregation was outraged, to say the least. The evening after the decision, someone fired three shots into Mariano's bedroom while he was sitting out on the porch. He reconsidered his decision and let the lay committee carry out the procession and *festa*, much to the pleasure of parishioners.[12]

The issue of lay control was important in the nationality parishes because the immigrants had played such critical roles in founding the first parishes; both Old and New World realities reinforced the idea of local sovereignty. The immigrants had settled in areas where no ethnic churches existed, had sacrificed greatly to purchase property and build chapels and parochial schools, and had recruited their own priests, usually without much assistance from American church leaders. Indeed, the process of establishing the first immigrant nationality parishes resembled the work Protestants had done in founding their own churches. The idea of working together without outside stimulus or assistance and establishing one's own institutions was very American, an approach coinciding closely with the values of democracy, individualism, and self-reliance. But there was also an Old World dimension to the dispute, for there the nobility had often exercised great authority in local parishes. In Hungary, for example, members of the nobility had often endowed local churches and patronized them financially. Their families then controlled power in the parish, creating a form of lay control.

Early in the 1900s, Magyar nobles had managed to replace Slovak-nationalist priests with "Magyarone" priests in many Slovakian villages. Slovak nationalists had resented such power then, but once in the United States they saw themselves as the patrons of the Slovak-nationality parishes, especially after sacrificing as a group to establish them. Slovak laymen, through "trustee committees," budgeted parish finances, directed the use of parish property, collected weekly dues from parishioners, and appointed as well as removed parish priests. Clerical salaries were paid from those lay-committee budgets. In 1916, for example, at SS Cyril and Methodius Parish in Bridgeport, Connecticut, the bishop of Hartford appointed Father Gaspar Panik as the new pastor, even though the lay committee opposed the nomination. When Father Panik showed up to assume his position, more than a hundred people demonstrated in front of the church, invaded and looted the rectory, and forced Father Panik to hide in the attic. Not until the police came and arrested several of the demonstrating parishioners was Father Panik able to leave the attic safely.[13]

The lay-control disputes led to the independent church movements when immigrant committees came into conflict with diocesan officials over management of the nationality parishes. In 1913, for example, there were more than five thousand Italians living in Hackensack, New Jersey, but they had no nationality parish, and the closest Catholic church was St. Mary's, an Irish and Polish church nearly two miles away. Despite repeated applications, Bishop John O'Connor had decided against establishing a nationality parish there. When Father Antonio Lenza organized St. Anthony's as a separate parish anyway, Bishop O'Connor suspended him as a priest and at the same time tried to defuse the controversy by agreeing to form St. Francis, an Italian-nationality parish, and urging all the Italians to attend the approved parish. Eventually, Father Lenza established the Independent Italian Catholic church, naming himself in 1919 as "Vicar General of the Italian Diocese of St. Anthony of Padua." In Sharon-Farrell, Pennsylvania, Croatians struggled to build an ethnic parish after purchasing property in 1912. They began constructing a church in 1914 but did not want to place it under diocesan control. When Father Leon J. Medic, a Franciscan Croatian, became resident pastor he convinced most of the parishioners to surrender jurisdiction, but a disgruntled minority bolted and formed the Independent Croatian Catholic church, a parish that survived until 1928. In 1912, Slovak immigrants in Homestead, Pennsylvania, established St. Anne's Independent Slovak Catholic church when the bishop refused to oust their pastor. The same problem developed in Passaic, New Jersey, in 1924; so some parishioners established the National Czechoslovak Catholic church and affiliated with a mother church recently established in Prague, Czechoslovakia.[14]

The most significant of the independent church movements developed in Polish and Lithuanian immigrant communities at the turn of the century. In the Old World, peasants had often taken the parish for granted; it had always existed in the village and its maintenance required very little sacrifice. But the decline of the Atlantic economy and the nuclear family had given rise to the formation of occupational and kinship societies, which amounted to new forms of power in the peasant villages. Those societies made the journey to the United States and often played leading roles in the construction of Roman Catholic chapels, schools, hospitals, and orphanages. Poor workers made great financial sacrifices, and as they transplanted the church their sense of lay power became even stronger. They were hardly a group of passive peasants waiting for fate to manipulate their lives. In the new parishes, the priests had to delegate authority to immigrant parishioners, and that too gave the parishioners a sense of power in church affairs. When diocesan officials, especially Irish ones, tried to take control of the new parishes, the immigrants and their societies were usually upset and sometimes rebellious.

In addition to the question of lay power, a struggle for power in the immigrant communities developed between the "religionists" and the "nationalists." Most Roman Catholic clergy insisted that Catholicism preempted all ethnic nationalisms—that being Polish or Czech or Lithuanian or Slovak was synonymous with being Catholic. These "religionists" claimed that the American church should exercise complete and direct control over all local parishes, including the nationality parishes. Immigrants might play an active role in parish administration, but ultimate power rested with the bishop, who owned parish property, supervised the parish budget, and directed the parish priests. Claiming that Roman Catholicism was the only conceivable religion for "true Poles" or "true Slovaks" or "true Ukrainians," religionists expressed these views through local parish societies and national organizations like the Polish Roman Catholic Union, Lithuanian Roman Catholic Alliance, or the Croatian Catholic Union.

On the opposing side were the ethnic "nationalists," intellectual descendents of the refugees of 1848 who yearned for independent nations in eastern Europe and worked to raise the political consciousness of peasant immigrants. The nationalists' loyalties transcended religion to embrace anyone who shared their patriotism—Catholics, Uniates, Eastern Orthodox, Protestants, and Jews. Nationalists also insisted that lay parishioners in the ethnic parishes, not the diocesan bishops, control local church property and finances. On the national level, they formed such groups as the Polish National Alliance, the Lithuanian Alliance of America, and the Slovenian National Benevolent Society.[15]

Finally, there was a strong resentment caused by the feeling that the American church was too slow in naming ethnic priests to the hierarchy, and that the hierarchy therefore was too Irish in composition. The appointment of ethnic bishops did seem a convenient way out of the struggle between the "religionists" and the "nationalists" because even if parish property reverted to diocesan control, it would still be technically in the hands of the ethnic group itself. The appointment of ethnic bishops also reinforced a major principle of the nationalist argument: that Roman Catholics could also be ethnic nationalists—Poles, Czechs, Lithuanians, Italians, Slovaks, Slovenes, Croatians, Rusins, Magyars, Maronites, Melkites, Ukrainians, French Canadians, and Germans. Precedents had already been established. Father John Henni had become the unofficial leader of German Catholics in the United States when he was ordained bishop of Milwaukee in 1844 and while he served as bishop and later archbishop. Archbishop Michael Heiss took over the archdiocese of Milwaukee in 1886 and played the same role.

The ordination of Louis de Goesbriand as bishop of Portland in 1852 had done the same for French Canadians. Father Frederic Baraga, a Slovenian missionary who served on the American frontier for twenty-five years as a traveling priest, was appointed bishop of northern Michigan and Wisconsin in 1853. Reverend Stephen Ortynsky, a Ukrainian from Galicia, ordained bishop in 1907, led the Ruthenian immigrants. In 1907 Pope Pius X named Father Joseph M. Koudelka, a Bohemian, as auxiliary bishop of Cleveland. To satisfy the large Polish population of Chicago, Pope Pius X also installed Paul Rhode, a Prussian Pole, as the auxiliary bishop of the archdiocese in 1908. Reverend Edward Koslowski was named auxiliary bishop of Milwaukee in 1913, and Rhodes became bishop of Green Bay in 1915. The appointment of ethnic bishops continued. In 1924, Bishops Constantine Bohachersky and Basil Takach headed the Ukrainian and Rusin sees. In 1966 the church created apostolic exarchates for the Maronites and Melkites. By 1972 Bishop Francis Zayek was serving as the Eparch of the St. Maron diocese, governing all Maronite parishes, and by 1976 Bishop Joseph Tawil headed the Eparchy of Newton, Massachusetts, governing all Melkite parishes in the United States.[16]

While the controversies over lay power, "religionists" versus "nationalists," and ethnic bishops were raging, strong independent church movements emerged from the Polish, Lithuanian, Slovak, and Italian communities. In 1895 Father Antoni Kozlowski organized an independent Polish parish in Chicago, and during the next two years several other independent parishes formed and established their own synod, naming Kozlowski as their bishop. That same year, Father Stephen Kaminski became bishop of a group of independent Polish parishes in New York. The most powerful of the independent groups began in the 1890s when Polish nationalists at Sacred Heart of Jesus parish in Scranton, Pennsylvania, began demanding more lay authority from their German pastor and Irish bishop. In 1897 Father Francis Hodur, a former assistant pastor at Sacred Heart and a fervent Polish nationalist, led the other nationalists in creating the Polish National Catholic church.[17]

By 1904 more than twenty-five independent Polish parishes existed in the upper Midwest and Northeast, and at a synod that year they elected Father Hodur as bishop of the Polish National Catholic church in America. Rejecting papal infallibility and Roman Catholicism as the only institutional manifestation of God on earth, they translated the Latin Rite into the Polish vernacular, included Polish national holidays on the religious calendar, openly called for Polish independence, and affiliated with the Old Catholic church of Utrecht. Most members of the Polish National Catholic church lived in Chicago, Detroit, Buffalo, Cleveland, and Scranton, and they numbered approximately 20,000 in 1910. Bishop Kozlowski's synod had joined the Polish National Catholic church in 1907, as did Bishop Kaminski's group in 1914. Similar developments were occurring in the Lithuanian, Slovak, and Italian communities. Isolated independent Lithuanian parishes developed in Pennsylvania, Illinois, and Massachusetts, and just before World War I they formed the Lithuanian National Catholic church. A special diocese for the independent Slovak parishes, like the one at Passaic, New Jersey, was established at the same time. By 1919 Father Lenza had affiliated his independent Italian Catholic churches with the Polish National Catholic church, naming Bishop Hodur as his "bishop protector" and permitting him to bless and dedicate churches and confirm children. In 1964 the Lithuanian National Catholic church merged formally with the Polish National Catholic church, by which time there were more than 250,000 members in more than 160 parishes. Although concessions to lay power, the appointments of ethnic bishops, and the creation of Poland, Lithuania, Czechoslovakia, Hungary, and Yugoslavia after World War I had prevented the national church movement from seriously damaging the church, it did represent the most serious schism in American Catholicism.[18]

The independent church movement also reflected deep-seated rivalries between different ethnic groups, usually between the Irish hierarchy of the American church and the traditions of recent immigrants. Although Irish clerics had grudgingly accepted the nationality parishes, they had a much more difficult time adjusting to immigrant piety, liturgies, and local traditions, especially if they differed markedly from Irish Catholicism. Each new immigrant group had trouble with the Irish hierarchy, but the difficulties of Italians and Ruthenians were the most visible—Italians because of their magical, unorthodox *clientismo* and Ruthenians because of the Uniate tradition. Competitive rivalries between various ethnic groups sharply defined Roman Catholicism in the United States and may even have stimulated devotional levels in some groups while alienating others.

The Irish-American clerics had mixed feelings about Italians. They knew the Italians needed the ministrations of the church, but at the same time the Irish viewed the Italians as an ignorant, superstitious people without any sense of genuine piety. Coming from a culture marked by intense ethnic persecution and a recent Catholic devotional revolution, the Irish were extremely devoted to the church and cherished a rational, ascetic piety and a highly personalized relationship with God. To them, the magical folk religion of southern Italians, with its world of ghosts, witches, spells, and cures, was immature and sacrilegious, an external display of superstition scandalizing to God. When, for example, the Irish witnessed *lingua strascinuni,* a form of penance in which the Italian worshiper honored a patron saint by crawling on hands and knees with his tongue dragging along the floor of the chapel, they became enraged at what they considered an outrageous display of ignorance. They felt the same way about the entire array of occult practices.[19]

Nor did the Irish have any respect for the *clientismo* Italians brought from the Mezzogiorno. Since the nineteenth-century devotional revolution, Irish Catholics had de-emphasized the worship of client saints in favor of personal relationships with God. They believed in personal piety and visible fidelity to the church on a day-to-day basis as the measure of spiritual commitment. For Irish Catholics, that meant daily personal devotions, regular attendance at Mass and confession, enrollment of children in parochial schools, and financial sacrifice for the parish. As far as the Irish were concerned, Italians attended Mass irregularly and confession rarely, preferred public to parochial schools, and were stingy in their financial support of the parish. A 1914 editorial in the Catholic journal *America* argued that true piety

> does not consist in processions or carrying candles, in prostrations before a statue of the Madonna, in processions in honor of patron saints or villages, but true piety consists in the daily fulfillment of the religious duties exacted of us by God Almighty and His church and it consists in a love for that church and her ministers. In these points, no matter how heavy the candles, no matter how many lights they carry, the Italian immigrant seems very deficient.[20]

When large numbers of Italian immigrants began flocking to the mining towns of the Intermountain West, Irish clerics there, already fighting their own battles to establish the church, were angry and embarrassed at what they saw in the Italian communities. Several editorials in the *Intermountain Catholic* during 1899 and 1900 revealed the Irish frustration:

> The Italian people, with rare exceptions, are ... in a state little better than Paganism.... In Utah and Colorado there are several colonies of Italians. In the former they are under the direct ministration of Bishop Scanlan.... In Colorado the Italians are well cared for by Bishop Matz, who takes especial interest in providing priests capable of ministering to them in their own tongue. That the results obtained from the Italian missions in these parts may not be all that is desired, it is clearly not due to lack of efficient and intelligent administration, but rather to a want of spiritual fervor among the Italians themselves.[21]

For the Irish, the Italian *festa* was the perfect symbol of all that was wrong with Italian piety. No annual spiritual event could compensate for an entire year of religious apathy. The fireworks, brass bands, carnivals, public begging, crawling, and bizarre forms of penance—*lingua strascinuni,* candle-carrying, personal mortifications, and the pinning of money to patron statues—could not make up for the lack of commitment to the church in daily affairs. Indeed, the *festa* was proof positive of how far the Italians had drifted from "true religion." In their frustration, some church leaders tried to eradicate the more "obnoxious" manifestations of Mezzogiorno religion as a means of "civilizing" the immigrants. Another editorial in *The Intermountain Catholic* said: "The average modern Latin . . . comes to America, neither controlled, dominated, or influenced by high civilization or the ideals of Christianity; he is a fit subject for civilization and Christianization."[22] In many dioceses, bishops outlawed the *festa* and procession, occult practices, strange forms of penance, brass bands in ceremonies, and certain funeral arrangements, and tried to destroy the spirit of *clientismo* by removing from churches all the statues of competing village saints. Priests often segregated Italian children in parochial schools and mixed parishes and condemned Italian immigrants from the pulpit. Not surprisingly, the Italians were frequently alienated from the American church, remaining nominally Roman Catholic but less committed institutionally than many other groups.[23]

The attitudes of the American hierarchy also helped drive thousands of Rusins and Ukrainians out of the church altogether. The ethnic rivalries of these groups, of course, had also played a significant role in defining religious loyalties. Between the nomination of Stephen Ortynsky as the Ruthenian bishop in 1907 and the appointment of Basil Takach to a Rusin see in 1924, Rusins had felt dominated by Ukrainian values and discriminated against by Irish bishops. But even as they were struggling between themselves, the Rusins and Ukrainians were also fighting to maintain the Uniate tradition within the church. Irish-American prelates, interested in transforming the church from a "foreign" to a "native" institution, wanted to impose the Latin Rite on Rusin and Ukrainian immigrants. To these prelates, the commitment to a married clergy, the Julian calendar, the Slavic liturgy, and the synodal church governing system were all threats to the "Americanization" of Catholicism in the United States. Even after the Cahensly and "Americanist" controversies of the 1890s, Irish-American church leaders remained committed to the "Latinization" of Eastern-Rite immigrants.[24]

The problem first surfaced in the 1880s when large numbers of Rusin immigrants began arriving in the United States. Father John Volansky, the first Uniate priest, came in 1884 to serve the Rusins in Shenandoah, Pennsylvania, but for five years he encountered extraordinary resistance from Irish priests and church leaders incapable of accepting that he was married and ecclesiastically independent. Other Rusin priests encountered the same hostility, usually failing to be installed as pastors after presenting their credentials to Latin Rite bishops. In 1890, at the insistence of an American hierarchy intent on integrating Eastern-Rite Catholics into local Latin Rite congregations, Rome ordered the Metropolitan of L'viv to stop sending married priests to the United States. The first defections occurred quickly, with Father Alexis Toth, a Rusin priest hoping to work at St. Mary's Parish in Minneapolis, taking his whole congregation into the Russian Orthodox church when Bishop John Ireland refused to install him as a pastor in the diocese of Minneapolis/St. Paul.[25]

Over the next forty years, Rome periodically reiterated its prohibition of married priests, and Irish-American priests worked to convert Ruthenians from the Julian to the Gregorian calendar and from the Eastern to the Latin Rite. Church authorities also opposed the establishment of independent Uniate sees. Defections from the Roman Catholic church continued among Ruthenian immigrants. The great beneficiary was the Russian Orthodox church, since the conversion to Orthodoxy demanded no change in clergy, liturgy, calendar, church organization, or ownership of church property, as long as title still remained in the hands of a lay committee. By 1907, 65 Ruthenian parishes had followed Father Toth into the Russian Orthodox church, and between 1907 and 1915 another 160 did so. The immigrants also turned to several branches of the Ukrainian Orthodox church.

In 1917, as World War I rekindled Ukrainian nationalism, a group of Ukrainian priests and laity in Kiev organized the Ukrainian Orthodox church and declared its independence from Moscow. Ukrainians in the United States quickly organized an American branch of the church, and thousands of dissatisfied Ukrainian immigrants joined them. Another Ukrainian Orthodox church was established in the United States as an affiliate of Constantinople, and in 1932 its members named Father Joseph Zuk, a former Uniate priest who had converted to Eastern Orthodoxy, as their first bishop. In 1929, when Rome restated its opposition to a married Uniate clergy in the United States, a Rusin rebellion occurred. By 1936, 40 Rusin parishes had seceded from Roman Catholic jurisdiction and established the American Carpatho-Russian Orthodox Greek Catholic church, selecting Father Orestes Chornock as their leader. The patriarch of Constantinople recognized them in 1938 and appointed Chornock as bishop of the Carpatho-Russian Orthodox diocese.

By 1965 there were a number of churches organized by the Ruthenian immigrants, with memberships of 280,000 in Ukrainian-Catholic parishes, 300,000 in Rusin-Catholic parishes, 400,000 Ukrainians and Rusins in Russian-Orthodox parishes, 135,000 in several Ukrainian-Orthodox denominations, and 100,000 in the American Carpatho-Russian Orthodox Greek Catholic church.[26]

Interethnic clashes were not confined only to the Irish. Germans and Poles, for example, often confronted one another in the cities of the upper Midwest. Germans had moved into Detroit in large numbers in the 1840s, settling on the east side and building two ethnic parishes—St. Mary's in 1843 and St. Joseph's in 1856. In 1870 the German-born Caspar Borgess became bishop of Detroit. There were more than three hundred Polish families worshiping at St. Mary's and St. Joseph's, but strife between them and the Germans was mounting, especially when St. Joseph's decided to segregate the Poles. The Poles then petitioned for their first nationality parish, which was constructed in 1872 and dedicated to St. Albertus. But during the next two decades, the Poles waged a bitter struggle for identity in Detroit. Between 1872 and 1887, Bishop Borgess dismissed four Polish priests—Szymon Wieczorek, Teodor Gieryk, Alfons Dombrowski, and Dominik Kolasinski—for what he considered financial indiscretions, moral turpitude, and pro-Polish political activity. Polish immigrants viewed the dismissals as discriminatory attacks by the "German" bishop. Borgess interdicted St. Albertus several times for what he considered open rebellion against church authority and on a number of occasions forbade Polish parishioners from attending Mass at neighboring German or Czech parishes. Indeed, by the 1880s and early 1890s, Polish resentment toward diocesan officials in Detroit led to periodic riots requiring the intervention of local police.[27]

A similar struggle erupted in Chicago between the Poles and Archbishop George William Mundelein. When Paul Rhode became auxiliary bishop of Chicago in 1907, the Poles had looked to him for spiritual leadership. But on the death of Archbishop James Quigley of Chicago in 1915, the Vatican announced Rhode's appointment to the diocese of Green Bay. When Mundelein, a German American, was appointed to the Chicago archdiocese, the Polish community felt betrayed. Mundelein tried to be solicitous, but the resentment of the community was overwhelming. The Polish Clergy Association of Chicago demanded more ethnic recognition from Mundelein, and in 1920 it submitted the *I Pollachi* memorial to the Vatican, insisting on the appointment of more Polish bishops, condemning Mundelein's "Americanization" program, and insisting that nationality parishes were for the "exclusive" use of the immigrant group. Mundelein was incensed, and after clearing his response with several other Roman Catholic leaders, including James Cardinal Gibbons, he announced:

> For generations the Catholics of the United States have repelled the unjust accusation of disloyalty to the American Government and of subserviency to foreign potentates. Should it become known that the Polish priests of the United States appealed to the Polish Government to bring pressure on the Holy See in favor of their pretensions . . . the Poles of this country would be accused of unfaithfulness to our Government; and the American Church would be charged with subjection to foreign powers. Non-Catholics would calumniate us as hindering the unification of the Nation, with whom our country may one day be at war. The consequences would be serious for the Catholic religion.[28]

Thus after nearly a century of large-scale immigration, the growth of the Catholic church into the largest denomination in the country, and the experiences of the nationality parishes, some church leaders were still preoccupied with the immigrant church and the role of Catholicism in American life.

Despite the ethnic disputes of the late nineteenth and early twentieth centuries, the immigrant church had indeed become an integral part of American life. What had saved the church from schism, of course, was its doctrinal uniformity across ethnic lines. The various nationalities had feuded constantly over questions of language, nationalism, culture, church property, and clerical appointments, but they had not really been forced to deal with differences over theology, salvation, and destiny. The subcultures within Roman Catholicism were not doctrinal; a fundamental consensus about theology gave the church its greatest resource in preventing schism. Millions of immigrants had given the church an institutional base in tens of thousands of parishes, schools, monasteries, orphanages, and hospitals, while the doctrinal purity and ecclesiastical enthusiasm of the Irish had given the church a distinct identity.

But the Irish background, as well as the political fears of earlier

Anglo Catholics, had also given the American church a social paranoia with roots in the brutalities of the Irish past, Anglo-Protestant discrimination against English Catholics, and the pains of the urban ghettoes of the United States. Desperate to ease the discrimination and eliminate the "foreign" image of the church, many nineteenth-century prelates had turned to "liberal Catholicism" and "Americanism" to make the church acceptable to Protestants. The Cahensly controversy and Pope Leo's condemnation of Americanism in 1899 were both reflections of that dilemma for American Catholics, as were the rhetorical battles between such "liberals" as James Cardinal Gibbons of Baltimore, Archbishop John Ireland of St. Paul, and Bishop John Lancaster Spaulding of Peoria, and such traditionalists as Archbishop Michael Corrigan of New York and Bishop Bernard McQuaid of Rochester.

Although Rome had certainly exaggerated the significance of "Americanism," the nineteenth-century liberals had been too paranoid about the threat of the new immigrants, too heavy-handed in their approach to ethnic assimilation, and too willing to join Anglo Protestants in Americanizing the newcomers. Pope Leo XIII's declaration of 1899 as well as the proliferation of nationality parishes had temporarily ended the controversy over the place of the immigrants in the church. But even then the approach to the immigrants depended on the attitudes of the local bishop, who exercised almost complete power inside his diocese. In Connecticut, for example, Bishop Michael Tierney's episcopate between 1894 and 1908 was marked by an unusual measure of cooperation and tranquility because he believed in the nationality parish and readily supported immigrants in establishing them. His successor, John Nilan, however, who presided in Connecticut between 1910 and 1934, was more committed to Americanization and had repeated disputes with immigrant parishioners.[29]

But when a new wave of anti-Catholicism swept through the United States during World War I and the 1920s, the controversy resumed. This time, however, a new generation of church leaders—people like George Cardinal Mundelein of Chicago, William Cardinal O'Connell of Boston, Denis Cardinal Dougherty of Philadelphia, John Cardinal Glennon of St. Louis, and later Francis Cardinal Spellman of New York—reacted differently to the crisis. American born but Roman trained, they consolidated the administration of the church, worked to "Americanize" the immigrants without the paranoia or heavy-handedness of the past, and "put the church on the map" by making Roman Catholicism an acceptable, integral part of American society. In Chicago, for example, Cardinal Mundelein constructed the lavish St. Mary of the Lake Seminary in the 1920s, with the exterior of the library modeled after Thomas Jefferson's University of Virginia and the interior a duplicate of the Barberini Palace in Rome; raised huge amounts of money for Catholic charities; consolidated church finances to reduce the disparities between affluent and poor parishes; and cultivated personal relations with prominent Protestant and Jewish attorneys, financiers, and politicians. Mundelein was vigorously patriotic during World War I and had a very high profile as a promoter of Liberty Bonds.[30]

By the 1930s, because of the efforts of church leaders Mundelein and O'Connell, American Catholicism had acquired a self-confidence unknown in earlier years, commensurate with its new status as the largest church in the United States. The ethnic controversies, difficult as they had been, had not destroyed or permanently fragmented the church. Indeed, the development of the nationality parishes had preserved immigrant devotion to the institutional church while the consolidating Americanization campaigns of the 1920s and 1930s, along with the normal forces of acculturation and assimilation, had reassured native Americans that Roman Catholicism was not really a threat to the future of the nation. When the National Origins Act of 1924 stopped the mass immigration from eastern and southern Europe, some of the pressure eased for the church, not only because the demand for nationality parishes declined but because the concern of native Americans about the relationship between immigration and Catholicism was no longer as intense as in the past. After 1924 the secular forces of American life managed to subtly achieve what an older generation of liberal Catholics and "Americanizers" had tried to force: the assimilation of the Roman Catholic immigrants.

9

The Hispanic Catholics

For decades the church had struggled with the nationality issue, moving back and forth between Americanization and pluralism, trying first mixed parishes, then ethnic parishes, and eventually moving back to mixed parishes. By the mid-1920s, with immigration restriction laws in place and anti-Catholicism rampant, a new generation of church leaders like George Cardinal Mundelein in Chicago and Francis Cardinal Spellman in New York began de-emphasizing the nationality issue, portraying Roman Catholicism as an institution capable of absorbing the "new immigrants" and acculturating them to American society. But after 1924, just as European immigration declined dramatically, immigration from Mexico, Puerto Rico, and later Cuba began rising. From 78,000 people in 1838, the Hispanic-American community would grow to more than 20 million people by 1984. Including undocumented workers, there would be 15 million Mexicans living in the United States. Because Puerto Rico, as a commonwealth partner of the United States, was exempt from immigration laws, as many as 2.5 million Puerto Ricans would be occupying northeastern ghettoes by the early 1980s. Between the Castro revolution of 1959 and the exodus of 1980, more than 1 million Cubans settled in the United States, most in Miami and the Southeast. The vast majority of the Hispanic immigrants were Roman Catholics, and once again church leaders faced the task of absorbing a large, alien population. By the time the Hispanics began arriving in large numbers, the golden age of the nationality parishes was over, at least in terms of the establishment of new ones. Church leaders returned once again to the idea of the mixed parish as the best way of incorporating the newest wave of immigrants.[1]

Like the Catholicism of the eastern and southern Europeans,

Hispanic Catholicism differed substantially from the religious traditions of the Irish. Hispanic Catholicism emerged from the Spanish conquest of New World indigenous societies. Despite major differences in customs, history, and racial background, the Cubans, Puerto Ricans, and Mexicans all mixed Spanish and American Indian values. Since the voyages of Columbus until the Spanish American War of 1898, Puerto Rico and Cuba were colonies of Spain, as was Mexico between the arrival of Cortés in 1519 and the end of the revolution in 1821. Hispanics inherited from Spain a spiritual individualism which viewed the soul as the most important ingredient of character. It was a romantic individualism in the tradition of Don Quixote, emphasizing honor, self-respect, integrity, individual courage, and personal self-expression. From American Indians Hispanics learned to trust one another, live in a kind of spiritual communalism, and feel comfortable with the rhythms of nature. A fourth group of Hispanic Catholics, the Filipinos, did not come from Spanish and American ancestry, but they too shared a religious culture fusing native values with Spanish Catholicism.[2]

When the Spanish empire first began expanding into Latin America and the Philippines in the sixteenth century, the *conquistadores* had an overpowering conviction that Roman Catholicism was the one true faith and that it was their solemn moral duty to teach and then impose it on the native peoples they encountered. Spaniards made no distinctions between church and state or religion and community; indeed, they built New World communities, or *pueblos*, where the Catholic faith and Spanish language were rigidly communicated to indigenous people. In the pueblos, Spaniards organized towns around the concept of peoplehood. The true meaning of life could be realized only within the context of those communities. The Spanish colonies in Mexico, Puerto Rico, Cuba, and the Philippines were all organized around that principle. At the center of community life, structurally as well as spiritually, were the town plaza and its church where people met, celebrated, and worshiped. The church building dominated the plaza, signifying that God was a member of the community along with everyone else. Richard Rodríguez, recalling his parents' descriptions of those Mexican communities in the 1930s, said:

> The steps of the church defined the eternal square where children played and adults talked after dinner. He remembers the way the

> church building was at the center of town life. She remembers the way one could hear the bell throughout the day, telling time. And the way the town completely closed down for certain feastdays. He remembers that the church spire was the first thing he'd see walking back to town. Both my parents have tried to describe something of what it was like for them to have grown up Catholic in small Mexican towns. They remember towns where everyone was Catholic.[3]

Since virtually everyone was Catholic, community identity was synonymous with church identity. Being a Roman Catholic really meant being part of that Roman Catholic *pueblo*, a birthright rather than the fruits of any individual spiritual or emotional experience. Again, Richard Rodríguez remembers that

> I was *un católico* before I was a Catholic. That is, I acquired my earliest sense of the Church—and my membership in it—through my parents' Mexican Catholicism. It was in Spanish that I first learned to pray. I recited family prayers—not from any book. And in those years when we felt alienated from *los gringos*, my family went across town every week to the wooden church of Our Lady of Guadalupe, which was decorated with yellow Christmas lights all year long.[4]

But a Roman Catholic identity did not imply devotion to the institutional church. Unlike the church of Ireland or French Canada, which had struggled for survival in a hostile environment and inspired intense loyalty among parishioners, the Latin American church had no political competition for years. Roman Catholic authority was at the very center of political life. There was no rivalry with foreign cultures, religions, or politics to sharpen Catholic identity or attract people to the institutional church as the vehicle for their survival. In Latin America, Catholic identity was not an intense fidelity to the church, its clerics, and its sacraments, but an individual sense of belonging to a larger community of Catholic people. Religiosity and devotion to the church were not necessarily synonymous for most Hispanic Catholics.

True piety did not depend on regular attendance at Mass and confession, reception of the sacraments, donations of money, obedience to church teachings in politics and family life, or support of the clergy. Indeed, a Hispanic Catholic could be quite indifferent toward the sacraments, even quite hostile to formal church teachings and alienated from church clerics, and yet still see himself as a good Catholic, a valuable, functioning member of the Catholic *pueblo*. In their communities, Hispanic Catholics attached a spiritual dimension to "La Raza," or the people, valuing the quality of *personalismo* in which intimate, personal relationships and internal stability transcended all impersonal, bureaucratic relationships. *Personalismo* on a spiritual plane left Hispanic Catholics with a profound sense of faith in *los santos*—the Catholic saints, who, in return for prayers, lighted candles, devotional promises, and roadside and fireside shrines, would provide assistance, protection, and direction. The church sometimes seemed bureaucratic to the Hispanic Catholic, and as such contradicted the cult of *personalismo*. Instead, Hispanics approached divinity through the medium of *los santos*, not through the sacraments or the priesthood.[5]

In Mexico, peasants were profoundly religious people in the nineteenth century, and like many eastern and southern Europeans, they did not separate the natural and supernatural worlds. Throughout the entire range of life, the Mexican peasant interpreted the world as a balance of opposites—a teetering scale of pleasure and pain, creation and destruction, health and sickness, acceptance and rejection, hope and despair, and life and death. At the top of this world, making sure that all suffering was eventually relieved and all prosperity eventually humbled, was God. In everyone's life, achieving a harmony between extremes was the only way of surviving. Lack of balance, disharmony, or a life of emotional extremes was certain to precipitate illness, misfortune, and pain. Mexican religion, both formal Catholicism and older folk traditions, was geared to achieving that cosmic balance, making sure that the natural world and the supernatural were always functioning on the same plane.[6] In dealing with the challenges of life, the Mexican peasants worked hard at controlling their environment, but true courage, or *machismo*, was not so much a matter of control as it was a question of understanding and accepting reality and of using the medium of *los santos* for necessary assistance.[7]

Like the *contadini* of southern Italy, the Mexican peasants were Roman Catholics without much formal loyalty to the institutional church. As a *mestizo* people racially despised for generations in Mexico by *peninsulares* (Spaniards born in Spain) and *criollos*

(Spaniards born in Mexico), Mexican peasants had a strong resentment of Europeans. Throughout the history of New Spain, most ranking clerics of the church were *peninsulares* and *criollos*; peasants often felt little affection for them. Usually allied with the Spanish elite controlling politics and economic power, the church was a conservative, propertied force in Mexico, controlling vast amounts of land while peasants often starved.[8] Many peasants saw the church as an adversary, and periodically throughout the nineteenth and twentieth centuries they attacked church property and expelled priests from the countryside. In the American borderlands of Texas, New Mexico, Arizona, and California during the nineteenth century, most Catholic clergymen were French, German, or Irish missionaries who spoke little Spanish and disdained Hispanic culture. One Mexican parishioner, when asked about the church, replied:

> These priests are good and educated men and we must respect them. But they do not understand everything. Their learning is from books. Any man can become a priest. It is not the best life and some undertake it as a form of penance. . . . When one wants help from God, one should go to someone who knows him. The priest's duty is to say mass. He runs the machinery of the church. He does not see into the trouble of one's soul.[9]

Many peasant immigrants to the United States also came from areas in Mexico where priests and parochial schools were few. Whether from open hostility or indifference, the Mexican peasants pouring into the Southwest after 1911 had a substantial distance from the church.

But while maintaining an emotional distance from the clergy and comfortably avoiding many authoritarian prohibitions of Roman Catholicism, Mexicans nevertheless considered themselves spiritual Catholics. Usually uninformed about theology and often unwilling to accept pastoral admonitions to donate money and render obedience, the peasants still functioned within a Catholic emotional world. Most made sure their children received the sacraments of baptism and confirmation and were faithful in praying the rosary. When visiting priests reached rural ranching communities, Mexican peasants received them with open arms, readying infants for baptism, youths for instruction in the catechism, and unwed couples for marriage. Temporary altars, crucifixes, *santitos* (images of saints), and confessionals appeared. In their homes, however humble, the peasants maintained elaborately decorated altars, replete with *santitos,* statues of the Virgin Mother, flowers, candles, drawings of deceased relatives, and votive figures. In the presence of that home altar, peasant families confronted the vicissitudes of life.[10]

Like the peasant villagers of southern and eastern Europe, Mexicans and Mexican Americans built their social life around the Catholic calendar, with *fiestas* and celebrations intermittently relieving the drudgery of daily existence. Beginning January 17 with the feast of St. Anthony the Abbot, when peasants decorated and paraded pets and farm animals past the church, the peasants went on to celebrate religious events like *Candelaría* (Purification) in February, Holy Week in April, All Saints' Day in November, Our Lady of Guadalupe on December 12 (Mexico's patron saint day), and *Posadas* during Christmas. They closed the year with the Day of Innocents on December 28, a memorial celebration of King Herod's massacre of children during his search for the infant Jesus. In between these religious *fiestas,* Mexican peasants also celebrated the days of St. Anthony, St. John, St. James, Santa Anna, St. Peter, and Santa Cruz.[11]

The frequent observance of saints' days reflected the universal appeal Catholic saints had for Mexican peasants. The peasants' devotion was similar in intensity to the *clientismo* of the southern Italians. Although their belief in *La Raza* convinced them of God's divine approbation, they too felt the need for intermediaries between people and heaven. Their unwillingness to rely always on priests to direct their relationship with God reinforced the need for saints. The Virgin of Guadalupe was their favorite, with a pilgrimage to her basilica in Mexico City the devotional peak of one's life. The Virgin Mother intervened with God, averted danger, cured illnesses, ended drought, and helped maintain the precarious balance of life. Mexican peasants also turned to particular saints to work out particular problems. The Virgin of San Juan helped people with family difficulties; St. Christopher, the patron saint of travelers, helped migrant workers; St. Anthony the Abbot protected farm animals; and St. Martin the Horseman helped bring prosperity.

Mexican peasants also had a folk Catholicism that blended European and Indian traditions. Even their most sacred religious devotion, that to the Virgin of Guadalupe, was inseparably connected to the indigenous past; for centuries before the appearance of the Virgin in 1531, a female goddess had appeared at the same site to Aztec worshipers. The Aztec emphasis on collective security (once sought through human sacrifice) survived in the commitment to *La Raza,* which guaranteed community life in the present while formal Catholicism sought to guarantee individual life in the future. Folk Catholicism intimately linked peasants to the continuum between the natural and supernatural worlds, giving them some sense of control over their environment. While formal Catholicism often preached passivity and resignation to the forces of the universe, folk religion gave peasants power, relieving their guilt about any personal failures to fulfill church expectations while leaving them in direct contact with divine power. The religion of *La Raza,* though hundreds of years removed from its Aztec beginnings, was essentially a *mestizo* faith emphasizing communalism in the present and individual salvation in the next world, without any heavy theological overtones about exactly what merited eternal life.

Older religious rituals, much to the dismay of many Catholic priests, had merged with formal ceremonial occasions. Even though succeeding generations of foreign priests urged peasants to abandon their "superstitions," the peasants held fast to them as the only way of surviving tragedy and externally imposed authority. On St. John's Day in June, for example, which peasants called *El Día de Bañar* (Day of Bathing), the celebrants ritually immersed themselves in a pond, river, lake, or tub as an atoning purification. On the same day women dampened their hair, then kneeled and spread their hair over the doorsill while members of a religious procession cut it off with hatchets. Festival parades with bands of violinists, fireworks, gunfire, and people walking barefoot or on their knees were common. On All Souls' Day, when the family gathered at the cemetery to commemorate the dead, peasants decorated the graves with flowers, images and pictures of saints and of the dead, bottles and oyster shells, and old personal mementos. A whole range of folktales mixed with Catholic theology to explain the peasant world. Mexican *tejanos,* for example, annually rejoiced at the story of San Miguel, the patron saint of El Paso valley, who appeared with a flaming sword at the tower of the parish church to ward off an attacking band of Civil War marauders.

Faith in divine intervention was the core of peasant folk religion. Peasants had enormous faith in miracles—the willingness of

God to intervene in individual affairs, usually for the good of an entire community, at the request of pleading patron saints and often through the medium of particularly gifted men and women. Among Mexican peasants, the most gifted people functioning outside institutional Catholicism were the *curanderos,* or healers. Since illness and misfortune were rooted in an imbalance between man and nature, usually through sin and disobedience, which witches *(brujas)* could exploit, the powers of the *curanderos* had spiritual and supernatural overtones. An old *tejano* peasant once remarked:

> Witches cannot harm the good. A pure person who has followed God's way is safe from them. A witch cannot affect flesh that is pure. But each sin puts a bit of evil in a man. It is through this evil that the witches work. If you have no sin in you, then you are safe. But where can you find a member of *La Raza* who has not at some time sinned? It is our fate.[12]

Curanderos mixed the popular beliefs and empirical remedies of both Spanish and Indian culture, using natural herbs and plants as well as chants, hexes, and blessings to restore balance and heal sickness. Some *curanderos* whose powers were particularly strong achieved the status of sainthood among Mexican peasants. An elderly man referred to as the "God of Hosts" reportedly healed the sick, cured the blind, mobilized paraplegics, and fed thousands of people with a few tortillas in northern Mexico in 1861. Teresa Urrea apparently healed thousands of people in El Paso in 1896 after spiritual voices called her to spend her life administering to the sick. The *curandero* Don Pedrito Jaramillo wandered for years throughout south Texas curing thousands of people in the 1880s and 1890s. After his death Mexican and Mexican-American peasants placed his picture among the pantheon of saints adorning family altars and frequently prayed to him for health and well-being. These, of course, were some of the "superstitions" church leaders wanted the peasants to abandon.[13]

Religious life among Cuban immigrants was even more complex. Like Mexico, Cuba was overwhelmingly Catholic, enjoyed a strong *pueblo* identity, and lacked strong commitments to the institutional church. There was also a class dimension to Cuban Catholicism in which different levels of piety and devotional observances separated peasants from elites, a distinction not as clear among

Mexican Catholics, at least among those coming to the United States. The Cuban immigrants came to America in two waves: an upper-class migration beginning in 1959 when Castro came to power and a peasant migration in the late 1970s and early 1980s. Their religious backgrounds contributed even more variety to American Catholicism.

In the Spanish colonial empire, the church was responsible for the moral and spiritual guidance of the people, but the Catholic clergy was under imperial direction. Church and state in Cuba did not really separate until after 1898, when the independence movement triumphed during the Spanish-American War. Spain had enjoyed a papal grant of power allowing the king to appoint, assign, and dismiss priests and collect tithes. Highly dependent on the governing classes, the church became a conservative force identified closely with the interests of the elite. Because of its upper-class bias, links to the conservative forces of the Spanish Crown, and intense opposition to the independence movement, the church alienated large numbers of Cubans, who equated it with corruption, conservatism, and authoritarian control. When Fidel Castro came to power in 1959, there were only two hundred parishes serving 6 million people on the island. Only seven hundred priests worked in those parishes. While Ireland had one parish for every 3,000 people and one priest for every 450 people, Cuba had only one parish for every 30,000 people and one priest for every 8,500 people. Even Mexico had one parish for every 14,500 people and one priest for every 3,700 people.[14]

The Cuban church for the most part served the needs of the urban middle and upper classes. Cuban priests almost always came from the upper classes. Traditionally, well-to-do Cubans had been more committed to the church, more likely to attend Mass as a family, to contribute financially, and to obey pastoral teachings. During the nineteenth century, the church had come under the influence of Jansenist morality and had accepted the importance of internal faith as well as external observances of piety. Those values persisted into the twentieth century, giving a small number of Cuban Catholics a kind of piety not unlike that of the Irish, Basques, or French Canadians. When Fidel Castro came to power and expropriated large amounts of property while converting the economy to socialism, large numbers of upper-class Cubans headed for the United States. Unlike immigrants from Mexico, Puerto Rico, and Central

America, they were more than nominal Catholics, more likely to identify with the institutional church.[15]

But the Cuban migration of the 1970s and early 1980s was quite different—a movement of peasants and workers rather than of the well-to-do. Not only were these peasants usually nominal Catholics enjoying a *pueblo* identity without feeling much loyalty to the church itself, they were also more likely to have a syncretic faith mixing formal Catholicism with traditional African folk beliefs. Unlike Mexico, where few Africans settled, Cuba had large plantations and large numbers of slaves. Blacks were a significant part of the population, totaling perhaps 17 percent by 1960 and outnumbering whites in several regions. Among large numbers of Cuban blacks as well as lower-class whites and those of mixed blood, religious beliefs revolved around syncretic Afro-Catholic rituals. Although the educated Cuban upper classes believed that the cults were based on barbaric superstitions, the lower classes, especially Africans, were drawn to them. It was often difficult to distinguish Roman Catholicism from such cults as Santería, Abakua, Mayombería, Regla de Palo, and Regla Conga.[16]

The largest of the Afro-Cuban religions was Santería, several closely related faiths distinguished by the ethnic backgrounds of their devotees. The most influential of the Santería cults was Lucumi, a group fusing the Yoruba language of West Africa with Spanish. Others included the Arara from Dahomey and *vodún* spiritualism from Haiti, a combination of French and Fon cultures. All of the Santería cults mixed selected Catholic rituals with African mythology, identifying themselves nominally as Catholics, equating Catholic saints with various African deities, and interpreting Catholicism as the Spanish-community version of Santería. Among the Lucumi, Yoruba gods and Catholic saints were treated as replicas of one another, known as *santos* in Spanish and *orishas* in Yoruba. St. Barbara was the same person as Shango, the god of war, while St. Francis of Assisi was equated with Orunmila, the god of destiny. Elegua guarded the gates of Heaven for Yorubans and was the same as St. Peter in Cuban Santería. The most important of the *orishas* was Odudua, identified with the Virgin of Carmen, to whom the Lucumi sacrificed white chickens every month. Each believer also had a patron saint to bring protection and prosperity—Yemaya, the goddess of the sea, for sailors; Ogun, the equivalent of John the Baptist, for blacksmiths and soldiers; or Oshun, the patroness of lovers. Santería rituals combined such Catholic practices as lighting candles and reciting the Lord's prayer and the rosary with chants, drumming, animal sacrifices, secret oaths, visionary trances, and spiritual possessions. The Afro-Cuban cults accompanied many peasant immigrants to America.[17]

Although not Hispanic Catholics, Haitian immigrants often accompanied the second wave of Cubans to the United States in the late 1970s and 1980s. Like lower-class Cuban Catholicism, Haitian religion retained powerful African roots and a strong voodoo connection. From the mid-1600s, when they were first transported as slaves from Africa to Haiti, they were forbidden to practice tribal religions. Forced converts to Roman Catholicism, the Haitians refused to abandon African voodoo, instead fusing the two into a single religion. Afro-Haitian Catholicism acknowledges God as the creator of heaven and earth, the *Gran Met,* a deity powerful but remote who delegated the mundane management of human affairs to intermediary spirits called *loa.* Haitians saw those spirits everywhere, in trees, ponds, rivers, waterfalls, caves, springs, lakes, valleys, or groves. Competition between good and evil spirits is the essence of life, and voodoo Catholicism maintains harmony in the world. Every July 16, Haitians celebrate the Vyej Marik, or the apparition of the Virgin of Miracles, Our Lady of Mount Carmel, on top of a palm tree at Ville Bonheur. The annual pilgrimage brings tens of thousands of people to the village—priests and nuns, rich and poor, voodoo practitioners, and wealthy businessmen—all to propitiate the *loa* Legba (St. Peter), known as the master of roads and pathways, make ritual stops at sacred trees, and to wash themselves in the sacred Saut d'Eau waterfalls of the Tombe River. Such voodoo spirits as Danbala Wedo, the snake symbol, or Aida Wedo or Ezili Freda possess the bodies of the worshipers. On the next morning, the pilgrims return to the village square to hear the standard Catholic Mass delivered from the church balcony.

Ever since their first attempts to convert the African slaves, Roman Catholic authorities in Haiti have attempted to suppress the Old World religion. Periodically over the centuries, the church has waged a political campaign against African-Catholic syncretic beliefs, the most recent one in 1941 when the Haitian government spearheaded an "antisuperstition" crusade involving destruction of temples and sacred natural settings. To the French and Irish priests serving in Haiti during the seventeenth, eighteenth, nineteenth, and twentieth centuries, the mixture of formal religion and voodoo was the epitome of sacrilege. The drinking of bull and chicken blood at religious ceremonies, the identification of St. Jacques with the African god of war Ougou Feray, the mud baths, and the hexes and charms all alienated the priests, but the traditions survived and came into the dioceses of the American church, especially in Florida, with the wave of Haitian immigrants in the early 1980s.[18]

A similar mix occurred in the Philippines. In order to secure part of the Asian spice trade, gain economic access to China and Japan, and convert the Filipinos to Christianity, Spain expanded into the Philippines in 1565. Unlike the conquest of Mexico, that of the Philippines was bloodless. The Philippines was a geographical quagmire of seven thousand separate islands, only eleven larger than one thousand square miles, and even those were marked by rugged mountains and jungles. Geographical particularism, political decentralization, and complex linguistic diversity characterized Filipino society and made for little organized resistance to Spanish colonization. But that regional diversity also made imposition of a single culture throughout the archipelago almost impossible. Although Spanish political control of the islands lasted from 1565 to 1898, cultural domination was never so complete; indeed, the natives managed to "Philippinize" Spanish culture and convert it to their own uses. Filipino Catholicism was a prime example.[19]

In preconquest Filipino society, a variety of gods, goddesses, and rituals governed the cycle of religious life. Although most Filipino ethnic groups had some notion of a supreme being—Bathala in the Tagalog language or Laon in Baseyan—responsible for creating the earth, it was not a deity playing a direct role in everyday affairs. As in most peasant societies, Filipino religious beliefs combined the world of natural objects and living things with spirits and with formal, institutional devotions. Filipinos worshiped nature, offering devotion to mountains, caves, rivers, the sun, the moon, and the stars as well as to such animals as crows, sharks, and crocodiles. They also worshiped a world of spirits. A large pantheon of deities and spirits ready to interfere in people's lives animated Filipino religion. The good spirits were known as *anitos* and the bad spirits as *diwatas.* Only a complicated series of ritual prayers, promises, and sacrifices could placate the wrath of *diwatas* or stimulate the generosity of *anitos.*[20]

Spain then imposed Roman Catholicism on this world of spirits.

The church tried to convert the entire Filipino society and to make Christianity an integral part of daily life. Spanish clerical and political officials required a whole range of daily devotions from parishioners in the *cabecera* villages where churches stood and priests resided. In most of those villages, women and children met each day at the large cross in the main plaza and recited the rosary, and at sunset children often chanted the rosary while walking through the streets. Most Filipinos, however, lived far away from those central villages, in rural areas where priests and churches were few and far between. The natives proved highly selective in their approach to Catholicism, adapting it to local circumstances and endowing it with a unique devotional content. Filipinos combined an external devotion to formalized ritual with a general indifference to theological and institutional subtleties; accepted magic and continued to be devoted to the spirits of ancestors and to the world of nature; had a powerful belief in miraculous cures; maintained a conspiracy of silence in which they refused to pass on to Spanish priests any news or evidence of "paganism" or religious unorthodoxy; and received infrequently the sacraments of the church.

But while seldom participating in conventional observances of the Catholic faith, rural Filipinos readily accepted the *fiesta* system to celebrate Holy Week, Corpus Christi, and local patron saints' days. Although most Filipinos rejected the seventeenth- and eighteenth-century attempts of Jesuit priests to introduce flagellation rituals as forms of penance, the practice did take root among a minority and persisted into the twentieth century. Forms of such penance ranged from walking on one's knees the length of a rough marble church floor to marching long distances with paid assistants whipping bare backs with rope-bamboo lashes. Most Filipinos readily accepted sensuous observances like candlelight parades, processional floats, the smell of incense, loud music, Gregorian chants, and elaborate pageantry. Because Filipino society had long been kin-oriented, Filipinos also quickly adopted the principle of coparenthood *(compadrazgo)* or godparenthood. During the eighteenth and nineteenth centuries, the elaborate ceremonies of Spanish Catholicism overpowered pagan rituals, eliminating, for example, the pre-Hispanic pattern of ritual drinking of alcoholic beverages. But in the process of absorbing Spanish Catholicism, Filipinos created a folk Catholicism of their own. In the past they had appealed to *anitos* and *diwatas*, but now they performed the same rituals for

Catholic saints. No single cult of mass appeal such as that of the Virgin of Guadalupe or of the Black Madonna of Czestochowa appeared, but Filipinos did have locally or regionally powerful saints capable of protecting and nourishing them, such as the Black Nazarene of Quiapo, Manila. In Filipino Catholicism, the miraculous powers of the supernatural permeated folk religion, providing a cultural unity previously unknown in the archipelago.[21]

A major schism, similar to the independent church movements in the United States, divided Filipino Catholicism after the Spanish American War of 1898. As the drive for Filipino independence gained momentum in the 1890s, resentment of the church's close relationship with Spanish authorities grew more intense. When armed rebellion erupted in 1896, Emilio Aguinaldo, the leader of the independence movement, appointed Gregoria Aglipay, a Filipino priest, to head the Philippine Independent church. By 1898 the church claimed more than 1 million members. Aguinaldo told the Catholic clergy to pledge allegiance to Aglipay or be labeled traitors to the Philippines. The Filipino independence movement had long looked to the day when Spanish power would be eliminated, but after 1898 the United States became the imperial enemy. When American officials and military personnel began arriving in the archipelago, Aguinaldo turned his wrath on them, enveloping the islands in a bitter guerrilla war between 1899 and 1902. At the same time, when Vatican officials accepted U.S. demands to appoint American rather than Filipino clerics to the church bishoprics, Aglipay's Philippine Independent church gained even more momentum. Dennis Dougherty, later the Cardinal Archbishop of Philadelphia, became bishop of the diocese of Nueva Segovia in the Philippines in 1903 and had to deal with the Aglipay schism, which by 1904 claimed more than one-quarter of the population and half the property of the Roman Catholic church in the Philippines. Although membership in the Philippine Independent church peaked and then declined after 1905, many Filipino immigrants brought its teachings with them to the United States.[22]

Finally, like the other Hispanic Catholics, the Filipinos too had a rich, syncretic folk religion, but it was complicated by the ethnic and linguistic background of the islands. When the Spaniards first arrived in the sixteenth century, they encountered hundreds of separate ethnic and linguistic groups but succeeded in superimposing Roman Catholicism on 90 percent of them. Naturally, folk religions emerged that fused the secular and spiritual worlds as well as ancient tribal religions and Christianity. Perhaps the best known of them was the *Guardia de Honor.* Originally founded in Central Luzon by the Dominicans as a confraternity devoted to the Virgin Mary, the Guardia slowly changed into a millennial cult led by "Baltazar," a charismatic figure who succeeded by 1900 in getting perhaps twenty-five thousand Filipinos to worship him along with the Virgin, Jesus, the Holy Ghost, and the Twelve Apostles. There were literally dozens of other folk religions throughout the islands, and many of them came to America with the formal Catholicism of the Filipino immigrants.[23]

In Puerto Rico, Spanish Catholicism went through similar stages: formal imposition on the native people, syncretic development of a folk religion, indifference to complicated theological questions and affairs of the institutional church, and the evolution of an overwhelming *pueblo* identity. The first Roman Catholic diocese in the New World was established at San Juan, Puerto Rico, in 1511, and until 1898, when Puerto Rico became an American territory, the diocese of San Juan was administered by a series of Spanish-born bishops. The only exception was Bishop Juan Alejo Arizmundi, a Puerto Rican native who presided over the diocese between 1803 and 1814. The lack of a native Puerto Rican clergy, the consecutive tenure of Spanish bishops, the close relationship between the church and the upper classes, and the opposition of the church to the nineteenth-century Puerto Rican independence movement all contributed to a sense of alienation among peasants. Although nominally Roman Catholic, they had little affection for or attraction to the institutional church.[24]

After 1898 church administration in Puerto Rico resembled that in the Philippines, with American priests and bishops replacing Spaniards. A clash of cultures occurred as Irish Catholicism confronted Hispanic values. The American church's emphasis on strict morality and obedience, the sacraments, the importance of parochial schools, the necessity of daily devotions, and the transcendence of religious asceticism contrasted sharply with the folk liberalism of Puerto Rican Catholicism. Irish-American administration did stimulate improvements in religious instruction, ritual devotion, church attendance, and the number of Puerto Ricans taking up vocations, but the church still failed to overcome the alienation of the masses.[25]

In several ways the alienation even increased. Irish-American priests staffed the parishes and parochial schools, and American-born bishops controlled the dioceses, creating a great distance between parishioners and church officials. It was not until 1961 that a Puerto Rican native, Luís Aponte Martínez, was ordained as bishop and assigned to an island diocese. Few American priests, nuns, or lay personnel spoke Spanish, and the parochial schools followed an American model, with little time given to Hispanic culture and history. Because the church insisted on rigorous administrative standards and on charging tuition, the parochial schools became elite institutions serving the upper class. During the 1940s and 1950s, as liberal and radical political movements appeared in Puerto Rico, American church leaders became identified with the forces of tradition and conservatism, opposing birth control and land reform. In 1960 the church endorsed the *Partido Acción Cristiana,* a conservative party opposed to the more liberal *Partido Popular.* The Catholic party received less than 10 percent of the vote, an indication of how large numbers of Puerto Ricans felt about the church. Americans had managed to assume completely the conservative role in church government, which the Spanish had vacated in 1898.[26]

But despite their nominal Catholicism, at least in a formal sense, which was a "womb to tomb" faith with little in between, the Puerto Ricans were highly religious, and most of them identified themselves as Roman Catholics. Most homes displayed a variety of holy pictures, crucifixes, and religious statues; children feared *el diablo* (the devil) and loved *Papá Díos* (Father God); people crossed themselves frequently and prayed regularly, usually to a favorite saint; participated in *fiestas* and processions of Holy Week, Christmas, Epiphany, and patron saint days; and frequently called on priests to bless homes, businesses, cars, and animals. And yet, attendance at Mass, communion, and confession remained infrequent; entering religious orders was rare; and financial support of the church was rather miserly. Such was the pattern of Hispanic Catholicism.[27]

Unlike the other Roman Catholic immigrants, the Mexicans, Puerto Ricans, Cubans, and Filipinos came after the zenith of the nationality parishes in the early 1900s. Bishops like Mundelein, O'Connell, Dougherty, and Spellman had turned to mixed, territorial parishes to assimilate the Hispanic immigrants into the church and larger society. Even without the "Americanization" commitments of the new generation of bishops, the Hispanic Catholics hardly produced enough ethnic priests to staff nationality parishes; nor were parishioner activity, financial resources, or financial commitments sufficient to support nationality churches. In Corpus Christi, Texas, in 1940, there were 147,000 Mexicans and only 14,000 Anglos in the diocese, but English-speaking priests outnumbered Spanish-speaking priests by 115 to 22. New nationality parishes were quite rare. The diocese of Miami, Florida, had been created in 1958, with Coleman F. Carroll as its first bishop. By 1960 there were 65 parishes and 308,000 Roman Catholics in the diocese, with the vast majority of the priests Irish American. In 1982, after more than twenty years of Cuban immigration, the Catholic population of the Archdiocese of Miami had reached nearly 900,000 people in 134 parishes. There were sixty-seven Spanish-surnamed priests in the diocese, with thirteen of them Cuban-born, and Augustin A. Roman, a Cuban native, serving as an auxiliary bishop for Archbishop Edward A. McCarthy. Bishop Roman was "Episcopal Vicar for the Spanish-speaking People" and supervised a number of diocesan societies for Cubans. But neither Bishop Carroll nor Archbishop McCarthy had turned to the separate nationality-parish model to handle the influx of Cuban immigrants. Puerto Ricans were not too different from Mexicans or Cubans. In the early 1960s, there were only 15,000 Puerto Rican children in New York parochial schools, less than 10 percent of those of school age, and only one native Puerto Rican priest in the archdiocese.[28]

The church's approach to the Puerto Ricans illustrated the demise of the nationality parish. During his tenure as Archbishop of Philadelphia between 1918 and 1951, Denis Cardinal Dougherty established 112 new parishes and 145 parochial schools, but he was like Mundelein in his opposition to nationality parishes. Ninety miles north, in New York, Francis Cardinal Spellman took the same position. In the 1920s a few Puerto Rican nationality parishes appeared—La Milagrosa parish in 1926 on 114th Street and Seventh Avenue and Holy Agony parish in 1930 at Third Avenue and 103d Street. But in 1939 Cardinal Spellman ended the practice, placing Puerto Rican immigrants in mixed parishes. He was not insensitive to their needs. He took St. Cecilia parish in East Harlem, for example, and turned it over to Spanish-speaking American priests who had worked in Puerto Rico, while leaving intact its designation as a territorial parish also serving remaining German and Irish parishioners. But Spellman generally worried about the wisdom of retaining nationality parishes, not only because they seemed to retard assimilation and to perpetuate the image of the church as a foreign institution, but also because they were so temporary. By the third generation, the English-speaking grandchildren of German, Slavic, and Italian immigrants were heading for the suburbs, leaving behind huge nationality churches with a few dozen elderly members. For Spellman, the inexorable forces of assimilation always destroyed the nationality churches; so why not move instead to integrated, mixed parishes serving elderly immigrants of an earlier generation as well as the young immigrants of the latest group? In a few generations, when earlier immigrants had left behind their elderly in the move to the suburbs and new immigrants filled the ghettoes, the church buildings, activity centers, and parochial schools would still be useful and available.[29]

A similar situation prevailed among Mexican Catholics in Los Angeles, where the American church hierarchy looked upon the immigrants with a mixture of concern, disdain, and fear. They very much wanted Mexicans to move into the institutional church, but they were concerned about the lack of Mexican priests, the detachment of the peasants from church ceremonies, and some of their devotional practices, and they were afraid that the immigrants would be vulnerable to evangelization by Protestants or Communists. German and Irish church leaders, conditioned to centralization in diocesan authority and devotion to the local parish, were disturbed that Mexican piety was so frequently divorced from the institutional church.[30]

Mexican Catholics were not, of course, totally indifferent or hostile to the church. They were members of the Catholic *pueblo,* and priests were necessary for the major spiritual rites of passage—baptism, confirmation, communion, confession, marriage, and extreme unction. Mexican immigrants settling in areas where there were no churches often exhibited the same lay initiative as other immigrants. At San José Parish in Nueces County, Texas, for example, they established three saints' societies in 1898 while another group from Tamualipas in Mexico formed a confraternity in 1904. Sixty families at La Cejita established six sodalities and confraternities between 1907 and 1916, and the next year asked the bishop to establish a parish for them. But while the Irish or Poles or French

Canadians placed great trust in the priest as a representative of God in everyday life and in the necessity of daily and weekly religious devotions and sacramentals, the Mexicans expressed much of their spirituality outside the network of priest and chapel.[31]

Because of divergent attitudes of clerics and immigrants, as well as the racial hostility of many Yankee and Irish Catholics, the church played no major role in mediating the collision between Anglo and Hispanic cultures or in assimilating the immigrants. Like the Irish and other immigrant priests in the late nineteenth century, clerical leaders in the Mexican communities did not want to trigger any twentieth-century reaction against the church; so they remained politically quite conservative on social issues. Still concerned about its image, the church was not about to do much to improve the social situation of the immigrants, at least beyond supporting the charitable institutions established in other dioceses. Consequently, the institutional church, so central to the lives of many European immigrant groups, was underdeveloped among the Mexicans. In 1930, for example, while there were 179 parochial schools, twelve orphanages, nine reform schools, seven homes for the aged, two rest homes, and nine hospitals for the 305,000 Catholics of the archdiocese of Baltimore, there were only twenty-seven schools, one orphanage, and three hospitals serving the nearly 170,000 Catholics in the diocese of Corpus Christi, Texas.[32]

Not until after World War II did church leaders, especially in Los Angeles, become particularly concerned about the Mexican immigrants and the need to Americanize them. Archbishop J. Francis McIntyre took his cue from Francis Cardinal Spellman in New York in attempting to absorb the Hispanic immigrants into the institutional church. McIntyre inaugurated a vigorous campaign to build parochial schools in the archdiocese of Los Angeles. In 1940, there were 98 parochial schools with an enrollment of 29,151 students serving a Catholic population of 317,000; by 1960 that had grown to 327 schools with 159,000 students serving 1,297,000 Catholics.[33] Many of those schools no doubt served the waves of eastern and midwestern Catholics settling in California after World War II, but by 1960 practically every parish in the barrios of East Los Angeles had a parochial school.

In the 1960s and 1970s, church leaders also began taking a closer look at Mexican-American economic problems. The National Catholic Welfare Conference had formed the Bishops' Committee for the Spanish-Speaking in 1943, but when César Chávez and the Farm Workers Organizing Committee began boycotting the growers of California and south Texas in the 1960s and 1970s, a number of church leaders became actively involved. Archbishop Robert Lucey of San Antonio had long expressed concern about immigrant poverty. Still, most church leaders took the high road, urging conciliation and compromise and a general spirit of equity and fairness for the workers. Because some parish priests did join the picketing and demonstrations, growers criticized the church, but since the church did not formally endorse the strikes, Mexican workers grew more alienated. It was all César Chávez could do to keep many of the immigrants from picketing diocesan headquarters in Los Angeles, San Francisco, and south Texas.[34] The church and Mexican Catholics had still not reached across that centuries-old institutional barrier.

The decline of the nationality parish coincided with the Hispanic influx and reinforced Hispanics' alienation from the church. In the nineteenth and twentieth centuries, the nationality parishes had helped maintain close communication between the immigrants and the church, providing immigrants with a strong institutional setting within which they could adjust to American society. Immigrants were able for a time to continue Old World rituals and holidays and meet with people familiar with Old World values. The buildings of the parish, along with the immigrants' identity as parishioners, left them with a sense of belonging in the community. Hispanic immigrants, because they had few native priests and settled in areas where active Catholic parishes were already functioning, did not enjoy those advantages, especially since they had no opportunities to establish their own parishes. Not until 1970, when Father Patricio Flores was ordained auxiliary bishop of San Antonio, was there a Hispanic bishop in the United States; by that time as well there were only fourteen hundred Hispanic priests in the United States, and only a third of them were American born.[35] The church hardly played the critical role in the lives of Hispanic immigrants that it had played in the lives of so many eastern and southern Europeans.

Hispanic apathy about the institutional church became a source of real concern to the American Catholic hierarchy, just as earlier Irish and German prelates had worried about the Italians and East Europeans. In the summer of 1985, Hispanic Catholics from 130 dioceses in the United States met in Washington, D.C., to discuss the problem. Termed III Encuentro, the meeting underscored the distance many Hispanics felt from the church. Archbishop Patricio Flores claimed there that Spanish-speaking Protestant evangelists were making real headway in the Hispanic community; that only 185 of the 1,500 Hispanic priests in the United States were American-born; that nearly 40 percent of Hispanic Catholics never attend Mass; and that only 1 percent of Hispanic youths were at all active in the church. In its 1983 Pastoral Letter on Hispanic Ministry, the National Conference of Catholic Bishops had expressed similar concerns, fearing that serious "leakage" was undermining the reality of the Catholic *pueblo* in the United States.[36]

10

Modernization and the Catholic Immigrants

In the peasant villages of the Old World, people had lived for centuries in "island communities" governed by nuclear families, subsistence economies, local markets, and personal relationships. They knew one another and felt secure in the overwhelming familiarity and predictability of everyday life. But changes in the Atlantic economy and migration to the United States had destroyed those traditional bases of emotional security. Finding themselves caught up in a new, complex economic world governed by international markets and impersonal relationships, the immigrants had been forced to build new institutions to restore their sense of security. In their workers' and emigrant aid societies, family associations, nationality parishes, parochial schools, sodalities, confraternities, and clubs, as well as in the foods they ate, holidays they celebrated, and cultural values they nurtured, the immigrants found symbolic associations to preserve some of the way of life they had left behind and to gain some control over their New World environment. All of the Catholic immigrants—Poles, Lithuanians, Czechs, Slovaks, Rusins, Ukrainians, Germans, Irish, French Canadians, Slovenes, Croatians, Italians, Melkites, Maronites, Mexicans, Cubans, Puerto Ricans, Spaniards, Portuguese, and Basques—established institutional ghettoes in the United States where they found stability and security.

Although ethnic loyalties created stability within individual groups, they often generated competition, fear, and instability for the society as a whole; so Americans constantly searched for ways of fulfilling their egalitarian ideals without dissolving their community. For more than three centuries, Americans have been preoccupied with their diversity, worried about whether the centrifugal forces of race, religion, language, and national origins would eventually split the country apart. The traditional and most rigid approach to diversity was "Anglo-conformity, " the conviction that American society would survive only if the newcomers adopted the values of the white Protestant majority. Such native American groups as the Know-Nothing party of the 1850s, the American Protective Association of the 1890s, and the Ku Klux Klan in the 1920s tried to force Protestant values upon the Roman Catholic immigrants. Even Yankee, French, and "liberal" Catholics in the nineteenth century had worked to "Americanize" the immigrants as quickly as possible in order to prevent the church from being identified as a "foreign institution." The immigrants, of course, resented Anglo-conformity. Surrendering their religion to Protestants or their language and spiritual values to American Catholics would have left them naked in a strange cultural environment, unable to interpret or adapt to the new values around them. So the idea of Anglo-conformity, though popular among some native American groups, was not at all a realistic approach to the problem of diversity.

The extreme opposite of Anglo-conformity was the idea of cultural pluralism. Accepting everyone's right to political and economic opportunity, cultural pluralists also proclaimed the right of each ethnic group to sustain its own identity. In the 1970s advocates of cultural pluralism exalted ethnic differences as the genius of American society, for although ethnic diversity guaranteed cultural conflict, it also prevented class conflict by dividing workers along cultural lines. Promoting equality and diversity, cultural pluralists were far more tolerant of ethnic differences than supporters of Anglo-conformity. For immigrant Catholics, the demise of "liberalism" and promotion of the nationality parishes in the late 1800s and early 1900s had marked the shift within the church from Anglo-conformity to cultural pluralism, just as the "Americanization" campaigns of Cardinals Mundelein and Spellman had reversed the trend in the 1920s and 1930s.

The middle ground in the debate over American diversity was the "melting-pot" ideal. The most naive proponents of this ideal were confident that a new culture would quickly emerge in the United States. English playwright Israel Zangwell described in 1909 what he thought was the American melting pot:

> There she lies, the great melting pot—listen! Can't you hear the roaring and the bubbling? There gapes her mouth—harbour

> where a thousand mammoth feeders come from the ends of the world to pour in their human freight. Ah, what a stirring and a seething—Celt and Latin, Slav and Teuton, Greek and Syrian, Black and yellow.[1]

By embracing every group and expecting the emergence of a new culture, the melting-pot ideology was more generous than Anglo-conformity and more in tune with notions of freedom and opportunity. The naiveté of the melting-pot ideal came in its assumption that the new culture would appear quickly, fusing every race, color, religion, language, and nationality group into a new whole. Now, more than seventy-five years since Zangwell's prediction, the melting he envisioned remains only a dream.[2]

In recent years, especially during the 1970s, Americans have flirted with the "ethnic revival," seeing in the civil rights and ethnic-power movements proof positive that diversity survives, that older patterns of race, religion, language, and national origins continue to govern social life in the United States.[3] But the melting pot is working nonetheless. At any given point in American history, the society seems quite diverse, apparently confirming the opinions of cultural pluralists about the continuing vitality of racial, religious, nationality, and linguistic differences. Despite appearances, however, the processes of modernization, acculturation, and assimilation have been inexorable, constantly working to transform minority values and loyalties and bring them in line with those of the larger society. Black people, for example, came from dozens of different tribal cultures in West Africa over the course of two centuries, but "melted" into an integrated cultural minority in the United States. Alex Haley notwithstanding, few American blacks can locate their tribal origins, so complete has been their assimilation with one another. Other ethnic melting pots have also been at work, bringing German-speaking people from all over western and central Europe together in the United States; stimulating large-scale intermarriage between Swedes, Norwegians, and Danes in the upper Midwest; and fusing the Scots-Irish and English settlers of the South. Each immigrant group has had to adjust Old World values and associate itself with larger groups, eventually undergoing a racial, religious, nationality, and linguistic accommodation. The speed and extent of assimilation have varied from group to group, but no group has been immune. While American society has remained culturally diverse from generation to generation, the nature of that diversity has changed at each stage, with older groups slowly mixing in with the larger society and new groups appearing isolated and distinct.[4]

The melting pot operated in several stages over the course of several generations, first introducing the immigrants to the rhythms and values of modern industrial society, then acculturating them and their children to the social values, language, and material artifacts of the United States, and finally assimilating them into the emotional relationships and social network of American society. At first, the immigrants experienced culture shock when their Old World customs and values were threatened with disruption in America. Desperately poor, they struggled for survival in an alien world of impersonal bureaucracies and complex economic relationships by creating a range of ethnic institutions. Such ethnic group leaders as priests, journalists, politicians, and society officers struggled to help their members adjust to modernism, survive economically, and preserve Old World cultural values.[5]

With the arrival of the second generation, contradictory forces developed within the ethnic communities. For most of the immigrants, culture shock soon gave way to acculturation, especially to material goods and the English language. Large numbers of the immigrants had moved into skilled blue collar jobs; a lower middle class of storekeepers, craftsmen, and civil service workers had emerged in the cities; and a tiny elite of educated intellectuals and professionals had appeared. But while the immigrants were diligently trying to preserve the past, the upwardly mobile second generation was trying to adjust to its new surroundings and success. Most of its members were not nearly as intense in their Old World loyalties as their parents had been. Indeed, the second generation often made a point of emphasizing American identity by disinheriting their past. Learning English, wearing American clothes, and asserting their American birth usually alienated them from their immigrant parents. Caught between the Old World and the New, between immigrant poverty and the economic promise of American life, they often felt guilty as well as self-conscious, unsure about their place or their identity. Richard Rodríguez recalled his own feelings in 1982:

> It mattered that education was changing me. It never ceased to matter.... "Your parents must be very proud of you." People

> began to say that to me about the time I was in the sixth grade. To answer affirmatively, I'd smile. Shyly I'd smile, never betraying my sense of irony: I was not proud of my mother and father. I was embarrassed by their lack of education.... I heard my father speak to my teacher and felt ashamed of his labored, accented words. Then felt guilty for the shame. I felt such contradictory feelings.[6]

In the next generation, increasingly large numbers of people had entered influential middle and professional classes. Economically successful, several decades removed from the Old World, and no longer plagued by internal doubts and self-consciousness, the grandchildren and great-grandchildren of the immigrants regained an interest in their heritage, wondering about Old World values, perhaps visiting Europe or Latin America or enrolling in language classes. They were conscious of their heritage but not desperate about it like the immigrants nor as afraid of it as the second and sometimes third generations. They were comfortable in their identity as English-speaking Americans with an "Old World" nationality. From those positions of security they were prepared to move beyond acculturation to assimilation—the voluntary social mixing with people from other nationality and language groups, which sometimes eventually led to the marriage bed, where culture and history fused.

What emerged out of modernization, acculturation, and assimilation was a series of melting pots based on race and religion. The nationality and linguistic dimensions of ethnic identity were usually the first to go, often in a few generations, but race and religion remained powerful and influential. By the third and fourth generations, the descendents of the Roman Catholic immigrants were expanding their network of social contacts, voluntarily reaching out to the descendents of other Catholic immigrant groups for friends, associates, working and business partners, and eventually wives and husbands. The vast majority of white immigrants married within racial lines, rarely venturing out to the black or Hispanic communities. Within the boundaries of race and color, they usually married within religious lines even while marrying exogamously in terms of nationality and language. Slowly and almost imperceptibly, Protestant, Catholic, and Jewish melting pots began appearing a few generations after the mass migrations from Europe had ended.[7]

But the emergence of a Roman Catholic melting pot was more than just a consequence of intermarriage among the immigrants and their descendents. Ever since those first English Catholics set foot in Maryland, church leaders had tried to transform the folk traditions and institutional commitments of immigrant Catholics. Centuries of worrying about having a "foreign" image as well as the twentieth-century drive to consolidate the church magnified the need to assimilate the immigrants to the values of American society and to those of Anglo-Irish Catholicism. In that sense the Catholic melting pot based on intermarriage was partly a product of the church's success in weaning the immigrants away from Old World traditions and in converting them to American-Catholic religious values. The transformation was a conscious and an unconscious process.

The origins of the melting pot extend back to the peasant villages of Europe, long before the immigrants found themselves in American ghettoes confronting a modern urban society. The great Catholic melting pot of the United States was but one dimension of a global transformation of political, social, and economic relationships—a "modernization" process resting on the emergence of an international economic market, a political system of organized, competitive interest groups, and a society of increasingly broad primary associations. Before industrialization triggered changes in the Atlantic economy, peasant life had revolved around nuclear families functioning for the most part in local, subsistence economies largely isolated from the outside world. The peasants' religious life had long fused the secular and the spiritual, with devotional practices intimately connected to local and regional shrines and local and regional saints. The separation between folk culture and formal religion was exceedingly small, if it existed at all. The peasants' values emphasized a strong sense of social place and social limitations, family economic cooperation, an expectation of economic survivalism rather than economic success, a powerful anti-materialism, and a modest fatalism about the possibilities of controlling the larger forces affecting one's life, except through the use of religion and magic. Finally, their primary social relationships were carefully confined in the peasant villages to neighbors who shared the same religion, language, and locale.

Long before the peasants emigrated, the modernization process had begun to threaten and challenge their way of life and its associated folkways, but the immigrants nevertheless brought those values with them to the New World. Italian families, for example, usually made sure that working patterns and occupation did not separate families, while Polish families maintained their view of fathers as rulers of the home. Croatians tried to nurture the extended kinship economic ties of the Adriatic *zadrugas* (communal farming arrangements), while many East European and Italian parents expected their children to go to work early to help support the family. In the United States, modernization completed its assault on peasant life, and by the 1970s one consequence was the emergence of the Catholic melting pot.[8]

A major change that modernization brought to peasant life was the rise of institutions and organizations transcending the nuclear family and then the village. The changes in the Atlantic economy eventually elevated the importance of the Roman Catholic parish to a point of significance well beyond its former role in Old World society. The general culture of Roman Catholic Europe had emphasized two closely related concepts—*paterfamilias* and *sacerdos.* For large numbers of Catholic peasants, the idea of *paterfamilias* conferred on the father a divine, absolute power in his home, an unquestioned right to rule his wife and children. Such power was to be tempered by Christian love, but of wife and children only total obedience was acceptable. What the father had in the home, priests had in parishes, and this was *sacerdos,* the role of God's representative, the individual with the power to conduct the altar sacrifice. The priest enjoyed an exalted role in the society. Believing firmly in both *paterfamilias* and *sacerdos,* most peasant Catholics, especially those from eastern Europe, respected authority and viewed power in rigid, hierarchical terms. Because of East European history and its competing religious ideologies, shifting political frontiers, and frequent invasions and wars, many peasants had also developed a kind of cultural pluralism, a sense that if their own faith was to survive they would have to let the religious cultures of others function as well. They recognized cultural differences and the right of people to be left alone with their own faith. Not surprisingly, the combined impact of *paterfamilias, sacerdos,* and cultural pluralism was an overpowering belief in the right to govern one's own community, to be left alone, to be free of external manipulation and cultural imperialism. In the United States, the nationality parish became the expression of that point of view, one way to protect the community from secular culture, Anglo Protestantism, and liberal "American" Catholicism.[9]

The nationality parish became the conscious way of preserving what had formerly been unconscious, psychologically given values. Immigration transformed the collective identity of peasant society and the role of the institutional church in their lives. Village social life had revolved around nuclear families bound up into larger kinship systems. The dividing line between the spiritual and temporal was exceedingly fine, and religion was not so much a separate church organization with approved beliefs as it was a folk culture animating the entire society. The institutional church was present in every village, but except in Ireland, Quebec, Lebanon, and Syria, it was not the central, moral foundation of peasant life. Economic institutions, family values, and religion were too closely integrated into an unconscious whole for the church to be dominant. Spiritual concerns filled the culture, but the parish itself was not necessarily the central dimension of peasant religion.

That situation changed during the migration when the peasants saw their communal world disintegrate. In the Old World village, everyone had played essentially the same agrarian role, and society had not been divided into competing interest groups. But in the migration, the peasants left behind their kinship-oriented and occupationally undifferentiated communal society for an occupationally integrated, highly differentiated urban society. Not only did the peasants suddenly find themselves working in a great variety of jobs that often competed with one another, but the whole process of making a living was removed from family life and traditional folkways and awarded to an external corporate or bureaucratic entity. Work, family, and faith, so closely integrated in the Old World, separated into different functions in the New World. The collective, culturally united peasant village was lost; so to preserve their value system the immigrants had to consciously substitute an associational or organizational entity for Old World communalism. Since it had possessed an institutional dimension in the Old World, the church became the foremost organization in the United States. It became the center of ethnic and religious life for many peasant immigrants, particularly for those like the Poles, Lithuanians, Irish, Germans, French Canadians, Basques, Rusins, Ukrainians, Slovaks, Syrians, and Lebanese who had possessed strong institutional loyalties to the church in the Old World. In the United States, the Roman Catholic parish, especially the nationality parish, played a much more important role in immigrant social life than it had in Europe.[10]

While helping the immigrants preserve some of their cultural values, the nationality parish also became an agent in their modernization by bringing together people from large numbers of Old World villages and supervising their associational life. The New World parish brought immigrants together into a single institution that transcended place and locale, which had been so important in peasant life. At Most Holy Redeemer parish in New York City, for example, immigrants came from all over German-speaking Europe. Most of them were southern Germans, with Bavaria accounting for about one-sixth of the parishioners, and there were also large concentrations of Rhinelanders and Austrians. Although they did not mix with the Irish in New York City, confining their marriage partners during much of the nineteenth century to other Germans, they nevertheless underwent an assimilation process, acquiring for the first time a sense of being German Catholics rather than provincial Catholics. In the Old World they had looked upon themselves as Bavarian or Silesian or Saxon Catholics, but at Most Holy Redeemer they became German Catholics. When groups such as the Slovaks or Italians came in chain migrations, there would be regional concentrations in the nationality parishes, but even then mixtures of Old World villages were inevitable. At St. Elizabeth's, a Slovak parish in Pittsburgh, there were immigrants from twelve different Slovak counties, with parishioners from Spis making up the largest group. They too began seeing themselves generally as Slovak Catholics after a few years in the United States. The peasant village, with its narrow perspective and restricted loyalties, was slowly being displaced.[11]

Just as village and even regional perspectives were giving way to national identities, the peasant family was experiencing a transition from nuclear to extended kinship systems. Industrialization and the rise of a global market had undermined peasant household economies, causing class and occupational interest groups rather than the nuclear family to be the primary unit of survival. To feed their families and provide basic economic needs, the peasants had been forced to broaden and formalize kinship ties beyond individual households through marriages, dowries, family apprenticeships, foster parents, godparents, and filial donations. With these extended family networks, large numbers of people were linked together in formal associations capable of assisting individual families in economic trouble. The new class and occupational focus of economic life forced peasants to reach out on another level in creating voluntary associations to organize trades, provide credit pools, and supply health, welfare, and life insurance.[12] At first confined to village boundaries and then, as mobility and economic interdependence increased, to groups of villages, these family and mutual benefit societies constituted a level of social and economic association that transcended the nuclear family and the peasant village. Once again, the narrow boundaries of the peasant village were breaking down in favor of larger visions.

Different ethnic groups, of course, dealt with these changes in different ways. Certain family values and historical traditions affected associational life and made for differences in the nature of community organization. One comparison of Czech and Mexican Catholics in south Texas reveals the power of different traditions. Both Mexican and Czech farmers had moved into Nueces County in the late nineteenth and early twentieth centuries, and both had taken up farming. But while the main focus of the Czech family was the lineal unit, the focus of the Mexican family was the lateral network of extended kinship relations. When Czechs formed mutual benefit societies, sodalities, and confraternities in their parishes, the organizations were closed corporations in which membership was confined to one or a few families, with loose coalitions connecting them. Mexican Catholics, on the other hand, formed fewer societies with larger memberships, consistent with the Hispanic sense of *La Raza.* The economic consequences of those values were dramatic, for while Czech societies evolved into corporate cooperatives, the Mexican organizations became trade unions of large numbers of workers.[13] But although associational life varied from group to group, the thrust of all of them was to broaden the range of peasant relationships and give the immigrants a much larger sense of community.

The immigrant associations and process of modernization they represented were carefully integrated into parish life. At first the organizations were confined to individual parishes and communities. Between 1870 and 1880, Czech immigrants in Chicago formed forty-nine mutual benefit societies, even though there were only three Czech parishes—St. Wenceslaus, St. John Nepomucene, and

St. Procopius. They quickly acquired a broader sense of community, forming the Czech Roman Catholic Benevolent Union of Chicago in 1884 and affiliating with the national Czech Roman Catholic First Central Union in the United States. The German Catholics had already created their Central Verein in 1855, uniting all the German mutual benefit societies. Poles held the first meeting of the Polish Roman Catholic Union in 1874, and Slovaks formed the First Catholic Slovak Union in 1890. Ukrainians and Rusins organized the Greek Catholic Union in 1892. Dedicated to the preservation of religion and faith among the ethnic Catholics, these associations provided immigrants, especially the leadership elites, with a cultural and political perspective much broader than the peasant family, village, or even the nationality parish.[14] Gaining that larger sense of community was essential to the modernization of immigrant culture.

The formation of a national vision out of village and regional loyalties proceeded at different paces among different groups, promoting or retarding the modernization process. Among the Irish and French-Canadian Catholics, the national perspective had already existed at the time of the migration because of Irish and Canadian history. Among other groups it arrived much more slowly. The Croatian Catholic Union, for example, did not form until 1921. The *bairrismo* of the Portuguese and the *campanilismo* of the Italians, which emphasized loyalties to Old World villages, and the tribal and linguistic differences among the Filipinos retarded the integration process. It was not until the 1960s, for example, that the first national organization of Italians appeared. But regardless of the pace, most Catholic immigrants acquired a sense of ethnic nationalism as opposed to village loyalties in the American parishes.[15]

It was a short jump from a national ethnic consciousness to political nationalism in the ethnic communities. Peasant immigrants often gained a sense of patriotic nationalism only after their arrival in the United States, not only because the migration and emerging associational life had thrown diverse people together but also because of the contrast between their own culture and those of the American cities. One early observer of Polish immigrants was amazed at how soon they shed their peasant apathy for an enthusiastic interest in Poland.

> Every Polish peasant, from whatever Polish province he comes, even from one of those which like Upper Silesia or East Prussia

> have been for a long time separated from the national body, when transferred to a strange soil among foreigners develops a Polish sentiment and a consciousness of his national character. This phenomenon is incomprehensible for those who saw the peasant at home without a consciousness of national duties. And yet it is quite natural. National consciousness originates in him spontaneously in a foreign country in consequence of the feeling of the striking differences between his speech, his customs, his conceptions from those of the people who surround him.... This plain man, formerly ignorant and passive for the national cause, will become an individual consciously and actively serving the idea which rests upon nationality.[16]

The immigrants were far more nationalistic in the United States than in the Old World. Except for the Italian and Jewish ghettoes in New York City, the immigrant communities in urban America were not monolithic enclaves inhabited by a single group. Instead, immigrants were surrounded by their own people as well as by people from other backgrounds. Social contacts in mixed neighborhoods, rather than diluting ethnic identity, actually sharpened it. Magyars, for example, had traditionally been the dominant ethnic group in Hungary and nurtured feelings of superiority toward Slovaks. When they found Slovaks living near them in Cleveland, they resurrected those same feelings, just as Slovaks continued to resent Magyar paternalism. Similar processes worked on Czechs and Germans, Ukrainians and Russians, and Magyars and Croatians. Old World villages had never been homogeneous, but they were certainly not the heterogeneous communities of the United States. The existence of dozens of other ethnic groups reinforced feelings of group identity among first-generation Catholic immigrants.

Earlier migrations also contributed to feelings of political nationalism among the new immigrants. Although large-scale peasant migration did not really begin until after 1870, smaller groups of East Europeans had immigrated earlier in the century. Four thousand Magyar political refugees had fled to the United States after the revolution of 1848. When he visited the United States, revolutionary Louis Kossuth received wide acclaim, generating tremendous sympathy for Hungarian freedom and democracy. Another Magyar refugee, Charles Tothvarady, established the first Hungarian newspaper in the United States. Thousands of Czech refugees, including

Vojta Naprstek, emigrated from Bohemia after the revolution of 1848. Naprstek settled in Milwaukee and established the liberal newspaper *Flug Blatter.* Thousands of Polish refugees fled to America in the 1830s and 1840s, and many of them, like Major Kaspar Tochman, toured the country speaking out for Polish independence. Paul Sobolewski, another refugee, founded the first Polish periodical in America in 1842. Usually well-educated and highly nationalistic, these early immigrants became the intellectual nucleus of the urban ethnic communities. Through their newspapers, emigrant aid societies, and political societies like the Czech, Slovak, or Croatian *sokols* or the Polish and Lithuanian *falcons* they created a highly politicized ethnic atmosphere in the United States, one that gradually affected the outlook of the later peasant immigrants.[17]

Although there were considerable debate and animosity between the "religionists" and the "nationalists" in the ethnic communities, they both grew out of the same phenomenon—the disintegration of parochial village and regional loyalties and the formation of national perspectives. A generation after the revolutionaries of 1848 had begun stimulating immigrant political nationalism, their "new immigrant" descendents were taking up the flag of independence. In the late nineteenth and early twentieth centuries, groups such as the Polish National Alliance, Ukrainian National Association, Ruthenian National Association, National Slovak Society, Czech Slavic Benevolent Society, Lithuanian National Alliance, and the Croatian National Alliance were integrating hundreds of local political associations and agitating for the liberation of their respective homelands. Both "religionists" and "nationalists" looked sympathetically on the idea of national independence in eastern Europe. Like their counterparts in Irish-American nationalism, the East European nationalisms imposed a different type of unity on the immigrant communities and pushed village loyalties further into the historical background.[18]

During World War I, East European nationalism intensified as the immigrants became more and more concerned about the fate of their homelands. Since most Catholic immigrants were blue-collar workers loyal to the Democratic party, they lobbied the Woodrow Wilson administration to employ American power at the Versailles peace negotiations to create new nation-states in eastern Europe. The Polish National Alliance campaigned vigorously to unite the Polish-speaking people of Germany, Austria, and Russia into a single country. They joyously celebrated the founding of modern Poland in 1918. Magyar immigrants asked President Wilson to separate Hungary from Austria in 1918 and grant her complete independence. Czech and Slovak Americans insisted on the creation of an independent Czechoslovakia in 1918. Croatian and Slovenian immigrants both wanted Wilson to help create an independent Croatia and an independent Slovenia, but they compromised on the creation of Yugoslavia in 1918, uniting the Croatians, Slovenians, Montenegrins, and Serbians in one country. Rusins managed to get Transcarpathia included in Czechoslovakia, while the Ruthenian National Alliance and Ukrainian National Alliance failed to get an independent Ukraine carved out of Russia. Throughout the twentieth century, those East European Catholic immigrants responded quickly to news from the Old World, and the process of nurturing that concern served to unite the various ethnic communities.[19] But while those campaigns certainly indicated a continuing vitality of ethnic identity in the United States, they were also proof that the modernization process was eliminating forever those Old World identities based on the nuclear family and the peasant village.

Finally, the parochial schools and ethnic press played roles similar to those of nationality parishes, benevolent societies, and political organizations in destroying village identities and bringing diverse people into larger and broader relationships. The existence of parochial schools and the ethnic press were signs of group vitality, but they also helped destroy the localist dimension of Old World culture. Although the schools and press tried to preserve the Old World language in order to protect the faith, there usually was no single vernacular among the immigrants but a variety of regional dialects. There were vast differences, for example, between Low German and High German, but in the German nationality parishes a language fusion occurred. Among the Polish immigrants there were many different dialects, but the curriculum in the parochial schools taught a standardized Polish using standardized texts. Children learned of Polish history, customs, and values and acquired a common sense of the past as well as a common written language. One Pole recalling his life in the village of Dzikov on the Vistula in Tarnobrzeg County, said:

> As for national consciousness, I have mentioned that the older peasants called themselves Masurians, and their speech Masurian.

> They lived their own life, forming a wholly separate group, and caring nothing for the nation. I myself did not know that I was a Pole till I began to read books and papers, and I fancy that other villagers came to be aware of their national attachment much in the same way.[20]

The common curriculum, common texts, and common language made the immigrant children Poles rather than villagers. The Polish press, by transmitting the symbols, values, and news of Poland as well as of the Polish-American communities, helped create a subculture that did not exist when the immigrants first arrived. More so than ever before in their lives or the lives of their parents, the immigrants had access to the world around them and acquired a common set of cultural values within their individual communities.[21]

The first stage, therefore, in the development of the Roman Catholic melting pot occurred in those nationality parishes and their associated institutions, which "liberals" and "Americanists" had once feared would only preserve the foreign church. As much as they were aimed at helping the immigrants maintain Old World values, the nationality parishes actually initiated the assault on the European past. During the nineteenth and twentieth centuries, the communal, localist world of the peasant villages had broken down and been replaced by a global economy operated by functional interest groups transcending regional and even national boundaries. Roman Catholic immigrants saw their peasant world disintegrate in the European villages, but it was in the associational life of the New World parishes, parochial schools, press, benevolent societies, and patriotic organizations that they acquired a new sense of community with hundreds of thousands and even millions of people. In the United States they discovered themselves to be Poles or Slovaks or Ukrainians or Croatians. Another generation would pass and their sense of community would expand again, this time making them Polish Americans or Slovak Americans or Ukrainian Americans or Croatian Americans. The boundaries of their village would continue to expand, each time incorporating more people into their primary world.

11

Acculturation and the Catholic Melting Pot

While acquiring new associational loyalties and identities as ethnic Catholics rather than village Catholics, the immigrants and their children were losing several other specific characteristics of the Old World cultures. The nationality parish and its related institutions, while presiding over the modernization of the peasant immigrants, was only a temporary way station, an aid to the transition from the peasant religious community of the Old World to the American-Catholic parish of the New World. The peasant immigrants encountered all the problems previous immigrants had found in the United States—the emphasis on the individual rather than the community, the emphasis on success and progress rather than on survival, the elevation of the material rather than the spiritual, the supremacy of secular rather than religious values in public society, the replacement of stability with every kind of mobility, the loss of the Old World language in favor of English, the liberation of women and children from patriarchal authority, and the transformation of diverse folk religions into larger denominational traditions. All this constituted acculturation as the immigrants adjusted to and accepted many American values. As they lost the Old World language, religious folkways, family values, and political loyalties in favor of American culture, their sense of community expanded once again, this time to include large numbers of white Catholics, regardless of their nationality background. They were slowly moving toward the Roman Catholic melting pot.

The immigrants first fought a losing battle over language. In the nineteenth century, German and French-Canadian Catholics had worried about language, convinced that its demise automatically implied loss of faith because adoption of English would inevitably bring Anglo-Protestant values. That the Irish had avoided losing Roman Catholicism even as they replaced Gaelic with English was of little consequence. To preserve culture and religion, the Germans and French-Canadians had worked diligently at language maintenance. Many new immigrants had similar concerns. For Poles, Lithuanians, Slovaks, Rusins, Ukrainians, Basques, Maronites, and Melkites, preservation of the mother tongue was essential to ethnic and spiritual survival. In their parishes and parochial schools, they invested tremendous emotional and financial energy in passing linguistic values on to their children. For a generation, the major function of nationality parishes was language maintenance because only if the language survived would religious testimony and piety also survive.

But it was a losing cause. The democratic individualism, secular values, ethnic diversity, geographic and occupational mobility, and mass culture of American society made acculturation a relentless process. Language was the first victim. English was the language of public society—government, public school, mass media, and the economic marketplace. To function in public society, the immigrants and their children had to learn English. Parishes, parochial schools, and ethnic societies tried to counter the public language in private settings, but by the time the second generation had established its own families, English had become the language of intimacy at home. For third generation children, English was the mother tongue, and whatever familiarity they had with the Old World language was a consequence of formal instruction at school. Even then, what connection they had with their grandparents' language was cultural rather than functional bilingualism.[1] The table below indicates the extent of language losses or language gains for various Roman Catholic immigrant groups between 1940 and 1960.[2]

The rate of language loss or gain varied from group to group and depended on several circumstances, including the strength of the nationality parishes and ethnic organizations, the extent of recent immigration, demographic residential patterns, occupational and geographic mobility, education, and levels of ethnic political nationalism. The anticommunist revolution in Hungary in 1956, which sent thousands of Magyar refugees to the United States, accounts for the very modest decline in the numbers of Magyar speakers in the country. Large-scale immigration of Ukrainians after World War II also explains the dramatic increase in the language.

Table 11.1
Native Language Losses and Gains, 1940–1960

Language	*1940 Total*	*1960 Total*	*Change*	*Percent*
French	1,412,060	1,043,220	−368,840	−26.1
German	4,949,780	3,145,772	−1,804,008	−36.4
Polish	2,416,320	2,184,936	−231,384	−9.6
Czech	520,440	217,771	−302,669	−58.2
Slovak	484,360	260,000	−224,360	−46.3
Magyar	453,000	404,114	−48,886	−10.8
Serbo-Croatian	153,080	184,094	+31,014	+20.3
Slovenian	178,640	67,108	−111,532	−62.4
Ukrainian	83,600	252,974	+169,374	+202.6
Lithuanian	272,680	206,043	−66,637	−24.4
Italian	3,766,820	3,363,141	−93,679	−2.5
Spanish	1,861,400	3,335,961	+1,474,561	+79.2
Portuguese	215,660	181,109	−34,551	−16.0

Because large numbers of Italians remained in the ethnic enclaves of New York City and the surrounding suburbs for several generations, the language survived there more successfully than other ethnic languages. But regardless of the differences in the pace of language loss, the transition to English was a common trend for most groups.

By the 1940s and 1950s, most of the children of the "new immigrants" had grown up and assumed places in public society, and they used English as their primary tongue at work and at home. Large numbers of American-born priests of immigrant parents were functioning in the nationality parishes, and while many older, foreign-born colleagues were unable to separate the language from the faith, the second-generation priests clearly gave priority to the latter and looked to the Irish experience as an example of how faith could survive language loss. Between 1908 and 1948, the number of foreign-born priests in the Archdiocese of Chicago dropped from 51 percent to 8 percent. To serve the English-speaking second generation, as well as nonethnic parishioners on the fringes of the ethnic neighborhoods, English-language sermons were introduced.[3] As time passed, the number of English-language sermons slowly increased and the number of ethnic-language sermons declined. Use of the Old World language in the nationality parishes was directly related to the power of ethnic loyalties as well as to the number of surviving immigrants. As the second and third generations became the majority in the nationality parishes, ethnic language sermons became less and less frequent. The following table ranks ethnic groups by language maintenance by dividing the total number of parishes in each group into the number of parishes using the mother tongue in at least half of their sermons in the early 1960s.[4]

Ukrainian	.86
Lithuanian	.80
Spanish	.77
Polish	.73
French	.61
Magyar	.58
Slovak	.54
Italian	.35
Rusin	.30
German	.13

The increasing use of English for sermons was paralleled in the nationality parochial schools. After World War I, increasingly large numbers of bishops followed the lead of people like George Cardinal Mundelein of Chicago in restricting the use of non-English curricula materials and mandating English as the language of instruction in parochial schools. During the nativist outbursts of the 1920s, several states prohibited foreign languages as instructional vehicles in both public and private schools. At the same time, state education boards were increasing the number of required subjects, thus reducing the time available for ethnic language, culture, and history courses. Just as American-born priests were coming to dominate the nationality parishes, so were American-born nuns filling the teaching staffs in parochial schools. Their academic preparation was better than that of their immigrant predecessors and their interest in Old World topics was substantially less. By 1945 the ethnic content of instruction in most nationality parish schools had disappeared.[5]

French Canadians, for example, had one of the strongest commitments to maintaining the language. From the very beginning of their migration they established a powerful network of religious, educational, cultural, and fraternal organizations, all passionately devoted to Roman Catholicism, Quebec, and the French language. As late as 1970 there were still 284 Catholic parishes with strong French-Canadian identities, along with 51 high schools and 195 elementary schools offering at least an hour of French instruction each day. But for all their efforts, French did not survive as the intimate language of personal, family, and religious life. Between 1940 and 1960, French Canadians sustained a loss of more than 25 percent of native speakers of the language. French became a cultural but not a functional tool in the descendents of the French-Canadian immigrants.[6]

The declining use of Old World languages was reflected directly in the fortunes of the immigrant press. During the early decades of the twentieth century, the circulation figures for daily ethnic-language newspapers were vital and increasing, but in the 1940s and 1950s the malaise and decline set in as the children of the immigrants turned to English-language publications.[7] The table below reflects those declines between 1910 and 1960. English had slowly displaced the Old World languages in the homes, parishes, parochial schools, and publications of the ethnic Catholics.

Table 11.2
Subscription Rates of Ethnic Language Newspapers

Group	*1910*	*1920*	*1930*	*1940*	*1950*	*1960*
French	43,000	41,000	32,000	25,000	8,000	3,000
Spanish	—	15,000	56,000	74,000	70,000	114,000
German	935,000	239,000	354,000	261,000	69,000	74,000
Magyar	27,000	72,000	98,000	98,000	52,000	43,000
Ukrainian	—	—	31,000	46,000	27,000	30,000
Italian	57,000	330,000	348,000	217,000	149,000	136,000
Polish	63,000	239,000	345,000	261,000	238,000	184,000
Czech	75,000	113,000	156,000	145,000	135,000	64,000
Other Slavic	—	184,000	254,000	200,000	101,000	74,000

In addition to losing their languages, the peasant immigrants also surrendered many traditional family values; indeed, the changes had already begun when the Atlantic economy undermined the nuclear family and forced peasants to reach out to one another in extended kinship associations. The peasant family was quite resilient, especially groups like the Italians, and even into the 1980s the ethnic roots of sexual roles, generational relationships, kinship networks, property control, and emotional expression were still visible. Differences in family values directly affected immigrant life, explaining why Italians remained aloof from secular and religious institutions, why *zadruga*-raised Croatians experimented with extended communal property ownership, or why Irish women played leadership roles in the home. But despite the vitality of peasant families, four generations of life in the United States inevitably altered Old World relationships, certainly not creating monolithic families but generating new family similarities that had not existed in Europe.

For all immigrant families, certain patterns emerged. The peasant tradition of *paterfamilias,* in which fathers ruled their homes with divine authority, slowly changed in the United States. Virtually every group of immigrants complained that their American-born children were unruly and lacking in proper respect for their elders. Immigrant men often registered the same complaint about their wives or the wives of their sons, especially in the 1960s and 1970s when changing social values opened new economic opportunities for women outside the home. Nor could Old World fertility patterns survive. In the economic atmosphere of urban America, children were liabilities; so family size gradually declined over the course of several generations. Because of geographic mobility in America, extended kinship ties, so recently forged in Europe, proved difficult to maintain. All these changes had specific influences on particular groups. Among Puerto Ricans, impersonal norms gradually replaced personalist values as the focus of individual and group relationships. Among Mexican-American families in Los Angeles, extended family living arrangements disappeared in favor of nuclear family arrangements. French-Canadian families experienced dramatic increases in illegitimate pregnancies and early marriages. Increasing rates of divorce affected Portuguese families. Few families were immune from change. The democratization and shrinkage of the family, the separation of work and home, the compulsory education of children, and the cult of individualism in the United States took their toll on all of the immigrants.[8]

In addition to losing the language and many family values of the Old World, the immigrants also gave up their political nationalisms, even though those loyalties had only been acquired after the migration. The process of gaining a conscious ethnic identity had introduced the immigrant villagers to large numbers of people, and the national liberation campaigns had peaked during World War I when each group worked so hard for the breakup of Austria-Hungary and for the political independence of its ethnic nationalities. But those passions faded after the war. The loyalties did not, of course, disappear. Irish Americans continued to send money to anti-British rebels in Northern Ireland into the 1980s, and French Canadians in New England kept a close watch on Quebec politics. Magyar Americans rose up in righteous indignation when the Soviet Union invaded Hungary in 1956 and when President Jimmy Carter decided in 1978 to return the crown of St. Stephen, the symbol of Hungarian independence, to Budapest and the communist government there. Still, the passions of the 1950s, 1960s, and 1970s could not match those of the early 1900s. The prevailing sense of accomplishment with the founding of Poland, Lithuania, Czechoslovakia, Hungary, and Yugoslavia, the end of large-scale immigration in the 1920s, the arrival of the second and third generations, and the loss of the Old World languages had all created a new distance between ethnic Catholics and their European relatives. Changing attitudes were soon reflected in the activities of ethnic organizations. In 1922, for example, the Union of Polish Priests met under the direction of Bishop Paul Rhode and consciously broke with the past by not discussing any Polish homeland issues, focusing instead on the need for Polish language maintenance in parochial schools, the appointment of more Polish bishops, the enrollment of more Polish children in ethnic organizations, and resistance to Americanization. Most other Catholic and immigrant societies, as well as such organizations as the National Catholic Welfare Conference, also made the shift in emphasis toward domestic issues, a focus that has persisted.[9]

Finally, in addition to surrendering language, certain family traditions, and nationalism, the immigrants lost many Old World religious folkways. The peasant tendency to imbue all of nature with spiritual and magical significance was central to Old World values. Every animal, tree, plant, river, stream, meadow, and mountain had a spiritual consciousness, and the peasants worked to maintain the balance of nature. Peasant life revolved around the cycles of nature, and a long series of sacred rituals were aimed at propitiating nature, preventing disaster, and guaranteeing survival. On the level of the supernatural, the peasant world was inhabited by mythological beings—devils, witches, water spirits, house ghosts, goblins, cloud-beings, and powerful animals. Finally, formal Catholicism reinforced both the natural and supernatural worlds of peasant religion by providing a cosmic rationale justifying contemporary events and promising other-worldly salvation for the obedient.[10]

But in the migration from peasant villages to urban ghettoes, the natural and supernatural worlds of immigrant religion changed. Spanish and Portuguese peasants, for example, had built special religious shrines at distinctive geographical sites marking village boundaries and symbolically limiting their temporal world. Those limits were lost, however, in the textile centers of New England where no particular geographical features circumscribed communities. Lithuanians in Chicago no longer appealed to St. George as the protector of farm animals because they no longer had farms. Among Czech immigrants in Cleveland, the forest ghosts (*hejka love*) so prominent in Old World superstitions lost their meaning in the urban forest of concrete and tall buildings. Village calendars had linked saints' days to agricultural events, making the acts of plowing, sowing, and harvesting spiritually significant. Rogation festivals had celebrated the bounties of life and the intimate relationship between people, nature, and God. But all those gradually declined in the United States, where the natural and supernatural layers of peasant piety were peeled away, eventually leaving only a rational, formal Catholicism that the church would soon transform.[11]

By the 1940s and 1950s, for example, Lithuanian folkways had changed substantially from Old World customs. Although many Lithuanian homes still had small shrines with national crosses, they no longer erected wayside crosses in America. Those would hardly have been appropriate, nor would they have survived in the crowded streets of the United States. Because so many Lithuanians lived in the cities, they no longer venerated bread as the staff of life or participated in religious harvest festivals. They discarded older traditions about the sacredness of the earth and the holiness of water. Lithuanian peasants had once venerated bees, trees, storks, cuckoos, larks, swallows, bears, and snakes, but not in America. Traditional fears of goats and toads as apparitions of the devil did not long survive the Atlantic crossing; nor did beliefs in *Aitvaras* (goblins) or *raganos* (witches). The use of Lithuanian charms, chants, and magical spells, which always ended with the sign of the cross, fell into disrepute. The adorning of homes with birth trees to commemorate Pentecost, special processions during Rogation Days, formal reciting of the rosary during October devotions, the annual blessing of grains on the feast of the Nativity of the Blessed Virgin Mary, the feasts of St. George and St. Agatha, and the singing of *valandos* (Little Hours of the Blessed Virgin Mary) all fell into disuse. Similar changes occurred in other Catholic ethnic groups.[12]

As the immigrant communities were shedding older religious folkways they also were giving up traditional patterns of governing the parish, a form of acculturation that for a time alienated them from the Irish hierarchy of the church and inspired countless internal disputes. Their faith in *paterfamilias* and *sacerdos* gave them faith in church authority, but they were still resentful when Irish or German bishops tried to control parish finances, limit the nationality parishes, or prohibit foreign languages in parochial schools. Their Old World experience with wealthy patrons controlling parish affairs left them feeling that since they had been responsible for establishing the nationality parishes in America, they were entitled to a good deal of lay participation in church affairs. That expectation fit perfectly into the American ethos. But there was no middle ground between *paterfamilias* and *sacerdos* on the one hand and lay power on the other. In the end, after the controversies over lay power and the appearance of the national Catholic churches, the church remained faithful to its own hierarchy, with bishops asserting the authority of their priesthood and the immigrants giving up hope of controlling church affairs. The appointment of ethnic bishops in some dioceses made acquiescence easier, but the principle of bishopric authority instead of lay authority was institutionalized. By the 1930s most of the bitter disputes over lay initiative had become only memories from the late nineteenth and early twentieth centuries.

The disappearance of older religious folkways, the acquiescence to bishopric authority, the conversion to English, and the demise of Old World political ties changed the nature of immigrant Catholicism, giving the immigrants a broader sense of community. In the Italian-nationality parishes, for example, the multitude of religious processions and feasts of all the village patron saints slowly declined, until most parishes celebrated only the feast day of their own patron, not the feast days of all the other parishes. By the 1940s and 1950s, English had replaced Italian as the language of most sermons and private liturgies. But at the same time that their language heritage was weakened, the Italian immigrants and their children acquired ethnic loyalties wider than those of the Old World *paese*. The immigrant groups also acquired, in some instances, a sense of national patrons they had never possessed in the Old World. Instead of their village patrons resting on the foundation of *bairrismo,* the Portuguese immigrants accepted a powerful devotion to Our Lady of Fatima in the 1920s and 1930s. The devotion to SS Cyril and Methodius, part of the spiritual lives of Slovak immigrants, became almost a cult in the United States as Slovaks throughout the country acquired a common religious perspective.[13] As a new generation of American-born priests rose to power in the ethnic communities during the 1930s and 1940s and laid to rest the disputes over lay initiative, a spirit of administrative and theological tranquility descended on the church. The second generation had few recollections of the jurisdictional struggles, and the end of the immigrant battle to secure parish independence eliminated one form of status competition that sharpened ethnic identity. Finally, the decline of the immigrant languages and triumph of English gave all Roman Catholics a common spiritual ground for expressing their faith. Those immigrants who had connected language and faith were right, for each language's subtle nuances and unique vocabulary constituted an independent religious persuasion. Richard Rodríguez, long after his English had somewhat alienated him from Old World culture, remembered:

> Standing beside my mother in the visiting room of a Carmelite convent, before the dense screen which rendered the nuns shadowy figures, I heard several Spanish-speaking nuns—their busy, sing-song overlapping voices—assure us that yes, yes, we were remembered, all our family was remembered in their prayers.[14]

As the immigrants and their children acquired one language, they also acquired one faith, since the vehicle for interpreting the spiritual world and expressing beliefs had become the same.

As immigrant culture changed, American Catholicism made steady inroads on ethnoreligious diversity. For generations the Irish-American hierarchy had worked to standardize religious education and worship, but immigration and nationality parishes had stalled their efforts. Much of the Irish frustration was inspired by the immigrants' distaste for the rituals and values of Gaelic Catholicism. Centuries of persecution and resistance in Ireland, along with the nineteenth-century devotional revolution, had given the Irish a powerful commitment to the institutional church. Deprived of state patronage as well as aristocratic philanthropy, the Irish church had also developed a long tradition of parish voluntarism—active participation by ordinary members in parish affairs. This was not to be confused with any anticlerical sense of lay control, for the Irish were devoted to their priests and participated in parish affairs under their direction. The traditions of institutional loyalty and widespread voluntarism made for regular, active participation of the vast majority of people in parish devotionals. Because of eighteenth-century Jansenism and nineteenth-century Victorianism, Irish Catholicism had also assumed a puritanical obsession with sin and sexual morality. Years of poverty, culminating in the Great Famine, had also pushed them to an appreciation of ascetic simplicity that respected internal piety and rejected complicated rituals and high church pageantry. In describing the religious tastes of Archbishop John Ireland in the late nineteenth century, Paulist priest Walter Elliott wrote: "He is a Celtic American through and through . . . quite content with catacombical public worship."[15] Irish immigrant priests and their American-born cousins nurtured those values in the United States and were quite startled by the different attitudes of many of the immigrant Catholic communities.

In particular, they could not understand the taste for elaborate pageantry and ritual among the German Catholics, or the anticlericalism of so many Czechs. The indifference of Hispanic and Italian Catholics toward the church—evidenced by their infrequent attendance at Mass and confession and by the dearth of boys taking vocations—was a source of unending frustration for the Irish, as were the folk "superstitions" and "pagan," "sacrilegious" rituals of many peasants. The Irish could not accept the married clergy and eastern rites of the Uniate Rusins, Ukrainians, Melkites, and Maronites. And the lay initiative impulses among Slovaks, Poles, and Lithuanians, as well as the independent national churches, stimulated years of jurisdictional struggle between ethnic parishes and Irish-dominated bishoprics.

Disturbed by the ethnic diversity so visible in the church, Irish bishops worked to "catholicize" worship and impose a universal system of rituals, rites, and values. It was a challenge. Most peasant immigrants had brought with them strong folk traditions that the Irish believed contradicted true piety. The worlds of natural and supernatural religion, which the peasant immigrants fused with formal Catholicism, were unacceptable to the Irish. Their own beliefs in ghosts and leprechauns had become part of a mythological past, victims of the Great Famine, the devotional revolution, and the English school system. Peasant beliefs in witches, ghosts, and animated spirits and in the power of magic and the evil eye irritated Irish-American clerics. Although those religious and folk traditions were eroding in the secular, urban environment of the United States, it was not happening fast enough to suit the Irish. While finally accommodating themselves to the Eastern Rite groups, the Irish managed to keep all married Uniate priests out of the country after 1890. They also managed to prohibit or restrict the Italian and Hispanic festivals, which the Irish found sacrilegious and demeaning. When Portuguese parishioners in Massachusetts and California joined the devotion to Our Lady of Fatima with Azorean bullfighting and dancing, the Irish clerics forced them to separate the two. In some dioceses, Irish-American bishops actually excluded Italian priests for fear they would reinforce peasant superstitions.[16]

The Irish also wanted to inspire a devotional revolution among immigrant peasants, one that internalized religion by emphasizing individual piety, obedience to the institutional church, and spiritual uniformity. To redirect individual piety, they campaigned against the excessive *clientismo* of many peasants—the tendency to approach God through the medium of various saints rather than through the priesthood and sacramental events. Many peasants were not intimately involved with day-to-day church affairs. Except for such rites of passage as baptism, confirmation, marriage, and extreme unction, church affairs were unimportant to some peasants, especially Italians and Mexicans, because they seemed unrelated to issues of survival in a hostile world. To guarantee survival, peasants had always turned to the saints, whose special gifts and special powers could influence the events of daily life. The Irish preferred a sacramental religion deemphasizing the powers of the saints in favor of individual obedience, respect for church authority, weekly attendance at Mass and confession, and daily devotions at home. The Irish had no inherent objections to the veneration of saints; indeed, they found the practice spiritually uplifting when combined with strong loyalty to the institutional church. At the same time, they tried to overcome peasant indifference to theology, working to imbue immigrants with a consciousness of sin and the realization that salvation depended on individual righteousness. True religion revolved around the individual relationship with God through the sacramental powers of the priesthood.

But for all their resentment of immigrant traditions, the Irish did not want the church to lose the immigrants. They feared the mass migration would trigger a new round of Protestant bigotry and that the church would have a difficult if not impossible time absorbing the immigrants. They worried that the immigrants, indifferent as many of them were, would be lost to the church in a disastrous "leakage," disappearing into the Anglo-Protestant world.[17] The Irish knew that the major Protestant denominations would stage great proselytizing campaigns to convert immigrant Catholics, and the church would have to be prepared to counter such evangelical crusades. The Irish passion to transform immigrant piety was not simply the paranoid, ethnocentric expression of a self-righteous elite; they genuinely wanted to "save" the immigrants for the church.

The Irish hierarchy used four techniques to standardize Roman Catholic piety, improve the image of the church, revitalize parishioner commitment, and stall Protestant evangelism.

First, the bishops felt the need to develop some national perspective in the American church. Because of the great distance from Rome, the decades of mission status under direction of the Propaganda, the poor internal transportation system in the United States as well as the size of the country, and the tradition of lay initiative in founding parishes and parochial schools, the American church had developed as a decentralized institution, with each diocese independent of the others and each bishop functioning as a power unto himself. Attitudes about church policy could differ widely from diocese to diocese, particularly concerning ethnic and cultural practices. To overcome these centrifugal forces and create a unified voice for American Catholicism, the American bishops began meeting together in periodic national councils where they discussed national problems and tried to "unite" on policies and administrative procedures and to assist one another. They held thirty-four major councils between 1829 and 1900, and in the process became the voice of American Catholicism.[18] Although the councils had no formal authority to reverse bishopric decisions in individual dioceses, they did provide a measure of consistency for the church.

Second, the Irish pushed the spirit of Catholic revivalism, a movement that spread throughout the country in the nineteenth century to combat ethnic diversity, religious apathy, and Protestant evangelism. Throughout Europe, a revival of Catholic piety was underway, and the American bishops picked up on the movement as a way of solving some of their problems. Many of them had already witnessed the potential of a devotional revolution of the kind that had swept through Ireland.[19] Religious orders—especially the Paulists, Jesuits, and Redemptorists—began sponsoring "missions" or revivals in parishes throughout the United States. In those revivals, the mission priests worked with two objectives in mind: to reclaim the devotion of immigrants drifting spiritually in the New World and to revitalize the faith of practicing, native Catholics. By generating a new spiritual vitality throughout the Catholic community, they hoped to achieve in America what the "devotional revolution" had achieved in Ireland.[20]

At revival meetings in urban, rural, immigrant, and native parishes, the traveling priests worked diligently for a conversion experience among parishioners. During the first week of the revival, they took a major theme of Irish Catholicism—a sense of human sinfulness and the threat of eternal damnation—and preached it repeatedly, constantly discussing sin, salvation, judgment, hell, and spiritual death. Their attempts to get people to recognize individual sinfulness and fear eternal judgment struck a responsive chord in the Irish-American community, as did the revivalist call for repentance, temperance, honesty, and sexual morality. The late nineteenth-century Victorian attitudes of Anglo-American culture also affected the immigrants and reinforced the message of the revival. Relief from guilt and the road to salvation lay inside the institutional church; so the mission priests urged all parishioners to return to the sacraments, especially the sacrament of penance. There people could receive forgiveness for their sins through the merciful, atoning sacrifice of Jesus Christ.[21]

To help parishioners maintain their newly discovered spirituality, the mission priests, with the full support of diocesan and parish officials, urged a variety of devotional exercises upon the audience. In addition to avoiding drunkenness, gambling, sexual impurity, and frivolous amusements, parishioners were to join actively in religious observations and spiritual associations. While Yankee Catholicism had been especially reserved and subdued, more concerned with the spirit of the commandments than with the letter of the law and with publicly displaying a reserved piety, the Irish-American church was promoting an active, visible religion, one that enveloped each parishioner in a psychological and institutional network.[22] The mission priests urged parishioners to join devotional confraternities, engage in Marian devotions through rosaries, support the cult of the Sacred Heart of Jesus, and fill their lives with holy pictures, holy medals, crucifixes, and scapulars. All these devotional acts, along with veneration of saints and relics and sacred processions, became the marrow of orthodox Catholic piety, a religious loyalty invigorated by the strength of Irish-Catholic values.[23] Catholic revivalism provided a pietistic unity transcending ethnic tradition and clerical persuasion.

Third, the Irish American and later the assimilated German American hierarchy closely associated themselves with Rome, not only in accepting Roman leadership but in accepting Roman devotions as well. New leaders of the American church, like George Cardinal Mundelein of Chicago or John Cardinal Glennon of St. Louis, wanted to make the church an acceptable institution in the United States, but they did not want to adopt the "liberalism" of predecessors like John Ireland or James Cardinal Gibbons who had become associated with Protestant values. The new bishops had no desire to tread on Pope Leo XIII's 1899 condemnation of liberal "Americanism." At the same time, they wanted to walk a tightrope between Yankee Catholicism and the attitudes of the famine Irish. They had no sympathy for the caution and trepidation of Yankee Catholicism; the church had arrived in the United States, and as the country's largest denomination deserved a place of prominence in public culture. But while achieving that prominence, they did not want to project the obnoxious militancy of the famine Irish. The church needed an image of confident security. So they centralized diocesan administration and demanded absolute obedience from parish priests, offered the same obedience to Rome, and then replaced the older, accommodationist Yankee Catholicism, the militant famine Irish Catholicism, and the nationality Catholicism with a Roman-based American devotion.

In Boston, for example, William O'Connell took over the diocese in 1907 and reversed nearly a century of episcopal leadership. Whereas Bishop John Williams had cultivated Boston Protestants, praised American democratic institutions, prized native-born and native-trained clergy, and maintained a distance and even suspicion of Roman authority in order to demonstrate the independence of American Catholicism, William Cardinal O'Connell felt no need to praise Yankee virtues. He wanted Roman-trained priests in diocesan leadership, rigidly adhered to Roman guidelines in diocesan administration, generously and freely supported Vatican financial needs, and constantly praised the virtues of Roman doctrine and leadership. He ruthlessly centralized diocesan authority, displaced both Yankee-Catholic and foreign-born Irish priests from positions of leadership, and then assumed an image of confidence and power in Boston. The needs to establish a powerful base for the church in America and to improve the social confidence of American Catholics without offending Rome had created a bureaucratic and sometimes dogmatic institution in Boston, and similar movements were appearing in Chicago, St. Louis, New York, New Orleans, and Philadelphia.[24]

As part of the new orientation to Rome and of the response to the need to bureaucratize church administration, the hierarchy undertook a crusade in the late nineteenth and early twentieth centuries to impose Roman devotions and schedules throughout the country. To create a universal devotional spirit, standard catechisms, manuals of rubrics, topical sermon schedules, sermon outlines, preprinted sermons, devotional tracts, missals, hymnals, prayerbooks, and parish decorations were distributed. Dedicated to revitalizing individual piety, the hierarchy urged the faithful to carry published Holy Cards, holy pictures, holy medals, scapulars, and crucifixes, as well as to place statues, devotional candles, holy pictures, and holy water fonts in their homes. Church authorities wanted standardized religious calendars through the country as well as routinized parish activities, including the same Ordo Missae during the year, the annual Forty Hours' devotion, missions, stations of the cross, the "May Crowning" of the Blessed Mother, and standardized weekly functions, including Mass on Sunday, Benediction of the Blessed Sacrament on Friday evening and Sunday afternoon, and Saturday confession. Throughout the country, especially in the territorial parishes, these devotional practices and calendars became more and more common.[25]

Finally, the fourth stage of the campaign to "Catholicize" the American church built on the traditions of Catholic revivalism, Roman authority, and Roman devotions. The new generation of bishops during the 1920s, 1930s, and 1940s returned to Americanization, if not "Americanism," as a major theme. But unlike an earlier generation of "liberal" "Americanist" bishops, the bishops experienced success rather than failure because of the new confidence of the church and because the processes of modernization and acculturation were already eroding immigrant culture and creating a larger Roman Catholic community. In the 1880s, when Archbishop John Ireland or Richard Gilmour spoke of Americanization as a way of strengthening the church and converting Protestant America, they were speaking directly to millions of first generation immigrants who wanted nothing more than to retreat into self-contained nationality parishes where they could survive the culture shock of migration. When Mundelein or O'Connell or Dougherty preached the same message, they were speaking to a Roman Catholic audience largely acculturated to American society.

George Cardinal Mundelein, for example, saw the nationality parishes as transitional devices, not permanent fixtures, of American Catholicism. In a 1920 address commending the Poles at St. Mary of the Angels Parish for their sacrifice in building a magnificent new church, he said:

> The people in this neighborhood were satisfied to contribute from their slender earnings in order that God's house might rise gigantic, majestic, and beautiful, while about it clustered their poorer and unpretentious homes. . . . It will stand here as a monument of the zeal, the deep faith and the generous spirit of self-sacrifice of the children of the Polish race in this great city. . . . We trust of the future harmonious relations that bind this our country to the Sister Republic of Poland: for which people have indeed given proof of "hands across the sea."[26]

But while praising immigrant devotion, Mundelein also wanted to push the immigrants and their children toward acculturation and assimilation. Shortly after taking over in Chicago, he changed the archdiocesan board of education and imposed English as the language of instruction in all parochial schools, with the immigrant languages confined to some catechism and reading classes. He also wrote a letter to Theodore Roosevelt arguing that

> there is hardly any other institution here in the country that does so much to bring about a sure, safe and sane Americanization of the children of emigrant people as do our parochial schools. My endeavor always will be to keep them up to the highest standard possible, so that they may be my monument rather than costly churches after I have gone, and the children that come from them be every bit as good American citizens as they are Catholics.[27]

Much to the dismay of Poles, Lithuanians, and Slovaks, Mundelein also declared a moratorium on new nationality parishes, opposed the appointment of ethnic auxiliary bishops, and even tried to begin assigning newly ordained ethnic priests to Irish and mixed parishes. Although he encountered a storm of protest from the nationality parishes, he generally received great praise from the native American press. Mundelein also displayed his patriotism by vigorously supporting the Liberty Bond programs during World War I, at the same time avoiding any connection with "Americanism" by rigorously adopting Vatican rules in diocesan administration and generously contributing to the "Peter's Pence" campaign for Vatican financial support.[28]

The standardization of religious piety and acculturation of the immigrants were part of much larger changes in American society. On the one hand, the forces of acculturation were gradually removing ethnic peculiarities from immigrant parishes, bringing them more in line with larger, native territorial parishes. Just as those changes were occurring, the processes of organization and centralization that had been at work in society since the early nineteenth century were consolidating American institutions into larger groups. Corporations, labor unions, and professional associations were assuming national dimensions, and the Catholic church was no different. The work of people like George Mundelein and William O'Connell had accelerated the process, but it had been underway nonetheless. From that acculturated, centralized staging ground, which consisted of the English language, American rather than Old World loyalties, and an increasingly standardized religious faith, the descendents of the immigrants were functioning comfortably in the larger society and were ready for ultimate assimilation into a Roman Catholic melting pot.[29]

12

Assimilation and the Roman Catholic Melting Pot

The modernization and acculturation of the Roman Catholic immigrants, as well as their gradual acquisition of a common devotional style, prepared a common ground for their assimilation into a larger religious association. The American-born, English-speaking descendents of the "new immigrants" had enough in common to begin meeting socially with one another. Out of those associations came the Roman Catholic melting pot, an unconscious product of the general forces of assimilation. The irony of it all was that even as the institutional role of the parish was becoming more important than ever, the influence of religion on people's lives would never be as strong as it had been in the peasant village. American values compartmentalized individual roles, destroying the sense of holistic unity traditional societies enjoyed. The prevailing belief in separation of church and state, the diversity of occupations, the abundance of ethnic and religious groups, the unprecedented geographical and vertical mobility, and the disintegration of extended and later nuclear families all served to divide the economic, political, social, and religious roles of community life. Never again would the peasants enjoy a society where job, family, religion, and neighbors shared so many of the same values and functioned as a collective whole.

The changes in traditional folkways, languages, families, and political loyalties slowly transformed the nationality parishes. What had been a parish of immigrant Slovaks, for example, became a Slovak-American parish in the second generation and an American parish of Slovak extraction in the third. By the 1930s and 1940s, the parochial schools in the nationality parishes were more concerned with instilling Roman Catholic values than Slovak Catholic culture and institutions. During the 1920s and 1930s, the older parish societies, originally formed in the Old World to provide collective support for the family-oriented peasant economies, were transformed from mutual aid, emigrant aid, and worker benefit organizations to parish social clubs offering insurance benefits and, finally, just to social clubs without such benefits. And while these subtle changes were occurring, the parish was remaining the organizational center of community life.

However, it was not necessarily a nationality parish any longer. As much as the immigrants may have wished it, the nationality parishes and immigrant neighborhoods were usually not permanent fixtures. They were always changing. Slowly but surely, as time passed and the second and third generations matured and began heading for the suburbs, the populations of the downtown nationality parishes began to decline. In Chicago, the children of the immigrants left the city and moved out to Belmont-Cragin, Avondale, Brighton Park, Archer Heights, Oak Lawn, Skokie, Marquette Park, or Park Ridge. Because the consolidating bishops like George Cardinal Mundelein opposed establishing nationality parishes in the suburbs, the children and grandchildren of the immigrants found themselves living in mixed neighborhoods and attending mixed territorial parishes. After World War II, the nationality parishes gradually declined in population and number. The 1982 *Catholic Directory* lists only 1,608 nationality parishes, down from 2,006 in 1940. If the Uniate parishes are removed from consideration, the number of nationality parishes dropped from 1,658 in 1940 to 1,091 in 1982. Since social life still revolved around the parish, the move to the suburbs amounted to a major step toward the Catholic melting pot, for in the ethnically mixed suburban churches, parochial schools, and parish societies, widespread social assimilation occurred.

The rate of disintegration of the nationality parishes varied widely, depending on historical commitments of individual groups to the institutional church and the demographic composition of the immigrant community. Between 1940 and 1982, all the ethnic groups lost nationality parishes, except the Rusins, Ukrainians, Melkites, and Maronites. The liturgical commitments, Uniate tradition, and national identities of these groups had always been strong, and as they moved into new areas, they worked hard to establish new parishes. It was also easier for them to do so. Because they had separate eparchies headed by bishops or eparchs sharing their ethnic identity and committed to expanding their administrative power, the Eastern Rite Catholics did not encounter the opposition of "Americanist" or consolidating bishops to new nationality parishes. So between 1940 and 1982 the number of their nationality parishes increased, fed also by post–World War II waves of immigration from the Ukraine. Czech parishes, on the other hand, almost disappeared between 1940 and 1982, primarily because Bohemian immigrants had long possessed ambivalent feelings about the church. Their children and grandchildren were not nearly as inclined to perpetuate the nationality parish as the descendents of some of the other ethnic Catholics.[1]

Survival of nationality parishes was closely related as well to demographic trends. Where chain migrations took place, ethnic neighborhoods had smaller population turnovers. For example, large numbers of Slovaks had immigrated to Pittsburgh to take jobs in the steel mills, but the neighborhoods there reflected Old World regional concentrations. In 1903, Slovak immigrants from Zemplin founded St. Gabriel Slovak Catholic church, and other Zemplin immigrants soon settled there. Slovak families from Spis settled near St. Matthew's Slovak Roman Catholic church. With large numbers of families from the same region of the Old World living in the same Pittsburgh communities, neighborhood identity was quite strong and the attraction of suburbs less pronounced. The same situation prevailed at St. Thaddeus parish in Detroit. But where groups were fewer in number and scattered widely, neighborhood identity was weaker and the tendency to make the move to the suburbs much stronger.[2]

The most well-developed ethnic community in America, both residentially and institutionally, was Chicago Polonia. Polish Catholics had been intensely nationalistic for two centuries, and when the associational revolution occurred in the United States, the immigrants became highly ethnocentric. There were fifty-seven parishes with a distinctly Polish flavor in Chicago, as well as hundreds of Polish societies. By 1920 there were 280,000 foreign-born Poles living in Chicago, and by 1945 they had been joined by nearly 500,000 children and grandchildren. In those parishes, they developed a highly collective yet personal religious atmosphere, transplanting the Old World liturgical calendar and guaranteeing an almost constant cycle of religious devotions. An important American historian has described that cycle:

> The Advent season was always climaxed by the traditional Christmas Vigil dinner (the *Wigila*).... In January, the feasts of the Circumcision and the Epiphany signalled the arrival of another cherished custom, the blessing of homes by the parish priest.... In February, the feasts of the Purification and of St. Blaise were accompanied by the blessing of the sacramentals ... and the blessing of throats; the Lenten season was accompanied by the *Gorzkie Zale,* the stations of the cross, and the celebration of the feasts of St. Casimir and St. Joseph. In late March and early April, one could expect the Holy Week services, the blessing of baskets *(Swiecone),* and the Resurrection sunrise mass; in May came the Marian devotions, when Holy Rosary sodalities throughout Polonia conducted their candlelight ceremonies at which time the "living rosary" was prayed; in June, on the feast of St. John the Baptist, the priest would ... bless swimming areas; in August, on the feast of the Assumption, thousands of Polish schoolchildren brought bouquets of flowers before the altar of Mary.... In September, these same schoolchildren could thaw the hardest of hearts singing "Happy Birthday" to the Blessed Mother; in October, many parishes conducted their "Forty Hours" devotions in honor of the Blessed Sacrament; in November, All Saints and All Souls day.[3]

There were also thousands of distinctly Polish ceremonies, songs, masses, and devotional practices, and a large membership in religious societies. At St. Stanislaus Kosta parish, they had dozens of them, including the St. Joseph Society for acts of mercy or service; the Living Rosary Sodality for prayers and devotions; the *Macierz Polska* for young men's social activities; the Polish Women's Association of Our Lady of Czestochowa; the Literary and Dramatic Circle for cultural activities; and the Polish Falcons or Polish Roman Catholic Union for patriotic and nationalistic programs. Within the boundaries of Chicago Polonia, the immigrants and their children had jobs, homes, schools, churches, charitable organizations, fraternal and social societies, and compatriots. To have readily left such a rich institutional life for the suburbs would have amounted to another migration and more culture shock. Instead, they stayed for years in the neighborhoods.

For a time, the church inside Chicago Polonia became an institution of resistance. When George Cardinal Mundelein promoted Americanization by halting formation of new nationality parishes, prohibiting ethnic languages in parochial schools, and drawing new territorial boundaries around predominantly Polish neighborhoods, many of the Polish clergy, including the highly orthodox Congregation of the Resurrection, actively discouraged movement out of the Polish neighborhoods. By maintaining an overwhelming Polish flavor to territorial parish activities, they also discouraged non-Polish movement into the neighborhoods. Retaining the Polish composition of the neighborhoods became the indirect method of perpetuating the nationality parish against the onslaught of the Irish-American hierarchy.[4]

But even though the Polish immigrant clergy had created a highly organized, living church in Chicago, and succeeded more than most other immigrant groups in preserving Old World values, they too were doomed in the long run. The secular forces of American life, especially the lure of good housing, jobs, quiet, cleanliness, and affluence in the suburbs, eventually pulled the children and grandchildren of the immigrants out of Polonia. Chicago Polonia reached its population peak in 1930 and its Old World devotional peak in 1950. But even then, the losses of language, nationality, family, and religious folkways, the spreading influence of Irish-Catholic devotional values, and the movement to the suburbs was undermining the community. By the late 1970s, the population of Chicago Polonia had dropped to only 150,000 people. The others had left for the mixed neighborhoods and mixed territorial parishes of the suburbs. In those mixed parishes, the Catholic melting pot ultimately began to emerge. In Chicago the Polish community was so large and the suburban migration so extensive that nationality parishes made it out to the suburbs of Calumet City, Evanston, Cicero, Chicago Heights, Berwyn, Argo, Lemont, North Chicago, North Riverside, and Bellwood, but the last one, St. Valentine in Cicero, was established in 1910. Although the Polish Catholic church in Chicago, as an ethnic institution, was still full of vitality in the metropolitan area in the 1980s, its decline had set in after World War II. And the Polish Catholic community in Chicago was the *best* case for the survival of the immigrant church. Among the smaller, more scattered, and less devout ethnic groups, the decline was even more significant.[5]

The immigrant communities also experienced dramatic changes in occupation and education, especially after World War II. For generations, the ethnic Catholics had been a blue-collar people, both institutionally and philosophically, valuing hard work as honorable and suspecting education and mobility for the threat they posed to religion and community life. While Anglo Protestants equated success with individual wealth and mobility, ethnic Catholics had opted for family stability and community integrity. By 1950, for example, nearly half of the Slovaks in Cleveland were still working at blue-collar jobs, living in the original neighborhoods, and praising the virtues of home, family, and community. They were alienated from the constant change and "progress" of Anglo America. "Success" for them was a religious and cultural issue rather than a social and economic one. If he wasn't careful, an individual could easily make huge sums of money while losing his family and his own soul.

But after World War II, besides moving to the suburbs, the children and grandchildren of the immigrants began looking at success in increasingly material terms, putting a new premium on educational achievement and occupational advancement. In a comparison of Catholic educational and occupational levels of immigrants' children with those of their parents in the late 1960s, Professor Harold Abramson noted dramatic changes over the course of a single generation. The extent of the changes, of course, varied from group to group, depending on how long each had resided in the United States, how large and demographically concentrated the population was, and how effective nationality parishes and community institutions had been. But for all the groups, increasing educational levels and white-collar jobs were replacing blue-collar and farm labor.[6]

This secondary assimilation into higher occupational and professional ranks had been a torturous process for many of the immigrant groups because the church had at first reinforced the antimaterialism and sense of social limitations endemic to peasant culture. The mid-nineteenth century was a period of intense reform in Protestant America. Issues undergoing transformation included temperance, abolition, women's rights, public education, and nativism.

Table 12.1
Occupational Mobility: Occupation

Ethnic Group	Father's Occupation			Son's Occupation		
	White collar	*Blue collar*	*Farm*	*White collar*	*Blue collar*	*Farm*
English	39	57	4	66	31	3
Irish	38	55	7	66	31	3
Italian	26	71	3	48	52	0
French Canadian	23	67	10	32	67	1
German	22	47	31	46	42	12
Lithuanian	19	74	7	45	55	0
East European	16	73	11	24	74	2
Hispanic	16	45	39	18	73	9
Polish	12	77	11	34	65	1
Total	24	62	14	43	54	4

Table 12.2
Occupational Mobility: Education

Ethnic Group	Father's Education				Son's Education			
	8th grade or less	*Some high school*	*High school*	*Post high school*	*8th grade or less*	*Some high school*	*High school*	*Post high school*
Hispanic	84	9	5	2	72	22	18	10
Lithuanian	80	14	0	6	22	21	21	16
Italian	83	10	3	4	20	32	31	17
East European	80	9	7	4	27	24	33	16
Polish	85	8	5	2	25	24	27	24
French Canadian	70	8	10	12	28	29	26	17
German	74	6	13	7	26	13	25	36
English	60	11	20	9	4	29	33	34
Irish	52	17	16	15	3	13	35	49
Total	74	10	9	7	22	23	29	26

Roman Catholics, for theological and social reasons, remained aloof from them. Church leaders in Europe had long promoted the status quo, treating poverty, misery, sickness, and death as God's will and urging the virtues of passivity, resignation, and pious acceptance. Those expectations, naturally, came to the United States with many of the immigrant priests. Socially, church leaders in America were extremely suspicious of American reform movements. Reform leaders were often Protestant ministers, and the movements for temperance, public education, and immigration restriction were laced with overt anti-Catholicism. Priests and bishops openly warned parishioners about the danger of the reform movements, putting them in the same light as such secret fraternal societies as the Freemasons.

For most nineteenth-century Catholic leaders, social reform was synonymous with Christian charity rather than social change. Individual philanthropy and parish charity to ameliorate suffering were perfectly alright, even admirable, but crusades to alter fundamental political, social, and economic relationships were not. Indeed, the church often pointed out the advantages of poverty: emulation of Jesus, freedom from materialism, humility, and the primacy of faith. The major vehicle for administering parish charity was the St. Vincent de Paul Society, a French-Catholic organization that spread throughout nineteenth and twentieth century Catholic America. The church also established a wide variety of hospitals, orphanages, and asylums in the nineteenth century to relieve suffering, but not to change the society.[8]

Not surprisingly, the Catholic social-work movement was somewhat retarded. In addition to being suspicious of social action programs, most church leaders were absorbed in dealing with mass immigration and assimilation. There were only fifty Catholic settlement houses to rival the more than five hundred established by Protestant and nonsectarian groups between 1885 and 1918. Concern about the religiosity of Italian and Czech immigrants as well as the fear that settlement houses like Jane Addams's Hull House in Chicago would entice immigrants away from the faith inspired the Catholic settlement-house movement. Late in the 1890s, under the direction of bishops Michael Corrigan of New York, Patrick Ryan of Philadelphia, John Ireland of St. Paul, James Cardinal Gibbons of Baltimore, and James Quigley of Chicago, the Catholic settlement-house movement began providing language training, child care services, job placement, religious instruction, health and sanitation information, and social centers for new immigrants. In 1897 Bishop William Elder of Cincinnati established the Santa María Institute for Italian immigrants, while at St. Rose Settlement House on Sixty-Fifth Street in New York the needs of Bohemian and Italian immigrants were met. The Guardian Angel Mission, L'Assunta House, and Madonna House served southern Italians in Chicago. In Detroit, the Weinman Club directed its services at Melkites and Maronites, while the German-Catholic Central Verein sponsored a settlement house for Magyars in St. Louis. Casa Maria Settlement on West Fourteenth Street in New York City assisted Spanish-speaking immigrants, while St. Elizabeth's worked with Polish Catholics in Chicago.

In addition to the St. Vincent de Paul Society and the settlement houses, other Catholic groups worked closely with the new immigrants. The immigrants, of course, had already formed thousands of benevolent societies as well as groups like the St. Raphael Society for Germans and Slovenes, Ancient Order of Hibernians for the Irish, the Italica Gens for Italians, and the Hungarian Catholic clubs for Magyars. In 1901, in an effort to coordinate the work of all the Catholic societies, church leaders established the American Federation of Catholic Societies. The Catholic Church Extension Society, founded in 1905, assisted immigrants in isolated mining camps in building chapels, while the Catholic Colonization Society began encouraging the urban poor in 1910 to consider relocating to rural, agricultural areas in the United States. Finally, in 1917, church leaders formed the National Catholic War Council to coordinate the work of all the Catholic settlement houses, emigrant aid societies, and national associations.[8]

The conservative philosophy was fine for a church tied to European monarchs and nobilities and for peasants enjoying little or no power, but American society was different. For years many Slavic immigrants were particularly antimaterialistic, bringing with them their European emphasis on balance and stability, often criticizing the American cult of money and wealth because it stimulated all sorts of social change. But in an Atlantic economy and American urban society where communal villages had broken down and new social cleavages had appeared based on occupation and income, the peasant fear of change was undermined. They too were becoming seduced by the American cult of progress and change and by the belief in power as a means of solving problems and guaranteeing justice. Equity and justice had often seemed ludicrous, irrelevant concepts in the fixed arrangements of European society, but in the United States they appeared possible and therefore worth struggling for.[9]

The debate between the "liberals" and "conservatives" in the 1880s and 1890s clearly showed how traditional the church was in the area of social change. For conservatives like Archbishop Michael Corrigan or Bishop Bernard McQuaid, Catholics should confine their social-work activities to charitable works. Some liberals like John Ireland were so upbeat about the virtues of American society that they denied the need for any real social change. Others like James Cardinal Gibbons feared that Catholic social activities would only inspire another round of nativism against the church. Liberals and conservatives might disagree on other matters, but the combined weight of their opinion rested solidly on the side of the social and economic status quo.[10]

The forces of social change in the Catholic community were coming from several directions, despite official opinion. By the time the Atlantic economy had destroyed village securities, the peasants had already moved to control economic forces by forming worker benefit societies in both the Old World and the New. Middle-class immigrants and ethnic Catholics had also initiated the nationalist movements to liberate their European homelands. The parish societies and national associations provided opportunities for status competition among a few of the immigrants, and one of the major consequences of these associations, beyond providing insurance or liberating the homeland, had been to confer status, respectability, and a sense of power and control on ethnic leaders. In those associations, the immigrants experienced their first taste of vertical mobility and interest group power, sensations that would only become more exaggerated in the United States.[11]

A second tradition of social change came out of the writings of people like Patrick Ford, Henry George, John Ryan, and Raymond McGowan, who advocated a variety of governmental and trade union solutions to the problem of poverty. Although generally recognizing the right of workers to organize and bargain collectively in the nineteenth and twentieth centuries, the church was afraid of the political implications of AFL strikes and boycotts, CIO class consciousness, and the radicalism of the International Workers of the World and the Molly Maguires.[12] The church felt comfortable with the labor conservatism of the French Canadians but often found itself staying neutral or even opposed to the labor agitation of the Irish. In spite of the temporizing of the church hierarchy, however, immigrant workers and their children slowly turned to the labor unions as a means of improving their situations. The days of peasant acquiescence and passivity were over as the immigrants flooded into the AFL unions in the 1890s and into the CIO unions in the 1930s and 1940s. The very act of joining those unions became a form of secondary association as the immigrants began rubbing shoulders with other ethnic Catholics.

Finally, many immigrants took power into their own hands through urban politics. By the 1880s the Irish had become a major force in American politics, having a power that grew out of their concentrated numbers and their experiences in organizational techniques gained in the political struggles of Daniel O'Connell's Ireland. In those urban machines of the Democratic party, they manipulated jobs, votes, contracts, and legislation, and as block chairmen, precinct captains, aldermen, and mayors they exercised power, gained respectability, and influenced the forces affecting their lives. With few exceptions, other Catholic immigrants followed them into the Democratic party, searching for the same power and control. The church adopted an equally careful view of Democratic politics, worrying about being too closely identified with any political point of view and generally insisting that priests be very circumspect in their political activity. But in nineteenth- and twentieth-century America, the urban political machines constituted another avenue for mobility and control. The theology of acquiescence was slowly yielding to the cult of power and progress, and the immigrants and their children were mixing with other ethnic Catholics to achieve them.[13]

From those three directions, with the sense of power and control they implied, the drive for progress swept through the ethnic Catholic communities. Groups of businessmen, professionals, intellectuals, and skilled workers had emerged in the ethnic communities and began to move into the American mainstream, if only in the most tentative way. Their social associations transcended nationality groups and brought them into contact with a wide variety of ethnic Catholics. Transnational groups like the Knights of Columbus thrived. The post-1945 educational and occupational changes accelerated those contacts, particularly in the mixed suburban parishes. Ethnic Catholics formed professional guilds and associations that had little or nothing to do with nationality backgrounds: the Catholic Alliance for Communication, the Catholic Press Association, the Catholic Nurses Club, the Catholic Actors Guild, the Catholic Writers Guild, the Catholic Dentists Guild, the Catholic Lawyers Guild, the Catholic Physicians Guild, and the Catholic Educators Guild. The Catholic melting pot also had its origins in those transnational professional, occupational, and political associations.[14]

From those social contacts in the mixed parishes and Catholic associations came the marriage melting pot. By the 1950s and 1960s, major changes were affecting immigrant marriage patterns. The tendency to marry outside the ethnic group was directly related to skin color, regional location, length of residence in the United States, socioeconomic status, and education. Ethnic Catholics with darker skins, like Mexicans or Filipinos, were far less likely than others to marry outside the group. Groups like Puerto Ricans, Mexicans, and French Canadians with ready access to the mother country were more likely to marry within their own group. Long-time residents of the United States, like the Irish or Germans, were more likely to marry outside their own group. The more well-to-do and better-educated Catholics, like the English or Irish, were more likely to marry exogamously than poor, uneducated Catholics. Spanish-speaking Catholics, who tend to be racially unique, close to their mother country, recent arrivals, poor, and undereducated were the least likely of ethnic Catholics to marry outside their ethnic group, while English Catholics, because of their opposite characteristics, were the most likely. One sampling of ethnic Catholics in the 1960s that compared the respondent's marriage with that of his or her parents indicated the following generational declines in endogamous marriages for the different Catholic groups.[15]

The impact of intermarriage on the nationality parish was critically important because when one partner did not speak the language of the nationality parish the couple would often move into a territorial parish. By 1957, for example, there were nineteen thousand French-Canadian Americans in the French-nationality parishes of Fall River, Massachusetts, and more than eleven thousand in the territorial parishes.[16] By the early 1970s, perhaps 55 percent of the Catholic population lived in endogamous marriages, with the Spanish speaking, Italian, and French Canadians significantly above that average and the Germans, English, and Irish significantly below it.

Table 12.3
Ethnic Intermarriage: Two Generations

Ethnic Group	*Endogamous Parents*	*Endogamous Respondent*	*Percent Change*
Spanish-speaking	96	88	−8
Italian	93	66	−27
Lithuanian	93	50	−43
Polish	89	50	−39
East European	86	39	−47
German	73	45	−28
Irish	65	43	−12
English	27	12	−15
Total	80	55	−25

Table 12.4
Ethnic Intermarriage: Three Generations

Ethnic Group	*First Generation*	*Second Generation*	*Third Generation*
English	—	—	100.0
Irish	33.3	57.5	74.4
German	55.6	77.4	59.5
French	46.7	27.1	60.7
Polish	—	57.8	64.9
East European	29.4	58.3	73.3
Italian	29.2	38.9	59.5
Hispanic	13.2	24.0	—

Although the decline of ethnic marriages was a strong indicator of assimilation and of the reality of the melting pot, the persistence of ethnic identity, even based on nationality, had far outlasted the predictions of most melting pot theorists, including Israel Zangwell as well as Ruby Jo Reeves Kennedy and Will Herberg. The persistence of ethnic national identities retarded the emergence of any general Catholic melting pot, but the fact that it was disappearing was no longer seriously in question. Another survey analyzing ethnic Catholic intermarriage rates by generation showed a growing pattern of exogamy as time passed.[17]

Equally significant was the rate of denominational intermarriage. Most ethnic Catholics marrying outside their nationality group nevertheless married inside their religious group, choosing other Catholics as partners. Of second generation Slovaks in Cleveland, for example, 61 percent married other Slovaks but fully 89 percent married other Roman Catholics. In the 1950s and 1960s, nearly 90 percent of Roman Catholics married other Catholics even if they did not marry someone from their own nationality group. Early melting pot theorists had exaggerated the pace and timing of assimilation as Herberg and others had exaggerated the timing of the emergence of the Catholic melting pot. The attraction of nationality loyalties were still exerting themselves, but the forces of acculturation and assimilation were inexorably undermining them. The Roman Catholic community in the United States was becoming just that—an integrated society offering a unique perspective on religion, politics, and society.[18]

The history of Holy Name of Jesus parish, a Polish congregation in Stamford, Connecticut, illustrates the process of modernization, acculturation, and assimilation. Established in 1903 to serve the needs of a Polish community, Holy Name was a classic immigrant parish during its first two decades. Twenty-nine immigrants had formed the Mutual Aid Society of King John Sobieski in 1898, joined the Polish Roman Catholic Union, organized the parish in 1903, completed the chapel in 1905, and started a parochial school in 1911. The atmosphere, liturgies, and parish organization all followed Polish models closely, and all but seven of the 537 marriages performed between 1903 and 1923 were endogamous between Polish Catholics. Parents commonly selected Polish religious names for their children.

During the interwar years, however, subtle signs of acculturation in the parish began to appear. New parish organizations were established—the Polish Business and Professional Club, the Youth Club, and the Holy Name Athletic Club—that were Polish in composition but secular in nature. Liturgical services retained their Polish village flavor and the parochial school taught Polish history and the Polish language, but English became the general language of instruction. Between 1923 and 1929 the number of exogamous marriages increased to 15 percent and to nearly 33 percent during the 1930s. Parents began turning to Anglo given names for their children in increasing numbers. Also in 1931, the parish formed the choir of St. Cecilia, a sure sign of acculturation to Irish-American Catholicism, because in Polish peasant churches the entire congregation had sung the responses to the mass. The social, communal act of congregational singing was giving way to the Irish practice of quiet, individual participation in the mass.

During and after World War II the pattern continued. More organizations like the Catholic Youth Organization, Boy Scouts, and veterans' societies appeared in the parish. English became the dominant language of the parish liturgies and organizations as well as of the parochial school. Endogamous marriages increased to nearly 50 percent, religiously mixed marriages to nearly 20 percent, and by the 1960s and 1970s, the third- and fourth-generation Polish Americans were leaving for the territorial parishes of the suburbs. New immigrants, primarily Spanish and French Canadians, began settling in the parish, giving it a multi-ethnic character, even though the statue of the Madonna of Czestochowa still presided in the sanctuary.[19] Similar processes were occurring throughout Catholic America. The forces of modernization had given the immigrants and their children a broader sense of community as well as a familiarity with organized interest groups and organized power; the forces of acculturation had given them a new language, family values, and devotional styles; and the forces of assimilation had thrown them together with other ethnic Catholics from all over the world. The transition from immigrant to ethnic Catholic to American Catholic was well underway by the early 1980s.

13

An Immigrant Catholic Legacy

Ever since large numbers of Irish immigrants began arriving in the 1820s, the Roman Catholic church has played a conspicuous role in American society, one distinguished by its theological and institutional differences with Anglo Protestantism. For years most Catholics felt quite conspicuous, caught between loyalty to the church and the centrifugal forces of democracy, individualism, and progress endemic to American culture. That tension left them feeling vulnerable, afraid of appearing "foreign" in a culture given to frequent nativism. Some of those fears finally began to wane after World War II. The election of John Kennedy in 1960, the deliberations of Vatican II, the steady decline of immigrant ethnicity, and the emergence of a large, ethnically mixed Roman Catholic community eased the nativist pressures, as did the prevailing secularism of American society. Nothing more clearly indicated the changing social climate than public reaction to the immigration of Mexicans, Cubans, Puerto Ricans, Haitians, and Asians during the 1960s and 1970s. The influx inspired a nativist concern about unemployment, welfare, and taxes, but there was no real fear about the fact that most new immigrants were Roman Catholics. The days of the Know-Nothing party, American Protective Association, and the Ku Klux Klan, at least in terms of its anti-immigrant nativism, were largely over.

By the 1980s, the church was the largest denomination in the United States, a fixed and even admired part of the social landscape, and Roman Catholics were accepted members of most communities. No longer preoccupied with religious sectarianism, Americans were focusing their energies on a broader series of social, economic, environmental, and foreign policy concerns. Within the church, many of the older immigrant sectarianisms had been laid to rest. Much later than they had planned, the "Americanists" like Bishop John Ireland and James Cardinal Gibbons had triumphed. The church had helped the immigrants absorb the shock of migration, adjust socially and economically to the New World, transcend nationality, and move into a larger Roman Catholic community. The church had ceased to be a community of immigrants. Hundreds of thousands of Catholics were immigrating each year, but they were entering a church of more than 55 million people, most of whom were English speaking and American born. This was a far cry from the early 1900s, when as many as 500,000 Catholics a year were entering a church numbering only 6 million people. The foreign image plaguing the church for so many years had disappeared.

The disappearance of the immigrant church and the emergence of an assimilated religious community had a dramatic effect on American Catholics, inspiring a gradual decline in piety, an ecumenical spirit capable of absorbing the Vatican II reforms, and several alternatives to traditional worship. Sociologists and historians have examined the challenges facing the contemporary church—"leakage" of members, serious declines in seminary enrollment, and defections of large numbers of priests—and have blamed the power of secular values and materialism, the rigidity of the church on social issues, and the competition of "more relevant" issues like Vietnam, poverty, civil rights, and ecology. But the decline of immigrant values and the rise of a Catholic melting pot were equally important in defining postwar piety, particularly in recruiting and maintaining priests, sustaining parochial school enrollments, and maintaining individual Catholic loyalties throughout a lifetime.

The most visible development among postwar Catholics was a serious decline in piety and institutional commitment. Opinion surveys in the 1960s and 1970s revealed a gradually increasing exodus from the church. By the late 1970s, approximately 17 percent of Catholics no longer identified with the church at all. Regular attendance at Mass declined from about 75 percent in the 1950s to only 50 percent in the late 1970s. In 1965 more than 180,000 nuns staffed church schools, hospitals, and charities, but that number declined to only 125,000 in 1980. Seminary enrollment dropped from nearly 50,000 to 13,000 in the same period, and many of those enrolled by 1980 were women ineligible for ordination. The number of Catholic colleges declined from 309 to 239; grade schools from 10,879 to 8,149; high schools from 2,413 to 1,527; and parochial school enrollment from 5.6 million to less than 3.2 million. The erosion of personnel, church attendance, charity and hospital work, and enrollment in the parochial schools became the greatest challenge facing the church.[1]

Although the declines were certainly related to the triumph of secular values, they were also connected to the disappearance of the immigrant church. The decline of the peasant economy in the Old World and the associational revolution in the New World had made the parish the most important institution for Catholic immigrants. Suddenly separated from family and religious life, they had given the parish a significance it had never possessed in the Old World, even among groups like the Irish and Poles, who were known for strong commitments to the institutional church. The nationality parish became the center of social and cultural life, and within that context immigrants worked to preserve their values in a strange society. The parish was the key to cultural survival and religious continuity; it is hardly surprising that immigrant loyalties to the church were so intense.

Such intensity could not survive assimilation because the immigrant sense of vulnerability did not survive. For many immigrant Catholics, language and faith were one and the same, and the first Poles, Germans, French Canadians, and Slovaks equally feared the loss of both. Their desire for ethnic language parishes, priests, and parochial schools reflected those convictions; when nationality parishes provided the institutional setting for the fusion of language and faith, they attracted immigrants dedicated to preserving the mother tongue. But as language loyalty eroded and the second and third generations realized that Roman Catholicism was not dependent on any linguistic tradition, the old connection between language and faith dissolved. While immigrant parents saw the parish as a means of preserving the language as well as the faith, children and grandchildren saw no connection, and the intense institutional loyalties growing out of language maintenance dissipated.

The decline in national loyalties played a similar role in undermining levels of religious activity, especially among groups like the Irish and French Canadians, who had fused nationality and religion, and among the Poles and Lithuanians, who saw the church as a means of political liberation. The church effectively lobbied for the liberation of Ireland or Quebec or Poland or Lithuania. Although "nationalists" had battled "religionists" over the nature of nationalism in the immigrant parishes, the church had still been identified with national independence. The desire to serve the mother country and liberate relatives left behind had inspired strong loyalties to the nationality parish. But by the 1920s, Ireland, Poland, Lithuania, Hungary, Czechoslovakia, and Yugoslavia had achieved independence just as the children and grandchildren of the immigrants were growing up without any recollection of the Old World. They did not possess the same concerns as their immigrant parents, and the church lost an important role that had attracted an earlier generation.[2]

The Rusin and Ukrainian experience illustrates the role of language and national loyalties in ethnic identification. Both groups had used Church-Slavonic or the vernacular as liturgical languages and campaigned for national liberation before World War I. But while Rusin ethnic loyalties waned after World War II, Ukrainians continued the struggle to maintain the language and liberate the homeland. Though the Ruthenian National Association succeeded in attaching Carpatho-Ruthenia to Czechoslovakia in 1918, the Ukraine remained dependent on the Soviet Union. Ukrainian Americans were still concerned about national liberation while Rusin Americans were generally satisfied. And while the flow of Rusin immigrants was limited after World War II, the flow of refugees from the Ukraine was steady and large. Rusin-American priests led a reform movement in the 1940s and 1950s to use English as the liturgical language, and the Vatican recognized that demand in 1955. There was little opposition in the Rusin community. It was different among Ukrainians. Some American-born Ukrainian priests also started a language-reform movement, and Bishop Joseph Shmondiuk agreed in 1965 to permit the use of English as the liturgical language. The reaction was immediate and intense, and Shmondiuk reversed himself, leaving Church-Slavonic and the Ukrainian vernacular as the liturgical languages. As late as 1984, when rumors began circulating that the Vatican, in an attempt to accommodate Soviet demands, wanted to restrict the vernacular in the Ukraine, suspend married priests, and rename the Ukrainian patriarch a bishop, a storm of protest emerged in the Ukrainian-American community. Ukrainian linguistic and national identities were still too strong.[3]

If the decline of language and nationality loyalties brought declines in religious commitment, so did the emergence of the Catholic melting pot. Intermarriage stimulated changes in ethnoreligious behavior. In the 1960s, ethnic commitments to attendance at Mass and monthly communion and to parochial education were consistent with historical experience. Those groups coming from European or American backgrounds with strong institutional commitments to the church maintained them, while those with weaker loyalties exhibited irregular attendance at Mass, communion, and parochial schools. Table 13.1 indicates various ethnic commitments to the institutional church in the 1960s.[4]

Table 13.1
Percent of Ethnic Religious Activity in the 1960s

Group	Weekly Mass		Monthly Communion		Catholic School	
	Father	*Mother*	*Father*	*Mother*	*Elementary*	*High School*
Irish	81	91	62	79	87	62
French Canadian	80	89	61	80	88	67
German	82	89	60	74	81	54
Polish	76	81	40	62	87	31
East European	66	76	31	52	68	37
Italian	39	71	23	61	35	14
Hispanic	36	58	24	55	35	9

But ethnic intermarriage brought significant declines in religious activity, especially among groups like the Irish and French Canadians who had been so devout. Table 13.2 indicates the change in religious activity in partners of endogamous ethnic marriages and in those of mixed ethnic marriages. The numbers listed are percentages derived by subtracting activity levels of endogamous partners from those of exogamous partners.[5]

Although intermarriage occasionally stimulated increases in religious activity, as with parochial education among Italians, the general trend was negative. The most consistent declines were among the Irish and French Canadians, groups that had been the most loyal supporters of the institutional church.

Table 13.2
Ethnic Intermarriage and Religious Activity

	Irish	*French Canadian*	*German*	*Polish*	*Italian*
Mass attendance: Mother	−10	−12	−24	+5	0
Mass attendance: Father	−8	−13	−6	−20	−4
Communion: Mother	−10	−26	−10	+15	−36
Communion: Father	−4	−9	+1	+1	+6
Catholic elementary school	−3	−15	+5	−11	+38
Catholic high school	+2	−13	+5	+12	+13

One irony of the decline in religious activity among Roman Catholics was the historical cycle it represented. In the United States, the combination of the nineteenth-century religious revivals in Europe, the American fusion of language, culture, and religion, and Irish-American revivalism and centralization had made most immigrants more faithful to the church in the United States than in the Old World. They were no longer the "nominal Catholics" many had been before the migration. But by the 1970s, the decline of the immigrant church, among other trends, was leading to the emergence of what Andrew Greeley has called "communal Catholics"—people loyal to Catholicism as a worldview but quite indifferent to the clergy, moral proscriptions, and institutional fidelity. These are people who see themselves as Catholics but accept birth control, abortion, divorce, married clergy, and situation ethics and who don't mind missing Mass, communion, and confession. Such a Catholic is not much different from the alienated, indifferent Catholic of pre-emigration Europe and Mexico.[6]

In addition to eroding religious activity, the decline of the immigrant church prepared the way for reception of Vatican II reforms. Between 1962 and 1966, church leaders from all over the world had convened in Rome and addressed themselves to the question of the place of Catholicism in contemporary life. Vatican II introduced a number of important changes to the church. After surviving several centuries in a pluralistic environment, American Catholicism possessed a unique faith in religious diversity, and at Vatican II Albert Cardinal Meyer of Chicago played a critical role in the successful Declaration of Religious Liberty. When Vatican II endorsed the collegiality of bishops to move away from the monarchical model of papal power, the American church was pleased, particularly since people like George Cardinal Mundelein in the 1920s and 1930s and Francis Cardinal Spellman in the 1940s and 1950s had consolidated church power at the diocesan level. Vatican II had also approved more lay priesthood power by expanding the role of lay deacons and parish assistants. Significant lay power had long been a characteristic of the immigrant American church.

The modern reform movement in Catholic seminaries as well as the devotional thrust of Vatican II had worked against popular, ethnically narrow paraliturgies and preoccupation with saints in favor of an ethical, sacramental religion, changes that Irish Catholicism had long been promoting. With the rise of ethical religion, the sermon came to play an increasingly important role in the Mass. Vatican II had also permitted more direct lay participation in the Mass and had slowly replaced the Latin Liturgy with the English vernacular in the United States. The introduction of English as the liturgical language was possible only in an assimilated, rather than an immigrant, church. Vatican II's de-emphasis on pomp and high church ceremonialism, once so central to German Catholicism, was accepted without much stress. There were, of course, some reactions to Vatican II. French Archbishop Marcel Lefebvre and his Society of St. Pius X continued saying the Latin Mass and gained a small following in the United States, and many immigrant traditionalists viewed Vatican II as an assault on the ethnically diverse church. But for most people, the recent decline of the immigrant church had prepared the American Catholic community for the Vatican II reforms.[7]

In addition to weakening religious activity and preparing the way for acceptance of Vatican II, the decline of the immigrant church also contributed to the growth of the Catholic charismatic movement in the 1960s and 1970s. The ethnic church of earlier years was slowly disappearing into the Catholic melting pot, but one group in particular—Hispanic Catholics—was remaining largely outside that melting pot and growing in size during the 1960s and 1970s. The McCarran-Walter Act had been amended in 1965, eliminating the old national origins system and stimulating a burst of immigration from southern Europe, Asia, and Latin America. Legal and illegal immigrants poured in from Mexico and Puerto Rico, and the Cuban revolution sent hundreds of thousands of people from Havana to Miami. Although the exact numbers are uncertain, Hispanic Catholics by 1980 probably totaled 25 percent of the church in the United States. Political oppression and poverty were also driving thousands of French-speaking Haitians into Florida. Of the immigrants from outside the Western Hemisphere in the 1960s and 1970s, Filipinos were the largest group and Italians second. Thousands of Portuguese continued moving into Massachusetts each year, becoming the largest ethnic group in the area, a change the Vatican recognized in 1970 when it named Humberto Madeiros to succeed Richard Cardinal Cushing as Archbishop of Boston.[8]

Although formal commitment to the church remained rather low among Hispanic Catholics, not from assimilation but from historical experience, the modern Catholic charismatic movement originated there. In its emphasis on the gifts of the spirit and aggressive lay participation in ritual life, the charismatic movement appealed to two groups in the American Catholic community: Hispanic Catholics whose connection to natural and supernatural peasant religion was still strong, and the descendents of the European immigrants who felt, in the disappearance of the immigrant church, a loss of community, authority, and identity. Searching for a new sense of community and spiritual direction within the church, they turned to the charismatic movement. Vatican II had openly claimed that the Holy Spirit is actively and continuously present in the affairs of the church, and charismatic Catholics claimed to have come personally in contact with that spirit. The gifts of healing, prophecy, and speaking in tongues were all physical manifestations of deep spiritual roots.

In 1949, Spanish Catholics developed a new spiritual movement known as *Cursillo de Cristianidad,* a series of intense, emotional weekend encounters between groups of priests, religious, and laity. At those weekend encounters, the priests and religious emphasized traditional Hispanic fidelity to the *pueblo,* the essentially communitarian nature of Catholic Christianity. During the 1950s, the *cursillo* movement spread to Hispanic Catholics in Texas, and from there to the descendents of European Catholics in the 1960s and 1970s. At about the same time, another pentecostal movement was emerging in the universities of the Northeast, where the children and grandchildren of the European immigrants were confronting a secular world. In 1966, some students at Duquesne University in Pittsburgh began organizing prayer and spiritual study groups where they actively sought the gifts of the spirit, and from there the movement spread out to other Catholic universities and state universities in heavily Catholic areas of the country. By 1980 there were more than 1 million charismatic Catholics in the United States organized into thousands of prayer groups. In the pentecostal movement, they rediscovered what they had lost when the immigrant church declined: strong leadership, spiritual certainty, social communalism, and active personal involvement in institutional religion.[9]

Another consequence of the decline of the immigrant church and the appearance of a Roman Catholic melting pot was the "white ethnic" movement of the 1960s and 1970s. Although some have viewed the rise of white ethnicity as proof of America's continuing diversity and of how "unmeltable" ethnic groups have become, the white ethnic movement was just the opposite—proof of how American the descendents of the immigrants have become, how unconcerned with nationality they are, and how they learned to view social and political reality through the lens of race, Catholicism, and Democratic interest-group politics. White ethnicity was a product of the melting pot, not proof of the permanence of diversity.

As successful as they were, Catholics were not far enough from their Old World roots to be complacent. Especially for those in the original settlements—Poles in Chicago, Italians in New York, Irish in Boston, Slovaks in Cleveland, or Ukrainians in Pittsburgh—the institutional ghetto was still visible, even though the ethnic-language newspapers were declining and ethnic associations losing membership. There also existed some doubt about how serious Americans were about cultural pluralism. John Kennedy's victory in 1960 had been perilously narrow even though the issue of religion had apparently been resolved. Although anti-Catholicism had not achieved its earlier vitality, older epithets like "polack" or "dago" or "bohunk" survived, as did the popularity of "Polish" or "Italian" jokes. A continuing prejudice against southern and eastern Europeans still lingered; so even in the 1980s many Catholics were uneasy about their place in American society.[10]

Economic uncertainty complicated their misgivings. Although younger Catholics in the 1980s had surpassed national averages in education and income, their parents remained in blue collar jobs. Memories of the Great Depression were still vivid, and the long-term problems in heavy industry and depression-level unemployment rates in the Northeast made economic security seem fragile indeed. Changes in the American economy, as it approached postindustrial maturity, were particularly threatening. Technological innovations were eliminating more blue collar jobs, and structural unemployment grew progressively worse. Labor unions were losing their power to influence politics and social affairs. For an immigrant people who prized work highly, long-term unemployment was psychologically devastating, to say nothing of its economic consequences. Businesses were relocating in the suburbs, city tax bases were eroding, and property owners had to bear the costs of education and social services. People who had struggled to buy homes found their property threatened by high taxes and escalating utility bills.[11]

Social changes were similarly bewildering. Most of the changes were inevitable transformations of Old World customs. Children of the immigrants had already sacrificed nationality and language, and now they witnessed the erosion of certain family values and community loyalties. Old World families seemed doomed. When both parents worked to make ends meet, children were naturally more independent and less responsive to parental authority. Life in an industrialized society made children economic liabilities rather than economic assets. In the old peasant villages children had had specific farming chores to perform, but in the American cities, with the obligations of school combined with social pressures, adolescents were economically dependent on parents for many years. Parents felt their families were breaking up. After World War II, when so many veterans moved from the ethnic neighborhoods to the cities of the South and West or to the suburbs, the extended family changed forever. Immigration from Europe had disrupted extended families, but total dispersal of the extended family became commonplace in twentieth-century America as children and grandchildren of the immigrants moved far away from home and returned only occasionally for holidays and short vacations. Parents realized that college education was important for prosperity and success, but at the same time, especially in the 1960s and 1970s, colleges seemed to be giving young people strange ideas. They became rebellious, too critical of traditional values and of the church, and were less likely to be as committed to the church as their parents had been. The two bastions of Old World culture, family and church, seemed threatened.[12]

The civil rights movement increased these fears, creating a social climate where "white ethnicity" flourished. Immigrant Catholics had never opposed the idea of civil equality; indeed, they had opened the doors of the CIO unions to blacks in the 1930s, served as the power base behind Hubert Humphrey's civil rights stand at the Democratic convention in 1948, and provided the margin of victory for the Civil Rights Act of 1964. But when the Black Power movement gained momentum, violence erupted in the streets, and the federal government turned to racial quotas and neighborhood engineering, immigrant and ethnic Catholics were outraged at what they considered a perversion of liberalism. A political coalition began to emerge between white Protestant Republicans who opposed a large federal government and ethnic Catholics who felt the federal government was becoming invasive and anticommunity. George Wallace's surprising support in the election of 1968 and Ronald Reagan's victories in 1980 and 1984 showed the power of that coalition.[13]

When it became clear early in the 1970s that civil rights legislation would not immediately bring equality, the federal government began focusing on *de facto* segregation, enforcing open housing laws, busing children across district lines to achieve racial integration, redesigning electoral districts to achieve racial balances, forcing employers to subordinate seniority rights and promote recently hired black and Hispanic workers, and imposing racial quotas on universities, local governments, and private businesses. But in attempting to right past wrongs, the federal government failed to understand the background of immigrant Catholicism and white ethnicity. Profoundly committed to homes, families, neighborhoods, and parishes as part of a peasant, immigrant heritage, ethnic Catholics felt threatened by expanding black ghettoes and the arbitrary busing of children. Insecure about their jobs in a troubled economy, they viewed union seniority rights as natural laws and fought even the suggestion of altering them. In college quotas and affirmative action programs for minorities, they saw roadblocks to their own vertical mobility. Even the Democratic party, their link to political power, deserted them in 1972 when Mayor Richard Daley's Chicago delegation failed to be seated at the presidential nominating convention because it did not meet racial, age, and sexual quotas demanded by liberal supporters of Senator George McGovern.

When blamed for black poverty and inequality, ethnic Catholics were quick to reply that they had not been around during slavery and were not responsible for segregation or black ghettoes. They had arrived in the cities at the same time as most blacks and had encountered a good deal of discrimination. They simply refused to be blamed, and instead of viewing the later phase of the civil rights movement as a legitimate campaign for equality, many saw it as an illegitimate attempt to destroy their neighborhoods. While blacks saw "law and order" as a euphemism for prejudice, white ethnics viewed it as a means of preserving neighborhoods from violence. When the Catholic parents of Detroit or Boston protested busing, or when labor unions sued to protect seniority rights, or when ethnic Catholics opposed the policies of Mayor Harold Washington in Chicago, it was not simply racism and prejudice but also a desperate attempt to preserve a way of life that was rapidly disappearing.

Ethnic Catholics insisted that racial and ethnic groups maintain themselves voluntarily. The government, they felt, should take a neutral position as it had with religions, neither promoting nor discouraging them. For white ethnic groups who valued community so highly, it was not the purpose of the government to sponsor residential, educational, or occupational dispersion programs, especially when there was little evidence of overt discrimination. Ethnic Catholics were committed to equality and pluralism, but not to a political system where the government obliterated communities, neighborhoods, and individual futures in the name of freedom. In those demands and expectations, the descendents of the immigrant Catholics found themselves occupying common ideological ground, regardless of their nationality backgrounds. Ethnic Catholics' class, racial, and residential situations had become more significant than national origins. They were white Catholics.[14]

Finally, the emergence of the Roman Catholic melting pot contributed to the waning anti-Catholicism in the United States. For centuries many native Americans had perceived the Catholic church as a foreign institution incapable of adjusting to social values in the United States. Time and again a new wave of Catholic immigration had triggered a new round of nativism. But by the 1960s and 1970s, even though millions of Hispanic Catholics were entering the country, the nativist reaction did not really have a religious dimension to it. For a few months in 1960, when John F. Kennedy was pursuing the presidency, the concerns about Roman Catholicism revived, but even they were short-lived, and his election proved more than anything else that one rather persistent theme in American social history was gone. With the vast majority of American Catholics native born and English speaking, and with most of the paraliturgies and folk elements of Old World religion disappearing, the church no longer seemed so strange and foreign.

Except for the Hispanic Catholics, the days of the immigrant church were over. In terms of family values, cuisine, and modes of emotional expression, as well as religious activity, older ethnic patterns still exerted some power, but like language and folk culture, even they were threatened by occupational and geographic mobility, education, and intermarriage. A Catholic melting pot was emerging out of the immigrant communities, simultaneously inspiring a decline of general religious commitment, liturgical and devotional reform, the pentecostal movement, white ethnicity, and the waning of anti-Catholicism. The challenge of the church in the 1980s and 1990s would be to retain a strong Catholic commitment in an increasingly secular and homogeneous religious society.

That immigrant church, however, had left an important legacy. Against many of the major themes of American history, immigrant Catholicism had offered clear alternatives, a set of values often leaving them apart from the larger society. Where most Americans had praised the virtues of democracy, immigrant Catholicism had offered instead the social efficacy of hierarchy and authority. While native Americans were defying egalitarianism, immigrant Catholics were often ignoring it, accepting instead a worldview of inequities as the natural order of things. Large numbers of Americans were traditionally preoccupied with the pursuit of perfection and faith in moral reform, but the immigrant Catholics were far more skeptical, unconvinced that society could ever be perfected because of the sinful nature of man. That of course led directly to the Catholic secession from the ideal of progress. While Puritan culture wanted to build the "City on a Hill," to push society forward in a progressive drive for redemption, immigrant Catholicism remained reluctant, afraid of what destruction "progress" might leave in its wake. While all of American history had celebrated individualism, immigrant Catholics had invested all their energies in the community and its corporate view of society. American history had also revolved around a relentless geographic mobility—the abandonment of old places for new places—but the Catholic immigrants had almost worshiped their homes and neighborhoods. They chose stability over mobility. While most Americans viewed work as a stepping stone to vertical mobility, the immigrant Catholics again chose stability, eschewing for a time material success and bringing to the United States a working class perspective, a sense of permanence about job and status that defied the shibboleths of success and progress. Finally, while native Americans had periodically embarked on assimilationist crusades, which the Catholic church occasionally endorsed, the immigrants stood up for pluralism within the church as well as for American society.

Because they had rejected centralized authority for some form of denominational or congregational autonomy, Protestants tended to be antiauthoritarian, suspicious of concentrated political or religious power. In their view of religion, sovereignty flowed up from the people through man-made bureaucracies rather than down to the people from a king or pope. Out of such beliefs came the individualistic ethos of Protestantism. Whether in the predestination of the Calvinists, the Inner Light of the Quakers, or the "saving grace" of the evangelicals, Protestants believed people could be saved outside the church because the personal relationship with God transcended all institutions. From that individualistic ethos came the Protestant view of success and community. The development of capitalism in premodern Europe had given rise to an ambitious entrepreneurial class who resented Catholic restrictions on business enterprise. Businessmen saw in Protestantism a liberating force. Eventually, Protestant theology not only liberated the entrepreneurial spirit from medieval restrictions but justified material success. Diligence and hard work were virtues indicating the potential of election and divine grace; success no longer required apologies. The striving for success permeated Protestant culture.

Protestant individualism also generated different visions of community. While in the older, Catholic view of society, the whole was more important than any of its parts, Protestants elevated the individual and argued that the community was only a tool to promote individual needs. When communities stopped meeting individual goals, people should leave. American society was as mobile geographically as it was economically, ready to sever roots and move to new opportunities, even if it meant leaving friends, family, and familiar places. To give themselves a temporary sense of community, these Americans became joiners, forming clubs and associations like the YMCA, YWCA, Masons, Odd Fellows, Elks, Lions, Eagles, Moose, Kiwanis, Optimists, Rotary, Salvation Army, Gideons, Daughters of the American Revolution, country clubs, chambers of commerce, and professional groups. The associations were overwhelmingly Protestant in composition.

Protestants also dominated American elites. They controlled the boards of directors of the largest banks, insurance companies, foundations, universities, and industrial corporations, and until 1945 they dominated the sciences, professions, and government. Even when they were not well-to-do, as in the case of many farmers and skilled workers in the AFL, they often supported conservative values, especially in social, moral, and political affairs. That was an irony of white Protestant history. Extremely flexible and adventurous in economic matters, and in the vanguard of the Industrial Revolution, they also favored prohibition, immigration restriction, and Sunday blue laws, and opposed gambling, prostitution, and parochial schools. Individualistic, independent, democratic, ruralistic, antiauthoritarian, opportunistic economically but conservative socially—these were the characteristics of Protestant society in the United States.[15]

In a society worshiping democracy, Roman Catholicism seemed a bastion of authority and centralized power. American society had long suspected centralized power, and Protestantism, capitalism, and states' rights had all served as the institutionalization of those fears. American Catholicism, while criticizing neither capitalism nor states' rights, nevertheless argued that hierarchical power was legitimate, that authority, as long as it came from God and was exercised righteously, was a perfectly natural way of ordering society, at least on a social and religious level. When Protestants worried that Catholic authoritarianism would filter into national politics, church leaders argued just the opposite, that politics and religion could remain separate, that church and state were not the same. Many Americans were not convinced, but Catholic leaders were still able to praise the virtues of political democracy as well as religious theocracy.

Nor were immigrant Catholics preoccupied with guaranteeing equality, equity, and perfection in society. Convinced from their Augustinian roots that human nature was weak and fallible and that transgression was an expected predicament easily handled in the confessional, immigrant Catholics had little faith in the perfectibility of man and extraordinary skepticism about the possibilities of eliminating sin. All Catholics, of course, were not the same. Irish Catholicism had picked up on some of the Victorian moralisms of nineteenth-century Anglo-Protestant culture, but few other immigrant Catholics possessed such intense concerns. Indeed, they usually resented and resisted the moral crusades of Anglo Protestants to prohibit such things as alcohol, gambling, dancing, and Sunday buying. These were hardly vices, only innocent entertainments rooted deep in human nature. To attempt to eliminate them in the name of perfection was ludicrous.

Immigrant Catholics, however, were not laissez faire purists complacently accepting the status quo. They too had passionate concerns about life in America, but instead of focusing on moral reform and the elimination of evil, they paid attention to economic issues, particularly to the amelioration of poverty, unemployment, and the problems of urban society. These were the primary focus of Roman Catholic reform, and the Irish immigrants had led the way because of their political talents. Despite poverty and lack of education, the Irish were culturally acclimated to political competition after centuries of struggle and oppression at the hands of the British Empire. Mass political action, including passive, direct, and violent activities, had gone on for years in Ireland. Building on that history, the Irish immigrants constructed their famous political machines between 1820 and 1900, epitomized by Tammany Hall in New York in the 1880s and by the Richard Daley organization in twentieth-century Chicago. Irish politicians attracted and maintained the loyalty of the poor immigrants through patronage—jobs in fire, police, sanitation, public works, and civil service departments in the major cities. Although often graft-ridden and the bane of moralizing Protestants, Irish machine politics contradicted laissez faire individualism by distributing food, fuel, and jobs to poor people. Skeptical about human nature, concerned with improvement rather than perfection, the Irish became the cornerstone of Democratic politics, which eventually became the New Deal of Franklin D. Roosevelt, the Fair Deal of Harry Truman, the New Frontier of John F. Kennedy, and the Great Society of Lyndon Johnson.

Millions of other immigrant Catholics usually accepted that Gaelic political posture, even while resenting Irish domination of the church. The origins of immigrant concern for economic survival were rooted in the workers' and mutual benefit societies that had sprouted in Europe and the United States when the Atlantic economy began changing. The deterioration of the peasant economy had placed great pressure on nuclear families, compromising their ability to support themselves; so they formed benevolent societies to provide economic assistance to one another. By 1910 there were thousands of those associations functioning in the Irish, French-Canadian, German, Italian, Polish, Czech, Slovak, Lithuanian, Croatian, Magyar, Slovene, Maronite, Melkite, Ukrainian, and Rusin communities. Among German Catholics, the *Unterstutzung-Verein* were mutual aid societies formed in the parishes to assist the sick and the poor, and in 1855 all the German-Catholic mutual aid societies had formed the Central Verein. By the early twentieth century, the Central Verein had become committed to social reform and was providing English-language schools, settlement houses, health and life insurance, day care centers, employment agencies, and welfare programs for German Catholics. In their political concerns, the immigrants expected government, on the local as well as the national level, to underwrite the objectives of those mutual aid societies. These were "bread and butter" issues, not the moralistic concerns of so many Protestants.

Most immigrant Catholics also followed the Irish into the Democratic party. Political behavior reflected cultural values. Ethnic groups supporting the Republican party were usually pietistic or evangelical in religion, while more formal, ritualistic groups tended to be Democrats; that is, the Baptists, Methodists, Presbyterians, Quakers, Scandinavian Lutherans, and Scandinavian and Dutch Calvinists in the North were often Republicans, while Roman Catholics and high church Lutherans were generally Democrats. Emphasizing formalism and priestly authority, the Catholics viewed the world skeptically, as if secular affairs were distinct from religious ones and man could do little to make the world perfect. Government should instead ensure that the standard of living was sufficient to make family and religious life fulfilling. Evangelical Protestants, on the other hand, felt an intense need to purify the world—to change people's minds and behavior by legislating morality. While the Republican party seemed bent on crusading to change America socially, the immigrant Catholics turned to the Democratic party because it opposed such crusades and respected the prerogatives of local communities and groups.

Evangelical Protestants were always advocating change in the name of progress while immigrant Catholics were always pursuing tradition and stability, afraid that a changing society would undermine their values. Protestants opposed parochial schools because they preserved Old World traditions and Catholic values. Catholics saw the public schools as "Protestant" schools: Protestant ministers on school boards, Protestant prayers repeated each morning, and the King James Bible used for instruction. Protestants supported prohibition as a means of purifying the world, but Catholics viewed liquor as a harmless diversion and opposed the temperance movement. Protestants supported Sabbath laws to close stores and taverns on Sunday, and the Catholics opposed them as unnecessary invasions of privacy. So while the Protestants in the Republican party worked to create a homogeneous America free of sin, the Catholics in the Democratic party tried to create a stable world where religious values could flourish in a timeless world.

Such cultural values dominated American politics until the turn of the century, but as industrialization continued its inexorable transformation of the social structure, economic issues became more and more important in defining political behavior. The ethnic cleavage in American politics acquired an ethnic base. The Whigs and then Republicans had traditionally reflected the interests of business and commerce and, in an economy just beginning to industrialize, of those skilled craftsmen who were still either small businessmen or the elite of the labor force in mining and manufacturing. Generally, businessmen of British descent believed the Republican party best represented their economic needs. In the 1860s and 1870s, when Dutch, German, and Scandinavian farmers poured into the Midwest, the Republican party had favored free land through the Homestead Act. So among businessmen, skilled workers, and northern farmers, the Republicans enjoyed strong support. For those people, the American dream of prosperity and success, of larger and larger farms and bigger and bigger businesses, seemed realistic, a promise the country was perfectly capable of achieving. To achieve that dream, they were prepared to sacrifice tradition and community in the name of technology, mobility, and change.[16]

Not so with immigrant Catholics. Unskilled and worried about mere survival rather than constant progress, they became a working-class people, struggling to make livings in the mines, mills, factories, smelters, and railroads of urban, industrial America. There was not the cultural passion, until recent years, to press always for economic betterment, to acquire higher education, or to climb the social ladder. Work was a necessary evil for the immigrant Catholics, a means of sustaining the family, not some manifestation of God's pleasure. Throughout the nineteenth and early twentieth centuries, the Catholic fear of progress and yearning for stability kept them confined to the lower rungs of the occupational ladder. By emphasizing acceptance of worldly status and limiting social life within the boundaries of the parish, church leaders reinforced economic inferiority. Revivals, catechisms, sermons, and parochial school curricula echoed that message again and again, urging people to contentedly accept what God willed for them economically while rejoicing in their spiritual salvation. This was not, of course, a fatalism linked to any Calvinist predestination; indeed, Catholics were supposed to work enthusiastically to support the church and attain salvation while not letting themselves be seduced by the Protestant attachment to money. The theological subculture of American Catholicism stimulated a gospel of economic acceptance, a value quite different from the prevailing ideologies of Anglo America.[17]

They did not, of course, passively accept low wages, long hours, and endless suffering. Generally accepting the permanence of working-class status but not of poverty, the immigrant Catholics poured into the available labor unions—the National Labor Union in the 1860s, the Knights of Labor in the 1870s, the American Federation of Labor in the 1880s, and the Congress of Industrial Organizations in the 1930s. During the 1930s, when the Great Depression once again threatened their survival, the immigrant Catholics aggressively demanded economic justice and joined that New Deal coalition that dominated American politics for a half-century, transforming the federal government into the underwriter of economic stability. But even within the context of modern union demands, immigrant Catholics clearly subordinated work rather than exalting it, rendering it a means not an end, a way of living and surviving while they worshiped and tried to prepare themselves and their families for eternal life.

Immigrant Catholic values also stood in sharp contrast to the individualistic ethos of American society. Ever since the sixteenth century, the whole thrust of Anglo-Protestantism had exalted the individual over society: salvation could be attained outside the institutional church, and freedom, both political and economic, could be attained only in the absence of government intervention. Large collections of people and power—government, church, and class—had become less significant than individuals. The Reformation, the rise of capitalism, and the development of classical political liberalism had released the individual from the chains of corporate society, justifying a whole range of values and public policies promoting individual progress. The American emphasis on geographic mobility, occupational advancement, and material success all rested on that liberation of the individual. Churches, schools, organizations, and communities were all subordinate to individual impulses, and the consequences had been an extraordinary economic energy, social vitality, philosphical pragmatism, and an unprecedented toleration for change.

But immigrant Catholicism, as well as its medieval predecessor, had always elevated the society and community above the individual, subordinating private impulses to the larger good. Catholics' faith in the corporate ideal—that the whole of society was greater than any of its parts—was a natural outgrowth of authoritarian theocracy. If God really manifested his will through his anointed stewards, then the institutional church carried the responsibility of integrating individual wishes with larger corporate needs. While Anglo Protestants viewed success and progress outside any institutional context, immigrant Catholics viewed them within the boundaries of the church. Charged to be "in the world but not of the world," Roman Catholics in the United States had struggled and sacrificed to create their own social world, a community of parishes, churches, schools, and societies where the individual could live out his or her life in security and stability. The immigrants saved their money, established their own savings and loan associations, and then purchased homes within the parish, creating a kind of religious neighborhood and social roots that relatively few Protestants experienced. Given the level of their attachment to those homes, parishes, schools, and associations, it is hardly surprising that they did not place too much faith or expectation in the idea that progress required geographic movement. While most Americans were usually quite prepared to uproot themselves and leave friends and families behind in an endless quest for "progress," the immigrant Catholics had a special reverence for a particular house on a particular street in a particular parish. When given a choice between individual aggrandizement and family and community stability, they usually opted for the latter.

Finally, immigrant Catholicism, even when struggling for survival against "Irish Catholic liberalism," was a beacon for pluralism in a larger society valuing assimilation and the melting pot. Out of their strong sense of neighborhood and community, their commitments to Old World cultures, and their fears of being religiously absorbed into Anglo-Protestant society came the immigrant Catholic commitment to pluralism—the virtues of being left culturally alone, politically tolerated, economically accepted, and religiously independent. They had always looked on assimilation as a danger rather than a virtue, something to be avoided at all costs because it would threaten the institutions, like the church or the family, they valued so highly. For them, the vitality of American society, and its prosperity and stability, had not resulted from its homogeneity but from its heterogeneity. For Catholics, out of all the cultural differences came an enormous energy, the ability to compromise, and the skills to change and adjust. In their differences, not their similarities, Americans enjoyed strength. Even in 1983, when more than one hundred American bishops visited the Vatican, Pope John Paul II expressed concern about pluralism in American Catholicism and about how deep the roots of the church were planted.[18] The church seemed too diverse to him, too divided in terms of liturgy and discipline, at least when compared with the internal unity of Polish Catholicism. After more than three centuries of development and wave after wave of immigration, and despite the emergence of the Roman Catholic melting pot, the American church, in the eyes of a Polish pope, still reflected its complicated ethnoreligious past.

Notes

Chapter 1. The Catholic Dimension in American History

1. Hector St. John de Crevecoeur, *Letters from an American Farmer* (New York, 1904); D. W. Brogan, *The American Character* (New York, 1956); Alexis de Tocqueville, *Democracy in America* (New York, 1956); Alistair Cooke, *The Americans* (New York, 1980).

2. See James S. Olson, *The Ethnic Dimension in American History* (New York, 1979).

3. For the best religious history of America, see Sydney E. Ahlstrom, *A Religious History of the American People* (New Haven, 1972). Also see Sydney Mead, *The Lively Experiment. The Shaping of Christianity in America* (New York, 1963).

4. See James Hennesey, *American Catholics. A History of the Roman Catholic Community in the United States* (New York, 1981) and John Tracy Ellis, *American Catholicism* (Chicago, 1959).

5. See Wallace Notestein, *The English People on the Eve of Colonization, 1603–1630* (New York, 1954); Peter Laslett, *The World We Have Lost* (New York, 1965); Carl Bridenbaugh, *Vexed and Troubled Englishmen, 1590–1642* (New York, 1968); Patrick Collinson, *The Elizabethan Puritan Movement* (New York, 1967); C. H. George and Katherine George, *The Protestant Mind of the English Reformation* (London, 1961).

6. See Bernard Bailyn, *The Ideological Origins of the American Revolution* (Cambridge, 1967); Stanley Elkins, *Slavery: A Problem in American Intellectual and Institutional Life* (Chicago, 1959); Louis Hartz, *The Liberal Tradition in America* (New York, 1955).

7. Martin E. Marty, *Righteous Empire: The Protestant Experience in America* (New York, 1970).

8. Mary A. Ray, *American Opinion of Roman Catholicism in the Eighteenth Century* (New York, 1936); Raymond J. Lahey, "The Role of Religion in Lord Baltimore's Colonial Enterprise," *Maryland Historical Magazine*, 72 (Winter, 1977), 492–511.

9. For an early description of Roman Catholicism in America, see Thomas O'Brien Hanley, ed., *The John Carroll Papers,* 3 vols. (Notre Dame, 1976), I, pp. 169–90. Also see Martin I. J. Griffin, "The First Mass in Philadelphia," *American Catholic Historical Researcher*, 12 (January, 1895), 38–40.

10. John Tracy Ellis, ed., *Documents of American Catholic History,* 2 vols. (Chicago, 1967), I, pp. 95–98.

11. Peter Guilday, *The Life and Times of John Carroll, First Archbishop of Baltimore, 1735–1815* (New York, 1922), pp. 225–27. Also see Thomas Hughes, *History of the Society of Jesus in North America, Colonial and Federal,* 4 vols. (New York: 1907–1917); Edwin W. Beitzell, *The Jesuit Missions of St. Mary's County, Maryland* (Abell, 1977); Mary Peter Carthy, *English Influence on Early American Catholicism* (Washington, D.C., 1959).

12. Peter Guilday, *John Carroll,* p. 832; Donna Merwick, *Boston Priests, 1848–1910* (Cambridge, 1973), p. 4; Mary Peter Carthy, *Catholicism in English-Speaking Lands* (New York, 1964), pp. 7–27, 45–50.

13. See Glenn R. Conrad, ed., *The Cajuns: Essays on Their History and Culture* (Lafayette, 1978); W. J. Eccles, *France in America* (New York, 1972); Naomi Griffiths, *The Acadians: Creation of a People* (New York, 1973); Elizabeth A. John, *Storms Brewed in Other Men's Worlds: The Confrontation of the Indians, Spanish, and French in the Southwest, 1540–1795* (College Station, 1975); Charles Gipson, *Spain in America* (New York, 1964); Audrey Lockhart, *Some Aspects of Emigration from Ireland to the North American Colonies between 1660 and 1775* (New York, 1976).

14. For general surveys of American immigration, see James S. Olson, *The Ethnic Dimension in American History*; Maldwyn Jones, *American Immigration* (Chicago, 1960); Philip D. Taylor, *Distant Magnet: European Emigration to the U.S.A.* (London, 1971); Maxine Seller, *To Seek America: A History of Ethnic Life in the United States* (Englewood Cliffs, 1977).

15. Ray Allen Billington, *The Protestant Crusade, 1800–1860: A Study of the Origins of American Nativism* (New York, 1938). Also see Michael Feldberg, *The Philadelphia Riots of 1844: A Study of Ethnic Conflict* (Greenwood, 1975).

16. See Andrew M. Greeley, *That Most Distressful Nation: The Taming of the American Irish* (Chicago, 1972); Lawrence J. McCaffrey, *The Irish Diaspora in America* (Bloomington, 1976); Joseph P. O'Grady, *How the Irish Became Americans* (New York, 1973).

17. James Hennesey, *American Catholics,* pp. 173, 207, 237.

18. John Higham, *Strangers in the Land: Patterns of American Nativism, 1860–1925* (New Brunswick, 1955).

19. See Joshua Fishman, ed., *Language Loyalty in the United States* (The Hague, 1966); Richard M. Linkh, *American Catholicism and European Immigrants (1900–1924)* (New York, 1975).

20. Will Herberg, *Protestant—Catholic—Jew: An Essay in American Religious Sociology* (New York, 1955).

21. See Harold J. Abramson, *Ethnic Diversity in Catholic America* (New York, 1973).

22. See Jay P. Dolan, *The Immigrant Church: New York's Irish and German Catholics, 1815–1865* (Baltimore, 1975), pp. 7, 55, 67, 114–15; John Bossy, "The Counter Reformation and the People of Catholic Europe," *Past and Present,* 47 (May, 1970), 52.

23. Gerald Shaughnessy, *Has the Immigrant Kept the Faith? A Study of Immigration and Catholic Growth in the United States* (New York, 1925), pp. 246–56.

Chapter 2. The Irish Background of American Catholicism

1. For general histories of Ireland, see J. C. Beckett, *A Short History of Ireland* (New York, 1966); Edmund Curtis, *A History of Ireland* (New York, 1968); T. W. Moody and F. X. Martin, eds., *The Course of Irish History* (New York, 1967).

2. See Michael Dolley, *Anglo-Norman Ireland* (Dublin, 1972); Kenneth Nicholls, *Gaelic and Gaelicized Ireland in the Middle Ages* (Dublin, 1972); J. H. Andrews, "A Geographer's View of Irish History," in T. W. Moody and F. X. Martin, eds., *The Course of Irish History,* pp. 17–29; A. J. Otway-Ruthven, *A History of Medieval Irèland* (London, 1968), pp. 1–14.

3. See John Watt, *The Church in Medieval Ireland* (Dublin, 1972); Margaret MacCurtain, *Tudor and Stuart Ireland* (Dublin, 1972). Also see Giovanni Costigan, *A History of Modern Ireland* (New York, 1969), pp. 19–29. For a look at the fusion of Catholic and Irish ethnicity, see Patrick O'Farrell, *Ireland's English Question* (New York, 1972).

4. For a background study of Irish customs, see Conrad Arensberg, *The Irish Countryman: An Anthropological Study* (Garden City, 1968); Emyr Estyn Evan, *Irish Heritage* (Dundalk, 1945); Sean O'Faolain, *The Irish* (Harmondsworth, 1969). Also see Andrew M. Greeley, *The Irish Americans: The Rise to Money and Power* (New York, 1981), pp. 130–41.

5. For a history of Irish nationalism, see Robert Kee, *The Green Flag* (New York, 1972). Also see Thomas N. Brown, *Irish-American Nationalism* (Philadelphia, 1966), p. 35.

6. Quoted in Edward M. Levine, *The Irish and Irish Politicians* (Notre Dame, 1966), p. 67.

7. See Giovanni Costigan, *A History of Modern Ireland,* pp. 46–49. Also see A. Clarke, "The Colonization of Ulster and the Rebellion of 1641," in T. W. Moody and F. X. Martin, *The Course of Irish History*, pp. 187–203.

8. See Mary Johnson, *Ireland in the Eighteenth Century* (Dublin, 1974).

9. Quoted in Lawrence J. McCaffrey, *The Irish Diaspora in America*, p. 110.

10. See Gearoid O'Tuathaigh, *Ireland before the Famine, 1798–1848* (Dublin, 1972).

11. Gustave de Beaumont, *Ireland: Social, Political and Religious,* 2 vols. (London, 1839), I, pp. 266–67.

12. See K. H. Connell, *The Population of Ireland, 1750–1845* (London, 1950). Also see W. F. Adams, *Ireland and Irish Emigration to the New World from 1815 to the Famine* (New Haven, 1932), pp. 334–409.

13. Quoted in Seumas MacManus, *The Story of the Irish Race* (New York, 1944), p. 607. For general histories of the Great Famine, see Cecil Woodham-Smith, *The Great Hunger* (New York, 1962); R. D. Edwards and T. D. Williams, eds., *The Great Famine: Studies in Irish History, 1845–1852* (New York, 1957).

14. For a typical Irish emigrant ballad, see the *Boston Pilot,* August 16, 1862.

15. Joseph P. O'Grady, *How the Irish Became Americans,* pp. 35–36.

16. For descriptions of the famine migration, see George Potter, *To the Golden Door: The Story of the Irish in Ireland and America* (Boston, 1960), pp. 113–60; Lawrence J. McCaffrey, *The Irish Diaspora in America,* pp. 59–70; Andrew M. Greeley, *That Most Distressful Nation,* pp. 33–42; Oliver MacDonagh, "The Irish Famine Migration to the United States," *Perspectives in American History,* 10 (1976), 357–446.

17. *Harper's Weekly,* October 21, 1871. Also see Dennis J. Clark, "The Irish Catholics: A Postponed Perspective," in Randall M. Miller and Thomas D. Marzik, eds., *Immigrants and Religion in Urban America* (Philadelphia, 1977), pp. 53–55.

18. See J. J. Slocum and G. Bourne, *The Awful Disclosures of Maria Monk* (New York, 1836), pp. 11–16, 167–83.

19. Ray Allen Billington, *The Protestant Crusade,* pp. 121–25. Also see Carlton Beals, *Brass-Knuckles Crusade: The Great Know-Nothing Conspiracy, 1820–1860* (New York, 1960) and Dale Knobel, "Paddy and the Republic: Popular Images of the American Irish, 1820–1860," Ph.D. dissertation, Northwestern University, 1976.

20. Gustave de Beaumont, *Ireland,* II, pp. 87–88.

21. For a discussion of that urban experience, see Dennis Clark, *The Irish in Philadelphia: Ten Generations of Urban Experience* (Philadelphia, 1974); Maldwyn Jones, *American Immigration,* p. 121; James S. Olson, *The Ethnic Dimension,* pp. 79–81; Robert Emmet Kennedy, *The Irish: Emigration, Marriage, and Fertility* (Berkeley, 1973), p. 82.

22. David Miller, "Irish Catholicism and the Great Famine," *Journal of Social History,* 9 (Fall, 1975), 81–98.

23. Jay P. Dolan, *The Immigrant Church,* pp. 11–27. Also see John R. G. Hassard, *Life of John Hughes, First Archbishop of New York* (New York, 1866).

24. Emmet Larkin, "The Devotional Revolution in Ireland, 1850–1875," *American Historical Review,* 72 (June, 1972), 625–52. For an analysis of religious understanding among one urban Irish community, see Sheridan Gilley, "The Roman Catholic Mission to the Irish in London," *Recusant History,* 10 (October, 1969), 123–45.

25. See Desmond Fennell, ed., *The Changing Face of Catholic Ireland* (London, 1968).

26. Emmet Larkin, "The Devotional Revolution," 627–28, 651–52.

27. Ibid., 625–52; David Miller, "Irish Catholicism," 81–98.

28. On the ascetic tradition, see John Hennig, "Old Ireland and Her Liturgy"; Jeremiah O'Sullivan, "Old Ireland and Her Monasticism," in Robert McNally, ed., *Old Ireland* (New York, 1965).

29. Sean O'Faolain, "The Priest," in *The Irish: A Character Study;* Ruth Clark, *Strangers and Sojourners at Port Royal. Being an Account of the Connections between the British Isles and the Jansenists of France and Holland* (Cambridge, 1932), pp. 204–19; Dale Van Kley, *The Jansenists and the Expulsion of the Jesuits from France, 1757–1765* (New Haven, 1975), pp. 6–36.

30. John C. Messenger, "Sex and Repression in an Irish Folk Community," in Donald S. Marshall and Robert C. Suggs, eds., *Human Sexual Behavior* (New York, 1970), pp. 14–19.

31. Emmet Larkin, "The Devotional Revolution," 649–52; Donald Akenson, *The Irish Education Experiment: The National System of Education in the Nineteenth Century* (London, 1970), pp. 346–72.

32. Emmet Larkin, "The Devotional Revolution," 644–45.

33. Jay P. Dolan, *The Immigrant Church,* pp. 45–47; Henry B. Leonard, "Ethnic Conflict and Episcopal Power: The Diocese of Cleveland, 1847–1870," *Catholic Historical Review,* 62 (July, 1976), 388–407; George F. Houck, *A History of Catholicity in Northern Ohio and in the Diocese of Cleveland from 1749 to December 31, 1900,* 2 vols. (Cleveland, 1903), I, pp. 427–30.

Chapter 3. The Triumph of Irish Catholicism

1. James Hennesey, *American Catholics,* pp. 91, 95, 99–100.

2. Emmet Larkin, "The Devotional Revolution," 351–52.

3. See Robert H. Lord et al., *History of the Archdiocese of Boston in the Various Stages of Its Development, 1604 to 1943,* 3 vols. (New York, 1944), III, pp. 98–99, 354, 406–08; Donna Merwick, *Boston Priests, 1848–1910. A Study of Social and Intellectual Change* (Cambridge, 1973), pp. 1–12. For a comment on the hospitable relations between Catholics and Protestants in early nineteenth-century Boston, see Joseph Paul Ryan,

"Travel Literature as Source Material for American Catholic History," *Illinois Catholic Historical Review,* 10 (January–April, 1928), 57–57; Thomas H. O'Connor, *Fitzpatrick's Boston 1846-1866: John Bernard Fitzpatrick, Third Bishop of Boston* (Boston, 1984), pp. 75–98, 232–39.

4. Emmet Larkin, "The Devotional Revolution," 651–52; Oliver MacDonagh, "The Irish Famine Migration," 360–91.

5. Quoted in Edward Wakin, *Enter the Irish-American* (New York, 1976), pp. 69–70.

6. Lawrence J. McCaffrey, *The Irish Diaspora in America,* pp. 85–91; Marjorie R. Fallows, *Irish Americans: Identity and Assimilation* (Englewood Cliffs, 1979), pp. 30–41.

7. For some specific trustee controversies, see Francis Joseph Magri, *The Catholic Church in the City and Diocese of Richmond* (Richmond, 1906), pp. 42–43; John H. Lamott, *History of the Archdiocese of Cincinnati, 1821–1921* (New York, 1921), pp. 322–23.

8. Quoted in John K. Sharp, *History of the Diocese of Brooklyn, 1853–1953. The Catholic Church on Long Island,* 2 vols. (New York, 1954), I, p. 18.

9. See Patrick Dignan, *A History of the Legal Incorporation of Church Property in the United States, 1784–1932* (Washington, D.C., 1933); Patrick Carey, "The Laity's Understanding of the Trustee System, 1785–1855," *Catholic Historical Review,* 64 (July, 1978), 357–76; James Hennesey, *American Catholics,* pp. 99–100.

10. See Timothy L. Smith, "Protestant Schooling and the American Nationality, 1800–1850," *Journal of American History,* 53 (March, 1967), 679–95; Stanley K. Schultz, *The Culture Factory: Boston Public Schools, 1789–1860* (New York, 1973).

11. Vincent P. Lannie, "Alienation in America: The Immigrant Catholic and Public Education in Pre-Civil War America," *The Review of Politics,* 32 (October, 1970), 503–21. Also see Donald H. Akenson, *The Irish Education Experiment: The National System of Education in the Nineteenth Century* (London, 1970).

12. "Pastoral Letter of 1843," in Peter Guilday, *The National Pastorals of the American Hierarchy* (Washington, D.C., 1923), p. 152.

13. See Jay P. Dolan, *The Immigrant Church,* pp. 100–102.

14. Michael Feldberg, *The Philadelphia Riots of 1844,* pp. 88–116.

15. James Hennesey, *American Catholics,* pp. 184–87.

16. Stephen Thernstrom, "Ethnic Groups in American History," in Lance Liebman, ed., *Ethnic Relations in America* (Englewood Cliffs, 1982), pp. 8–9.

17. James Hennesey, *American Catholics,* p. 187.

18. T. D. Sullivan, "The Irish-American," *Irish-American Almanac for 1875* (New York, 1874), p. 30.

19. See Thomas N. Brown, *Irish-American Nationalism*, pp. 1–23.

20. *The New York Herald*, January 26, 1866.

21. Thomas N. Brown, *Irish-American Nationalism*, pp. 38–42.

22. Ibid., pp. 43–51, 65–66.

23. Martin Ridge, *Ignatius Donnelly: Portrait of a Politician* (Chicago, 1962); James P. Rodechko, *Patrick Ford and His Search for America: A Case Study of Irish-American Journalism, 1870–1913* (New York, 1976); Francis G. McManamin, *The American Years of John Boyle O'Reilly, 1870–1890* (Washington, D.C., 1959); Sidney Fine, *Laissez-Faire and the General Welfare State: A Study of Conflict in American Thought, 1865–1901* (Ann Arbor, 1964), pp. 289–95.

24. Thomas N. Brown, *Irish-American Nationalism*, pp. 56–57.

25. Jay P. Dolan, *The Immigrant Church*, pp. 61–62; J. Brady, "Funeral Customs of the Past," *Irish Ecclesiastical Record*, 78 (November, 1942), 330–39; Constantia Maxwell, *Country and Town in Ireland under the Georges* (Dundalk, 1949), p. 348.

26. See Joan Bland, *Hibernian Crusade* (Washington, D.C., 1951); Jon M. Kingsdale, "The Poor Man's Club: Social Functions of the Urban-Working Class Saloon," *American Quarterly*, 25 (October, 1973), 473–81.

27. Emmet Larkin, "The Devotional Revolution," 650–52.

28. See Theodore Maynard, *The Catholic Church and the American Idea* (New York, 1953); Robert Cross, *The Emergence of Liberal Catholicism* (Cambridge, 1958); Christopher J. Kauffmann, *Faith and Fraternalism: The History of the Knights of Columbus, 1882–1982* (New York, 1982).

29. Frederick J. Zwierlein, *The Life and Letters of Bishop McQuaid*, 2 vols. (Rochester, 1927), II, pp. 119–53.

Chapter 4. The Great Debate: Language and Nationality in Roman Catholicism

1. Charles F. St. Laurent, *Language and Nationality in the Light of Revelation and History* (Montreal, 1896), p. 13.

2. Mason Wade, "The Culture of French Canada," in Julian Park, *The Culture of Contemporary Canada* (Ithaca, 1957), p. 368.

3. Mason Wade, *The French Canadians, 1760–1945* (Toronto, 1956), pp. 5, 25, 38–39.

4. Horace Miner, *St. Denis: A French-Canadian Parish* (Chicago, 1939), pp. 91–106, 111–41.

5. Mason Wade, "The French Parish and *Survivance* in Nineteenth Century New England," *Catholic Historical Review*, 36 (July, 1950), 163–89.

6. Anthony Coelho, "A Row of Nationalities: Life in a Working Class Community: The Irish, English, and French Canadians of Fall River, Massachusetts, 1850–1890," Ph.D. Dissertation, Brown University, 1980, p. 226.

7. Mason Wade, "The French Parish," 176.

8. Massachusetts Bureau of Labor Statistics, *Annual Report, 1880* (Boston, 1881), pp. 469–70.

9. Philip T. Silvia, Jr., "The 'Flint' Affair: French Canadian Struggle for Survivance," *Catholic Historical Review,* 65 (July, 1979), 414–35.

10. Wolfgang Kollmann and Peter Marschalk, "German Emigration to the United States," *Perspectives in American History,* 7 (1973), 499–554.

11. Ibid., 499–540; Jay P. Dolan, *The Immigrant Church*, pp. 68–69.

12. Colman J. Barry, *The Catholic Church and German Americans* (Milwaukee, 1953), pp. 293–94.

13. Ibid., pp. 3–5.

14. Quoted in La Vern J. Rippley, *The German Americans* (New York, 1976), p. 111.

15. Colman Barry, *The Catholic Church and German Americans,* pp. 293–294.

16. Ibid., p. 294.

17. Jay P. Dolan, *The Immigrant Church,* pp. 68–86.

18. See Frederick C. Luebke, "German Immigrants and Churches in Nebraska, 1889–1915," *Mid-America,* 50 (April, 1968), 116–30; Emmet H. Rothan, *The German Catholic Immigrant in the United States, 1830–1860* (Washington, D.C., 1946); Colman Barry, *The Catholic Church and German Americans,* pp. 44–85.

19. Quoted in Colman Barry, *The Catholic Church and German Americans,* p. 118.

20. James Cardinal Gibbons, *A Retrospect of Fifty Years,* 2 vols. (New York, 1916), II, pp. 148–55.

21. Richard M. Linkh, *American Catholicism,* pp. 2–15.

22. Colman Barry, *The Catholic Church and German Americans,* pp. 62–85.

23. Ibid., p. 67.

24. Ibid., pp. 296–312.

25. Ibid., pp. 131–37; John Meng, "Cahenslyism: The First Stage, 1883–1891," *Catholic Historical Review,* 31 (January, 1946), 389–413.

26. Colman Barry, *The Catholic Church and German Americans,* pp. 140–82; John Meng, "Cahenslyism: The Second Chapter, 1891–1910," *Catholic Historical Review,* 32 (January, 1947), 302–40.

27. Colman Barry, *The Catholic Church and German Americans,* pp. 185–87; Daniel W. Kucera, "A Historical Pronouncement: Wisconsin Bishops Protest the Bennett Law," *Social Justice Review,* 31 (December, 1940-January, 1941), 282–84, 318–20.

28. Thomas T. McAvoy, *The Great Crisis in American Catholic History, 1895–1900* (Chicago, 1957); *The Americanist Heresy in Roman Catholicism, 1895–1900* (Notre Dame, 1963).

Chapter 5. The East-European Catholics

1. For an early but still useful look at Slavic peasant customs, see Emily Balch, *Our Slavic Fellow Citizens* (New York, 1910).
2. Caroline Golab, *Immigrant Destinations,* pp. 67–100.
3. W. I. Thomas and Florian Znaniecki, *The Polish Peasant in Europe and America,* p. 162. Also see pp. 156–205.
4. See Caroline Golab, *Immigrant Destinations,* pp. 43–66; Johann Chmelar, "The Austrian Emigration, 1900–1914," pp. 275–380.
5. W. I. Thomas and Florian Znaniecki, *The Polish Peasant,* pp. 87–106.
6. Thomas Merton, *Seasons of Celebration* (New York, 1965), pp. 45–53.
7. See Josef J. Barton, "Religion and Cultural Change in Czech Immigrant Communities, 1850–1920," in Randall M. Miller and Thomas D. Marzik, *Immigrants and Religion in Urban America* (Philadelphia, 1977), pp. 8–10.
8. Ibid., pp. 9–16. Also see Karel D. Bicha, "The Survival of the Village in Urban America: A Note on the Czech Immigrants in Chicago to 1914," *International Migration Review,* 5 (Spring, 1971).
9. Norman Davies, *God's Playground. A History of Poland,* 2 vols. (New York, 1982); Oscar Halecki, *A History of Poland* (New York, 1961); Norman J. Pounds, *Poland between East and West* (Princeton, 1964); Martin Brakas, *Lithuania Minor: A Collection of Studies on Her History and Ethnography* (New York, 1976); Alfred E. Senn, *The Emergence of Modern Lithuania* (New York, 1959).
10. Robert A. Kann, *A History of the Hapsburg Empire, 1526–1918* (Berkeley, 1974); Carlile Macartney, *Hungary* (London, 1934); Robert Seton-Watson, *Racial Problems in Hungary* (New York, 1972); Andrew Janos, *The Politics of Backwardness in Hungary, 1825–1945* (Princeton, 1982).
11. Robert Seton-Watson, *A History of the Czechs and Slovaks* (Hamden, 1965); Samuel H. Thomson, *Czechoslovakia in European History* (Princeton, 1953); Peter Brock, *The Slovak National Awakening: An Essay in the Intellectual History of East Central Europe* (Toronto, 1976); Jozef Lettrich, *History of Modern Slovakia* (New York, 1955); A. H. Hermann, *A History of the Czechs* (London, 1975); Joseph M. Kirschbaum, *Slovakia in the 19th and 20th Century* (Toronto, 1973).

12. Carole Rogel, *The Slovenes and Yugoslavism, 1890–1914* (New York, 1977).

13. Francis H. Eterovich and Christopher Spalatin, eds., *Croatia: Land, People, Culture,* 2 vols. (Toronto, 1964); Ante Kadic, *From Croatian Renaissance to Yugoslav Socialism* (The Hague, 1969).

14. John A. Armstrong, *Ukrainian Nationalism* (New York, 1963).

15. For a general discussion of peasant religion as it related to the Poles, see William I. Thomas and Florian Znaniecki, *The Polish Peasant,* pp. 205–87.

16. Ibid., pp. 275–88.

17. R. F. Leslie, *Reform and Insurrection in Russian Poland,1856–1865* (Westport, 1969), pp. 232–51; V. Stanley Vardys, *The Catholic Church, Dissent, and Nationality in Soviet Lithuania* (New York, 1978), pp. 1–18.

18. V. Stanley Vardys, *The Catholic Church,* pp. 1–18.

19. Joseph Cada, *Czech-American Catholics, 1850–1920* (Chicago, 1964), pp. 1–5.

20. A. H. Hermann, *A History of the Czechs,* pp. 26–27, 36–46, 82–102, and Ludvik Nemec, *Church and State in Czechoslovakia* (New York, 1955), pp. 96–145.

21. Karel D. Bicha, "Settling Accounts with an Old Adversary: The Decatholicization of Czech Immigrants in America," *Social History-Histoire Sociale*, No. 8 (November, 1972), 45–50. Also see Emily Balch, *Our Slavic Fellow Citizens,* pp. 390–91.

22. J. F. N. Bradley, *Czechoslovakia* (Edinburgh, 1971), pp. 119–39; David P. Daniel, "The Protestant Reformation and Slovak Ethnic Consciousness," *Slovakia*, 28 (1978–1979), 49–65; Joseph A. Mikus, *Slovakia and the Slovaks* (Washington, D.C., 1977), pp. 148–52.

23. Karoly Viski, *Hungarian Peasant Customs* (Budapest, 1932).

24. C. A. Macartney, *Hungary: A Short History* (Chicago, 1962), pp. 76–87; Peter Hidas, *The Metamorphosis of a Social Class in Hungary during the Reign of Young Franz Joseph* (New York, 1977), pp. 21–29, 40–56.

25. Quoted in Irene Winner, *A Slovenian Village* (Providence, 1971), p. 196.

26. Carole Rogel, *The Slovenes,* pp. 75–89.

27. Francis H. Eterovich and Christopher Spalatin, *Croatia,* I, pp. 193–225. Also see Stella Alexander, *Church and State in Yugoslavia since 1945* (London, 1979), pp. 1–7.

28. Donald Attwater, *The Catholic Eastern Churches* (Milwaukee, 1937), pp. 76–92.

Chapter 6. The Mediterranean Catholics

1. Caroline Golab, *Immigrant Destinations*, pp. 57–59; Virginia Yans-McLaughlin, *Family and Community: Italian Immigrants in Buffalo, 1880–1930* (Urbana, 1982), pp. 25–54; Josef J. Barton, *Peasants and Strangers: Italians, Rumanians, and Slovaks in an American City, 1890–1950* (Cambridge, 1975), pp. 27–47.

2. See Andrew Rolle, *The Italian Americans: Troubled Roots* (New York, 1980); Erik Amfifheatrof, *The Children of Columbus: An Informal History of the Italians in the New World* (Boston, 1973); Humbert Nelli, *From Immigrants to Ethnics: The Italian Americans* (New York, 1983).

3. Richard Gambino, *Blood of My Blood: The Dilemma of the Italian Americans* (Garden City, 1974), pp. 39–50.

4. Denis Mack Smith, *Italy: A Modern History* (Ann Arbor, 1959), pp. 230–42.

5. For a history of Sicily, see Denis Mack Smith, *A History of Sicily: Modern Sicily after 1713* (New York, 1968).

6. Richard Gambino, *Blood of My Blood*, pp. 1–38; Constance Cronin, *The Sting of Change: Sicilians in Sicily and Australia* (Chicago, 1970), pp. 43–66, 85–89; Rudolph J. Vecoli, "Contadini in Chicago: A Critique of the Uprooted," *Journal of American History*, 51 (December, 1964), 404–17.

7. Rudolph J. Vecoli, "Cult and Occult in Italian-American Culture: The Persistence of a Religious Heritage," in Randall M. Miller and Thomas D. Marzik, *Immigrants and Religion*, pp. 26–27.

8. Rudolph J. Vecoli, "Prelates and Peasants: Italian Immigrants and the Catholic Church," *Journal of Social History*, 2 (Spring; 1969), p. 229.

9. For southern Italian folk religion, see Charlotte Gower Chapman, *Milocca, a Sicilian Village* (Cambridge, 1971); Ann Cornelisen, *Torregreca: Life, Death, Miracles* (New York, 1970). Also see Leonard W. Moss and Stephen C. Cappannari, "Folklore and Medicine in an Italian Village," *Journal of American Folklore*, 73 (April, 1960), 85–102.

10. Rudolph J. Vecoli, "Cult and Occult," pp. 27–28.

11. Charlotte Gower Chapman, *Milocca*, pp. 158–80; Rudolph J. Vecoli, "Prelates and Peasants," pp. 231–35.

12. Jean Becarud, "Spain," in M. A. Fitzsimons, *The Catholic Church Today: Western Europe* (Notre Dame, 1969), pp. 183–86; C. R. Boxer, *The Church Militant and Iberian Expansion, 1440–1770* (Baltimore, 1978), pp. 1–93.

13. William A. Christian, Jr., *Person and God in a Spanish Valley* (New York, 1972), pp. 118–29.

14. Ibid., pp. 44–99, 191–95.

15. See Daniel A. Gómez-Ibañez, *The Western Pyrenees: Differential Evolution of the French and Spanish Borderland* (Oxford, 1975).

16. William Douglass and Jon Bilbao, *Amerikanuak: Basques in the New World* (Reno, 1975), pp. 330–36.

17. Quoted in William Perkins, *Three Years in California. William Perkins' Journal of Life at Sonora (1849–1852)* (Berkeley, 1964), pp. 300–301.

18. William Douglass and Jon Bilbao, *Amerikanuak*, pp. 329–42, 364–67.

19. Sandra Ott, *The Circle of Mountains: A Basque Shepherding Community* (Oxford, 1981), pp. 82–102; William Douglass and Jon Bilbao, *Amerikanuak*, pp. 356–57.

20. Sandra Ott, *The Circle of Mountains*, pp. 89–96; William Douglass and Jon Bilbao, *Amerikanuak*, pp. 357–58. Also see William Douglass, *Death in Murelaga* (Seattle, 1969).

21. Antonio da Silva Rego, "Portugal," in M.A. Fitzsimons, ed., *The Catholic Church Today*, pp. 157–66; Leo Pap, *The Portuguese Americans* (New York, 1981), pp. 120–23.

22. Rodney Gallop, *Portugal: A Book of Folk-Ways* (London, 1936), pp. 126–58; M. F. Smithers, *Things Seen in Portugal* (London, 1931), pp. 144–48; Lyman H. Weeks, *Among the Azores* (Boston, 1882), p. 204.

23. Francis M. Rogers, *Americans of Portuguese Descent: A Lesson in Differentiation* (Beverly Hills, 1974), pp. 19–31.

24. M. F. Smithers, *Things Seen in Portugal*, pp. 144, 145, 147.

25. Quoted in Leo Pap, *The Portuguese Americans*, p. 143.

26. On the spirit of *bairrismo*, see Alvin R. Graves, "Immigrants in Agriculture: The Portuguese Californians, 1850–1970," Ph.D. dissertation, University of California at Los Angeles, 1977, p. 32.

27. Joyce C. Riegelhaupt, "Festas and Padres: The Organization of Religious Action in a Portuguese Parish," *American Anthropologist*, 75 (1973), 835–52.

28. Adrian Fortescue, *The Uniate Eastern Churches. The Byzantine Rite in Italy, Sicily, Syria, and Egypt* (New York, 1923) and N. Liesel, *The Eastern Catholic Liturgies* (Westminister, 1960).

29. Philip M. Kayal and Joseph M. Kayal, *The Syrian-Lebanese in America: A Study in Religion and Assimilation* (Boston, 1975), pp. 31–34.

30. Ibid., pp. 34–36.

Chapter 7. The Nationality Church

1. Francis C. Kelley, "The Church and the Immigrant," *Catholic Mind*, 13 (September 8, 1915), 471–84.

2. Sylvia June Alexander, "The Immigrant Church and Community: The Formation of Pittsburgh's Slovak Religious Institutions, 1880-1914," Ph.D. dissertation, University of Minnesota, 1980, pp. 281–97; *St. Nicholas Church in Second Street* (New York, 1933), p. 104; M. Martina Abbot, *A City Parish Grows and Changes* (Washington, D.C., 1953), pp. 66–80.

3. Jay P. Dolan, *The Immigrant Church,* pp. 87–98.

4. John L. Thomas, "Nationalities and American Catholics," in Louis J. Putz, *The Catholic Church U.S.A.* (Chicago, 1956), pp. 155–76; Emmet Larkin, "The Devotional Revolution in Ireland," pp. 649–52; Edmund M. Dunne, "The Church and the Immigrant," in C. E. McGuire, ed., *Catholic Builders of the Nation,* 5 vols. (Boston, 1923), II, p. 4; Charles Shanabruch, *Chicago's Catholics: The Evolution of an American Identity* (Notre Dame, 1981), pp. 78–80.

5. Quoted in Marie Conistre, "Education in a Local Area: A Study of a Decade in the Life and Education of the Adult Italian Immigrant in East Harlem, New York," Ph.D. dissertation, New York University, 1973, p. 273.

6. Silvano Tomasi, *Piety and Power: The Role of Italian Parishes in the New York Metropolitan Area* (New York, 1975), pp. 76–81; Edward J. Dworaczyk, *The First Polish Colonies of America in Texas* (San Antonio, 1936), pp. 157–62.

7. Mark Stolarik, "Lay Initiative in American-Slovak Parishes: 1880–1930," *Records of the American Catholic Historical Society,* 83 (September–December, 1972), 151–58; Sylvia June Alexander, "The Immigrant Church," pp. 350–51; Sister T. Lewandowska, "The Polish Immigrant in Philadelphia to 1914," *Records of the American Catholic Historical Society,* 65 (June, 1945), 67–101, 313–41; Richard M. Linkh, *American Catholics and European Immigrants,* pp. 103–08.

8. *The Official Catholic Directory, 1900* (New York, 1900), pp. 305–10.

9. Charles Shanabruch, *Chicago's Catholics,* pp. 233–38; Thomas Capek, *The Czechs (Bohemians) in America* (Boston, 1920), pp. 246–47.

10. The tables for Cleveland, Hartford, and Boston were taken from current parish listings in *The Official Catholic Directory, 1982* (New York, 1982) and Doris A. Liptak, "European Immigrants and the Catholic Church in Connecticut, 1870–1920," Ph.D. dissertation, University of Connecticut, 1979, pp. 424–28.

11. Josef J. Barton, "Religion and Cultural Change in Czech Immigrant Communities," pp. 3–12.

12. Ibid., pp. 3–12; Virginia Yans McLaughlin, *Family and Community,* pp. 110–11, 130–31; Sylvia June Alexander, "The Immigrant Church," pp. 209–12; Frank Renkiewicz, "An Economy of Self-Help: Fraternal Capitalism and the Evolution of Polish America," in Charles A. Ward, Philip Shashko, and Donald E. Pienkos, *Studies in Ethnicity: The East European Experience*

(New York, 1980), pp. 71–88; The First Catholic Slovak Union, *Slovak Catholic Churches and Institutions in the United States and Canada* (Cleveland, 1955); and Emil Lengyel, *Americans from Hungary* (Philadelphia, 1948), pp. 157–93.

13. Quoted in Victor Greene, *For God and Country: The Rise of Polish and Lithuanian Ethnic Consciousness in America* (Madison, 1975), p. 56.

14. See Paul Wrobel, *Our Way. Family, Parish, and Neighborhood in a Polish-American Community* (Notre Dame, 1979).

15. Ibid., p. 122.

16. Quoted in Silvano Tomasi, *Piety and Power,* p. 97.

17. Ibid., p. 77.

18. Ibid., p. 77.

19. Ibid., p. 99.

20. Ibid., p. 123.

21. Richard Gambino, *Blood of My Blood. The Dilemma of the Italian-Americans* (New York, 1975), pp. 213–44.

22. See *The Official Catholic Directory* for 1860, 1880, 1900, 1921, 1940, 1960, and 1982.

23. Betty Boyd Caroli, *Italian Repatriation From the United States, 1900–1914* (New York, 1974); Leo Pap, *The Portuguese Americans,* pp. 35–47; Philip M. Kayal and Joseph M. Kayal, *The Syrian-Lebanese in America,* pp. 60–71; LaVerne Rippley, *The German Americans* (New York, 1976), pp. 217–21; Colman Barry, *The Catholic Church and German Americans,* p. 3; Antanas Kucas, *Lithuanians in America,* pp. 57–61; Helen Z. Lopata, *Polish Americans,* p. 38; Johann Chmelar, "The Austrian Emigration," p. 316; Howard Stein, *An Ethno-Historic Study of Slovak-American Identity,* pp. 100–102; Karel D. Bicha, *The Czechs in Oklahoma,* p. 10; Emil Lengyel, *Americans From Hungary,* p. 183; Yaroslav J. Chyz, *The Ukrainian Immigrants in the United States,* pp. 68–69; Wasyl Halich, *Ukrainians in the United States,* pp. 12–25; John P. Fulton, "Demographic Profile of Ukrainian Americans," 379–82; and Walter C. Warzeski, "The Rusin Community in Pennsylvania," pp. 175–76; Gerald G. Govorchin, *Americans From Yugoslavia,* (Gainesville, 1961), pp. 62–64.

24. George Prpic, *The Croatian Immigrants in America* (New York, 1971), p. 192.

25. Karel D. Bicha, "Settling Accounts with an Old Adversary," pp. 45–60.

Chapter 8. Conflict and Consolidation in the Immigrant Church

1. Sidney M. Greenfield, "In Search of Social Identity: Strategies of Ethnic Identity Management amongst Capeverdeans in Southeastern Massa-

chusetts," *Luso-Brazilian Review,* 13 (Summer, 1976), 3–17.

2. Bohdan P. Procko, *Ukrainian Catholics in America* (Washington, D.C., 1982), pp. 19–52.

3. William Douglass and Jon Bilbao, *Amerikanuak*, pp. 335–36.

4. Edward Steiner, *On the Trail of the Immigrant* (New York, 1906), p. 227.

5. Bruce M. Garver, "Czech-American Freethinkers on the Great Plains, 1871–1914," in Frederick C. Luebke, ed., *Ethnicity on the Great Plains* (Lincoln, 1980), pp. 147–69.

6. Mark Stolarik, "Immigration and Urbanization: The Slovak Experience, 1870–1918," Ph.D. dissertation, University of Minnesota, 1974, p. 88.

7. Thomas W. Brown, *Irish-American Nationalism,* pp. 56–57.

8. Vela Vassady, Jr., "The 'Homeland Cause' as Stimulant to Ethnic Unity: The Hungarian-American Response to Karolyi's 1914 American Tour," *Journal of American Ethnic History*, 2 (Fall, 1982), 39–64.

9. Rudolph J. Vecoli, "Prelates and Peasants," 231–34.

10. Quoted in Silvano Tomasi, *Piety and Power,* p. 125.

11. Joseph Cada, *Czech-American Catholics,* pp. 27–29.

12. Silvano Tomasi, *Piety and Power,* pp. 141–43.

13. Mark Stolarik, "Immigration and Urbanization," pp. 75–93.

14. See Silvano Tomasi, *Piety and Power,* pp. 149–50; George Prpic, *The Croatian Immigrants in America,* p. 185; Mark Stolarik, "Immigration and Urbanization," pp. 78–88; Ludvic Nemec, "The Czechoslovak Heresy and Schism: The Emergence of a National Czechoslovak Church," *Transactions of the American Philosophical Society,* 65 Part I (1975), 3–78.

15. Victor Greene, *For God and Country: The Rise of Polish and Lithuanian Ethnic Consciousness in America* (Madison, 1975), pp. 66–84; Mark Stolarik, "Immigration and Urbanization," pp. 71–79.

16. Adele K. Donchenko, "Slovene Missionaries in the Upper Midwest," in Keith P. Dyrud, Michael Novak, and Rudolph J. Vecoli, *The Other Catholics* (New York, 1978), p. 11; Bohdan Procko, *Ukrainian Catholics,* pp. 18, 53; Charles Shanabruch, *Chicago's Catholics,* pp. 123–24; *The Official Catholic Directory, 1977* (New York, 1977), pp. 489, 782; Colman Barry, *The Catholic Church and German Americans,* p. 253. Also see Anthony J. Kuzniewski, *Faith and Fatherland: The Polish Church War in Wisconsin, 1896–1918* (Notre Dame, 1981).

17. Charles Shanabruch, *Chicago's Catholics,* p. 96; Joseph P. Gallagher, *A Century of History: The Diocese of Scranton, 1868–1968* (Scranton, 1968), p. 223.

18. Victor Greene, *For God and Country,* pp. 100–121; Theodore L. Zawistowski, "The Polish National Catholic Church: An Acceptable Alternative," in Frank Mocha, ed., *Poles in America* (Stevens Point, 1978), pp. 423–34; Silvano Tomasi, *Piety and Power,* pp. 149–52; Warren C. Platt, "The Polish National Catholic Church: An Inquiry into Its Origins," *Church His-*

tory, 46 (December, 1977), 474–89. Also see Gregory Swiderski, "Polish-American Polish National Catholic Bishops," *Polish American Studies*, 24 (January–June, 1967), 27–41; Lawrence Orzell, "A Minority within a Minority: The Polish National Catholic Church, 1896–1907," *Polish American Studies*, 36 (Spring, 1979), 5–32.

19. Silvano Tomasi, *Piety and Power*, pp. 141–51; Rudolph J. Vecoli, "Cult and Occult," pp. 32–33.

20. Quoted in Rudolph J. Vecoli, "Prelates and Peasants," p. 234. Also see Henry J. Browne, "The 'Italian Problem' in the Catholic Church in the United States, 1886–1900," *Historical Records and Studies,* 35 (1946), 46–62.

21. *The Intermountain Catholic,* October 12, 1899.

22. Ibid., May 19, 1900.

23. Quoted in Rudolph J. Vecoli, "Prelates and Peasants," pp. 260–68.

24. Stephen C. Gulovich, "Byzantine Slavonic Catholics and the Latin Clergy," *Homiletic and Pastoral Review,* 45 (1945), 517–27, 586–96, 678–80.

25. Keith S. Russin, "Father Alexis G. Toth and the Wilkes-Barre Litigations," *St. Vladimir's Theological Quarterly,* 16 (1972), 128–49.

26. Keith P. Dyrud, "The Establishment of the Greek Catholic Rite in America as a Competitor to Orthodoxy," in Keith P. Dyrud et al. *The Other Catholics,* pp. 190–225; Stephen C. Gulovich, "The Ruthenian Tragedy," *Homiletic and Pastoral Review,* 46 (1946), 574–84; "The Rusin Exarchate in the United States," *Eastern Churches Quarterly,* 6 (1946), 459–86; Walter C. Warzeski, *Byzantine Rite Rusins in Carpatho-Ruthenia and America* (Pittsburgh, 1971), pp. 114–26.

27. Lawrence D. Orton, *Polish Detroit and the Kolasinski Affair* (Detroit, 1981), pp. 161–95.

28. Quoted in Joseph John Parot, *Polish Catholics in Chicago, 1850–1920: A Religious History* (DeKalb, 1981), p. 211.

29. William Wolkovich-Valkavicius, "Lithuanian Immigrants and Their Irish Bishops in the Catholic Church of Connecticut, 1893–1915," in Keith P. Dyrud et al., *The Other Catholics,* pp. 1–55.

30. Edward R. Kantowicz, "Cardinal Mundelein of Chicago and the Shaping of Twentieth Century American Catholicism," *Journal of American History,* 68 (June, 1981), 52–68; James Gaffey, "The Changing of the Guard: The Rise of Cardinal O'Connell of Boston," *Catholic Historical Review,* 59 (July, 1973), 225–44.

Chapter 9. The Hispanic Catholics

1. James S. Olson, *The Ethnic Dimension,* pp. 377–78.

2. Ellwyn Stoddard, *Mexican Americans* (New York, 1973), pp. 73–

74, 85–88, 178–80. Also see Robert Ricard, *The Spiritual Conquest of Mexico* (Berkeley, 1966).

3. Richard Rodriguez, *Hunger of Memory* (Boston, 1982), p. 77.

4. Ibid., p. 81. Also see Joseph P. Fitzpatrick, *Puerto Rican Americans: The Meaning of Migration to the Mainland* (Englewood Cliffs, 1971), pp. 115–16; J. Lloyd Mecham, *Church and State in Latin America* (Chapel Hill, 1966), pp. 3–37.

5. Joseph P. Fitzpatrick, *Puerto Rican Americans,* pp. 117–18. Also see Isidro Lucas, *The Browning of America: The Hispanic Revolution in the American Church* (Chicago, 1981), pp. 55–57.

6. William Madsen, *Mexican-Americans of South Texas* (New York, 1964), pp. 15–17.

7. James Diego Vigil, *From Indians to Chicanos. A Sociocultural History* (St. Louis, 1980), pp. 69–86. Also see Robert Ricard, *The Spiritual Conquest of Mexico,* p. 276; Charles Bigson, *Aztecs under Spanish Rule* (Stanford, 1964), p. 404.

8. M. G. Navarro, "Mestizaje in Mexico during the National Period," in M. Morner, ed., *Race and Class in Latin America* (New York, 1970), pp. 145–55; Frederick A. Ober, *Travels in Mexico and Life among the Mexicans* (Boston, 1883), pp. 291–304.

9. Quoted in William Madsen, *Mexican-Americans of South Texas*, p. 58. Also see Robert A. Wilson, *Mexico: Its Peasants and Its Priests* (New York, 1856), pp. 192–95.

10. Isidro Lucas, *The Browning of America,* pp. 55–59; Arnoldo DeLeon, *The Tejano Community 1836–1900* (Albuquerque, 1982), pp. 138–41.

11. This discussion is taken largely from Arnoldo DeLeon, *The Tejano Community,* pp. 137–54.

12. Quoted in William Madsen, *Mexican-Americans of South Texas,* pp. 83–84.

13. See H. C. Arbuckle III, "Don José and Don Pedrito," in Francis Edward Abernathy, ed., *The Folklore of Texan Cultures* (Austin, 1974); Ari Kiev, *Curanderismo: Mexican American Folk Psychiatry* (New York, 1968); Ruth Dodson, "Don Pedrito Jaramillo: The Curandero of Los Olmos," in William M. Hudson, *The Healer of Los Olmos and Other Mexican Lore* (Dallas, 1951).

14. Eric Williams, *From Columbus to Castro: The History of the Caribbean, 1492–1969* (London, 1970); Frank Knight, *Slave Society in Cuba during the Nineteenth Century* (Madison, 1970), pp. 106–12; Fred Ward, *Inside Cuba Today* (New York, 1978), pp. 51–54.

15. Wyatt MacGaffey and Clifford R. Barnett, *Cuba: Its People, Its Society, Its Culture* (New Haven, 1962), pp. 197–204.

16. George Simpson Easton, *Religious Cults of the Caribbean* (San Juan, 1960), pp. 11–111, 157–200; Wyatt MacGaffey and Clifford R. Barnett, *Cuba,* pp. 205–10.

17. William R. Bascom, "The Focus of Cuban Santería," in Michael M. Horowitz, *Peoples and Cultures of the Caribbean* (Garden City, 1971), pp. 522–28.

18. Carole Devillers, "Haiti's Voodoo Pilgrimages," *National Geographic*, 167, (March, 1985), 395–408.

19. Keith Lightfoot, *The Philippines* (New York, 1973), pp. 55–81.

20. Ibid., pp. 25–54.

21. John Leddy Phelan, *The Hispanization of the Philippines: Spanish Aims and Filipino Responses, 1565–1700* (Madison, 1967), pp. 72–93; David Joel Steinberg, *The Philippines: A Singular and a Plural Place* (Boulder, 1982), pp. 67–74.

22. Pedro S. de Achutegni and Miguel A. Bernad, *Religious Revolution in the Philippines: The Life and Church of Gregorio Aglipay*, 2 vols. (Quezon City, 1960); Frank H. Wise, *The History of the Philippine Independent Church* (Dumaguete, 1965); Daniel F. Doeppers, "Changing Patterns of Aglipayan Adherence in the Philippines, 1918–1970," *Philippine Studies*, 25 (1977), 265–77.

23. David Joel Steinberg, *The Philippines*, pp. 70–73.

24. Joseph F. Fitzpatrick, *Puerto Rican Americans*, pp. 118–20.

25. Ibid., p. 120; Clifford A. Hauberg, *Puerto Rico and the Puerto Ricans* (New York, 1974), p. 143; Jerry Fenton, *Understanding the Religious Background of the Puerto Rican* (Cuernavaca, 1969).

26. Joseph Fitzpatrick, *Puerto Rican Americans*, pp. 120–21; Dorothy Dohen, *Two Studies of Puerto Rico* (Cuernavaca, 1966), pp. 61–87.

27. Kal Wagenheim, "Puerto Rico: A Profile," in Francesco Cordasco and Eugene Bucchioni, *The Puerto Rican Experience* (Totowa, 1973), pp. 95–102.

28. *The Official Catholic Directory, 1940* (New York, 1940), pp. 322–24; *The Official Catholic Directory, 1985* (New York, 1985), pp. 503–09; Nathan Glazer and Daniel Patrick Moynihan, *Beyond the Melting Pot: The Negroes, Puerto Ricans, Jews, Italians and Irish of New York City* (Cambridge, 1963), p. 104.

29. Joseph P. Fitzpatrick, "The Role of the Parish in the Spiritual Care of Puerto Ricans in the New York Archdiocese," *Studi Emigrazione*, 7 (October, 1966), 1–27.

30. Robert E. Quirk, "Religion and Mexican Social Revolution," in W. V. D'Antonio and F. B. Pike, eds., *Religion, Revolution, and Reform: New Forces for Change in Latin America* (New York, 1964), p. 62.

31. See Josef J. Barton, "Land, Labor, and Community in Nueces: Czech Farmers and Mexican Laborers in South Texas, 1880–1930," in Frederick Luebke, *Ethnicity on the Great Plains* (Lincoln, 1980), p. 200.

32. *The Official Catholic Directory, 1930* (New York, 1930), pp. 28, 305.

33. *The Official Catholic Directory, 1940,* p. 100; *The Official Catholic Directory, 1960* (New York, 1960), p. 127.

34. Patrick H. McNamara, "Dynamics of the Catholic Church: From Pastoral to Social Concern," in Leo Grebler, Joan W. Moore, and Ralph Guzman, *The Mexican-American People* (New York, 1970), pp. 449–78.

35. Isidro Lucas, *The Browning of America,* p. 39; Albert Carrillo, "The Sociological Failure of the Catholic Church toward the Chicano," *Journal of Mexican American Studies,* I (Winter, 1971), 75–83.

36. *Los Angeles Times,* August 15, 1985.

Chapter 10. Modernization and the Catholic Immigrants

1. Israel Zangwell, *The Melting Pot* (New York, 1909), pp. 198–99.

2. See James S. Olson, *The Ethnic Dimension,* pp. xvii–xxi.

3. See Nathan Glazer and Daniel Patrick Moynihan, *Beyond the Melting Pot;* Michael Novak, *The Rise of the Unmeltable Ethnic* (New York, 1971); Perry Weed, *The White Ethnic Movement and Ethnic Politics* (New York, 1973); Francis M. Wilhoit, *The Politics of Massive Resistance* (New York, 1973).

4. See Lawrence Levine, *Black Culture and Black Consciousness: Afro American Folk Thought from Slavery to Freedom* (New York, 1977); LaVerne Rippley, *The German Americans* (New York, 1976); Charles Anderson, *White Protestant Americans: From National Origins to Religious Groups* (Englewood Cliffs, 1970).

5. See Milton M. Gordon, *Assimilation in American Life: The Role of Race, Religion, and National Origins* (New York, 1964). Also see Andrew M. Greeley, *Why Can't They Be Like Us? America's White Ethnic Groups* (New York, 1975), pp. 53–59.

6. Richard Rodríguez, *Hunger of Memory,* pp. 52–53.

7. For the classic view, see Will Herberg, *Protestant—Catholic—Jew: An Essay in American Religious Sociology* (New York, 1955).

8. For a discussion of peasant values, see William I. Thomas and Florian Znaniecki, *The Polish Peasant,* pp. 87–287; Jack M. Potter, May M. Diaz, and George M. Foster, eds., *Peasant Society* (Boston, 1967); Ladislas Reymont, *The Peasants: Fall, Winter, Spring, Summer.* 4 vols. (New York, 1925).

9. See Daniel S. Buczek, "The Polish American Parish as an Americanizing Factor," in Charles A. Ward, Philip Shashko, and Donald E. Pienkos, eds., *Studies in Ethnicity: The East European Experience in America* (Boulder, 1980), pp. 157–59.

10. Vladimir C. Nahirny and Joshua A. Fishman, "Ukrainian Language Maintenance Efforts in the United States," in Joshua A. Fishman, *Language Loyalty in the United States* (The Hague, 1966), pp. 330–40.

11. See James S. Olson, *The Ethnic Dimension,* pp. 104–05; Jay P. Dolan, *The Immigrant Church,* pp. 73–74.

12. Josef J. Barton, "Religion and Cultural Change in Czech Immigrant Communities," pp. 6–15; "Eastern and Southern Europeans," in John Higham, ed., *Ethnic Leadership in America* (Baltimore, 1978), pp. 150–75.

13. Josef J. Barton, "Land, Labor, and Community in Nueces: Czech Farmers and Mexican Laborers in South Texas, 1880–1930," in Frederick Luebke, *Ethnicity on the Great Plains* (Lincoln, 1980), pp. 190–209.

14. Thomas Capek, *The Czechs (Bohemians) in the United States,* pp. 254–64; Josef J. Barton, "Religion and Cultural Change in Czech Immigrant Communities," pp. 16–17; *The Official Catholic Directory, 1887* (New York, 1887), pp. 68–69; Joseph John Parot, *Polish Catholics,* pp. 52–55; Daniel F. Tanzone, "Slovak Fraternal Organizations," *Slovakia,* 25 (1975), 68–71; Bohdan Procko, *Ukrainian Catholics,* p. 10.

15. George Prpic, *The Croatian Immigrants in America,* pp. 262–69.

16. Stanislaw Osada, *History of the Polish National Alliance* (Chicago, 1905), pp. 102–3.

17. Carl Wittke, *Refugees of Revolution: The German Forty-Eighters in America* (Philadelphia, 1952), pp. 92–110; Jerzy Jan Lerski, *A Polish Chapter,* pp. 98–125; Emil Lengyel, *Americans from Hungary,* pp. 37–64.

18. George Prpic, *The Croatian Immigrants in America,* pp. 180–81; Bohdan Procko, *Ukrainian Catholics,* pp. 45–49; Joseph John Parot, *Polish Catholics,* pp. 32–36; and Daniel F. Tanzone, "Slovak Fraternal Organizations," pp. 68–69.

19. See Joseph P. O'Grady, *The Immigrants' Influence on Wilson's Peace Policies* (Lexington, 1967).

20. Jan Slomka, *From Serfdom to Self-Government: Memoirs of a Polish Village Mayor 1842–1927* (London, 1941), p. 171.

21. Joshua Fishman, *Language and Nationalism* (Rowley, 1972), pp. 41–44; Thomas I. Monzell, "The Catholic Church and the Americanization of the Polish Immigrant," *Polish American Studies,* 26 (January–June, 1969), 11; Eugene Obidinski, "The Polish American Press: Survival through Adaptation," *Polish American Studies,* 34 (Autumn, 1977), 38–55; Lidia Woytak, "Polish Language Textbooks for English-speaking Students," *Polish American Studies,* 36 (Autumn, 1979), 74–83. Also see Charles A. Ward, "Intrafamilial Patterns and Croatian Language Maintenance in America," in Charles A. Ward et al., *Studies in Ethnicity,* pp. 3–12.

Chapter 11. Acculturation and the Catholic Melting Pot

1. See Nathan Glazer, "Ethnic Groups in America," in Monroe Berger, Theodore Abel, and Charles H. Page, eds., *Freedom and Control in Modern Society* (New York, 1954), pp. 165–68.

2. See Joshua A. Fishman, *Language Loyalty in the United States* (The Hague, 1966), p. 44.

3. See Stanislaus Blejwas, "A Polish Community in Transition: The Evolution of Holy Cross Parish, New Britain, Connecticut," *Polish American Studies,* 35 (Spring–Autumn, 1978), 23–28; Edward R. Kantowicz, *Corporation Sole: Cardinal Mundelein and Chicago Catholicism* (Notre Dame, 1983), p. 61.

4. Joshua A. Fishman, *Language Loyalty,* p. 135.

5. William J. Galush, "Faith and Fatherland. Dimensions of Polish-American Ethnoreligion, 1875–1975," in Randall M. Miller and Thomas D. Marzik, *Immigrants and Religion in Urban America,* pp. 92–97; and Edward R. Kantowicz, *Corporation Sole,* pp. 77–78.

6. Herve-B. Lemaire, "Franco-American Efforts on Behalf of the French Language in New England," in Joshua A. Fishman, *Language Loyalty,* pp. 253–79.

7. Joshua A. Fishman, Robert G. Hayden, and Mary E. Warshauer, "The Non-English and the Ethnic Group Press, 1910–1960," in Joshua A. Fishman, *Language Loyalty,* p. 53.

8. See Charles H. Mindel and Robert W. Haberstam, *Ethnic Families in America* (New York, 1976).

9. William J. Galush, "Faith and Fatherland," p. 94.

10. See Jan Slomka, *From Serfdom to Self-Government,* pp. 141–47.

11. William A. Christian, Jr., *Person and God,* pp. 44–77.

12. Leo J. Alilunas, *Lithuanians in the United States: Selected Studies* (San Francisco, 1978), pp. 103–20.

13. Nicholas J. Russo, "The Religious Acculturation of the Italians in New York City," Ph.D. dissertation, St. John's University, 1968, p. 341; K. Culen, "The Cult of SS Cyril and Methodius amongst the Slovaks in U.S.A. and Canada," *Slovakia,* 22 (1972), 98–112; Leo Pap, *The Portuguese Americans,* p. 200.

14. Richard Rodríguez, *Hunger of Memory,* p. 26.

15. Quoted in James Hennesey, *American Catholics,* p. 177.

16. Bohdan Procko, *Ukrainian Catholics,* p. 12; Leo Pap, *The Portuguese Americans,* pp. 200–201; Rudolph Vecoli, "Prelates and Peasants," pp. 262–68.

17. For a historical perspective on the problem of "leakage," see Gerald Shaughnessy, *Has the Immigrant Kept the Faith?* (New York, 1925);

The Metropolitan Catholic Almanac and Laity Directory 1850 (Baltimore, 1850), pp. 234–35.

18. Thomas T. McAvoy, *A History of the Catholic Church in the United States* (Notre Dame, 1969), pp. 124–25.

19. Kenneth Scott Latourette, *The Nineteenth Century in Europe: Background and the Roman Catholic Phase* (Grand Rapids, 1969), pp. 368–74.

20. For the best account of Catholic revivalism, see Jay P. Dolan, *Catholic Revivalism: The American Experience, 1830–1900* (Notre Dame, 1977).

21. For an account of the interplay between guilt, sin, persecution, and the Catholic identity of Ireland, see Emmet Larkin, "The Devotional Revolution in Ireland," pp. 649–52.

22. For Alexis de Tocqueville's surprised observations of the restraint of Yankee Catholicism in the United States, see his *Democracy in America,* 2 vols. (New York, 1945), II, p. 28.

23. Kenneth Scott Latourette, *The Nineteenth Century in Europe,* pp. 350–70.

24. Donna Merwick, *Boston Priests*, pp. 147–96. For a look at Romanization among the Irish Catholics, see Emmet Larkin, *The Making of the Roman Catholic Church in Ireland, 1850–1860* (Chapel Hill, 1980), pp. 482–92.

25. Dennis J. Clark, "The Irish Catholics: A Postponed Perspective," in Randall M. Miller and Thomas D. Marzik, *Immigrants and Religion in Urban America,* pp. 56–57.

26. Quoted in John Joseph Parot, *Polish Catholics,* p. 205.

27. Quoted in Edward R. Kantowicz, "Cardinal Mundelein of Chicago and the Shaping of Twentieth Century American Catholicism," *Journal of American History,* 68 (June, 1981), 64–65.

28. Edward R. Kantowicz, *Corporation Sole,* pp. 75–82.

29. See Nathan Glazer, "Ethnic Groups in America," in Monroe Berger et al., *Freedom and Control in Modern Society,* pp. 165–68.

Chapter 12. Assimilation and the Roman Catholic Melting Pot

1. *The Official Catholic Directory, 1982* (New York, 1982), passim.

2. Sylvia June Alexander, "The Immigrant Church," pp. 56–83; Jay P. Dolan, *The Immigrant Church,* pp. 40–41; Josef J. Barton, *Peasants and Strangers,* pp. 12–14.

3. Joseph John Parot, *Polish Catholics,* p. 221.

4. Alexander, "The Immigrant Church," p. 230. Also see Edward F. Kantowicz, *Corporation Sole,* pp. 65–83.

5. Joseph John Parot, *Polish Catholics,* pp. 215–38.

6. Harold J. Abramson, *Ethnic Diversity in Catholic America* (New York, 1973), pp. 41, 44.

7. See Aaron I. Abell, *American Catholicism and Social Action* (Notre Dame, 1963), pp. 1–24; James E. Roohan, "American Catholics and the Social Question," Ph.D. dissertation, Yale University, 1952, pp. 1–60; Daniel T. McColgan, *A Century of Charity: The First One Hundred Years of the Society of St. Vincent de Paul in the United States* (Milwaukee, 1951); Timothy Walch, "Catholic Social Institutions and Urban Development: The View from Nineteenth Century Chicago and Milwaukee," *Catholic Historical Review,* 64 (January, 1978), 16–32.

8. See Richard M. Linkh, *American Catholicism,* pp. 49–64.

9. John Bodnar, "Immigrants and Modernization," *Journal of Social History,* 10 (Fall, 1976), p. 10.

10. Timothy Walch, "Catholic Social Institutions," pp. 324–25.

11. David O'Brien, "American Catholics and Organized Labor in the 1930s" *Catholic Historical Review,* 52 (July, 1966), 323–49; Thomas N. Brown, *Irish American Nationalism,* pp. 178–82. Also see John Higham, *Ethnic Leadership in America,* pp. 64–90, 150–98; Helen Z. Lopata, *Polish Americans: Status Competition in an Ethnic Community* (Englewood Cliffs, 1976), pp. 47–62.

12. David O'Brien, "American Catholics," pp. 323–48.

13. Paul Michael Green, "Irish Chicago: The Multiethnic Road to Machine Success," and Michael F. Funchion, "Irish Chicago: Church, Homeland, Politics, and Class—The Shaping of an Ethnic Group, 1870–1900," in Peter d'A. Jones and Melvin G. Holli, *Ethnic Chicago* (Grand Rapids, 1981), pp. 8–39, 212–59; Thomas N. Brown, *Irish American Nationalism,* pp. 178–82; Robert D. Cross,"The Irish," in John Higham, ed., *Ethnic Leadership in America* (Baltimore, 1978),pp. 176–79; Donna Merwick, *Boston Priests,* pp. 191–96; Edward F. Kantowicz, *Polish American Politics in Chicago* (Chicago, 1975), pp. 45–56.

14. See the associated parish associations in the major dioceses during the 1950s and 1960s in any edition of *The Official Catholic Directory.*

15. Harold Abramson, *Ethnic Diversity in Catholic America,* p. 53.

16. See Herve-B. Lemaire, "Franco-American Efforts," p. 267.

17. Richard D. Alba, "Social Assimilation among American Catholic National-Origins Groups," *American Sociological Review,* 41 (December, 1976), 1039. Also see B. R. Bugleski, "Assimilation through Intermarriage," *Social Forces,* 40 (December, 1961), 148–53; Ruby Jo Reeves Kennedy, "Single or Triple Melting Pot? Intermarriage Trends in New Haven, 1870–1940, " *American Journal of Sociology,* 49 (January, 1944), 331–39; William Walkovich-Balkaricius, "Lithuanians of Worcester, Massachusetts: A Socio-Historic Glimpse at Marriage Records, 1910–1915 and 1930–1934," *Lituanus,* 26 (1980), 63–86; Richard M. Bernard, *The Melting Pot and the*

Altar: Marital Assimilation in Early Twentieth Century Wisconsin (Minneapolis, 1980).

18. Ibid.

19. Daniel S. Buczek, "Ethnic to American: Holy Name of Jesus Parish, Stamford, Connecticut," *Polish-American Studies,* 37 (Autumn, 1980) 17–59.

Chapter 13. An Immigrant Catholic Legacy

1. James Hennesey, *American Catholicism,* pp. 321–29.

2. Dorothy Dohen, *Nationalism and American Catholicism* (New York, 1967), pp. 163–92; Joshua Fishman, *Language and Nationalism,* pp. 52–55.

3. Stephen William Mamchur, "Nationalism, Religion, and the Problem of Assimilation among the Ukrainians in the United States," Ph.D. dissertation, Yale University, 1942, p. 46; Walter Warzeski, *Byzantine Rite Rusins,* p. 239; Vasyl Markus, "A Century of Ukrainian Religious Experience in the United States," in Richard Renoff and Stephen Reynolds, eds., *Proceedings of the Conference on Carpatho-Ruthenian Immigration* (Cambridge, 1975), pp. 105–28.

4. Harold J. Abramson, *Ethnic Diversity in Catholic America,* p. 108.

5. Ibid., p. 158.

6. See Andrew M. Greeley, *The Communal Catholic: A Personal Manifesto* (New York, 1976). Also see Edward Wakin and Father Joseph F. Scheuer, *The De-Romanization of the American Catholic Church* (New York, 1966), pp. 281–91.

7. James Hennesey, *American Catholics,* pp. 309–10.

8. Ibid., p. 313; Isidro Lucas, *The Browning of America,* pp. 141–46.

9. James B. Manney, "Before Duquesne: Sources of the Renewal," in Ralph Martin, ed., *The Spirit and the Church* (New York, 1976), pp. 21–41. Also see Edward D. O'Conner, ed., *Perspectives on Charismatic Renewal* (Notre Dame, 1975).

10. James Hennesey, *American Catholics,* pp. 330–31.

11. James S. Olson, *The Ethnic Dimension,* pp. 427–31.

12. See Christopher H. Mindel and Robert Habenstein, eds., *Ethnic Families in America: Patterns and Variations* (New York, 1976), pp. 15–40, 61–123, 192–218, 271–92, 323–46.

13. Andrew M. Greeley, *The American Catholic: A Social Portrait* (New York, 1977), pp. 50–68, 270–74.

14. See Michael Novak, *The Rise of the Unmeltable Ethnics* (New York, 1971), pp. 314–42; Thomas Sowell, *Ethnic America: A History* (New York,

1981), pp. 273–96; Richard Krickus, *Pursuing the American Dream: White Ethnics and the New Populism* (Garden City, 1976), pp. 354–98; Stanley Lieberson, *A Piece of the Pie: Blacks and White Immigrants since 1880* (Berkeley, 1980), pp. 363–94.

15. See Martin E. Marty, *Righteous Empire: The Protestant Experience in America* (New York, 1970).

16. Paul Kleppner, *The Cross of Culture: A Social Analysis of Midwestern Politics 1850–1900* (New York, 1970), pp. 369–76.

17. For a contemporary discussion of work and religious culture, see M. Mark Stolarik, "Immigration, Education, and the Social Mobility of Slovaks, 1870–1930," in Randall M. Miller and Thomas D. Marzik, *Immigrants and Religion in Urban America*, pp. 112–14.

18. "The Pope vs. the U.S. Church," *Newsweek* (October 10, 1983), p. 78.

Bibliography

Abell, Aaron I. *American Catholicism and Social Action*, Notre Dame: 1963.

Abernathy, Francis E., ed. *The Folklore of Texan Cultures*. Austin: 1974.

Abrahamson, Harold J. *Ethnic Diversity in Catholic America*. New York: 1973.

Achutegni, Pedro S. and Miguel A. Bernad. *Religious Revolution in the Philippines: The Life and Church of Gregorio Aglipay*. 2 volumes. Quezon City: 1960.

Adams, W. F. *Ireland and Irish Emigration to the New World from 1815 to the Famine*. New Haven: 1932.

Ahlstrom, Sydney E. *A Religious History of the American People*. New Haven: 1972.

Akenson, Donald. *The Irish Education Experiment: The National System of Education in the Nineteenth Century*. London: 1970.

Alba, Richard D. "Social Assimilation among American Catholic National-Origins Groups." *American Sociological Review*. 41 (December, 1976).

Alexander, Stella. *Church and State in Yugoslavia since 1945*. London: 1979.

Alexander, Sylvia June. "The Immigrant Church and Community: The Formation of Pittsburgh's Slovak Religious Institutions, 1880-1914." Ph.D. dissertation, University of Minnesota, 1980.

Alilunas, Leo J. *Lithuanians in the United States: Selected Studies*. San Francisco: 1978.

Amfifheatrof, Erik. *The Children of Columbus: An Informal History of the Italians in the New World*. Boston: 1973.

Anderson, Charles. *White Protestant Americans: From National Origins to Religious Groups*. Englewood Cliffs: 1970.

Arensberg, Conrad. *The Irish Countryman: An Anthropological Study*. Garden City: 1968.

Armstrong, John A. *Ukrainian Nationalism*. New York: 1963.

Attwater, Donald. *The Catholic Eastern Churches*. Milwaukee: 1937.

Bailyn, Bernard. *The Ideological Origins of the American Revolution*. Cambridge: 1967.

Balch, Emily. *Our Slavic Fellow Citizens*. New York: 1910.

Balkaricius, William Walkovich. "Lithuanians of Worcester, Massachusetts:

A Socio-Historic Glimpse at Marriage Records, 1910-1915 and 1930-1934." *Lituanus*. 26 (1980).

Barry, Colman J. *The Catholic Church and German Americans*. Milwaukee: 1953.

Barton, Josef J. *Peasants and Strangers: Italians, Rumanians, and Slovaks in an American City, 1890–1950*. Cambridge: 1975.

Beals, Carlton. *Brass-Knuckles Crusade: The Great Know-Nothing Conspiracy. 1820-1860*. New York: 1960.

Beckett, J. C. *A Short History of Ireland*. New York: 1966.

Beitzell, Edwin W. *The Jesuit Missions of St. Mary's County, Maryland*. Abell: 1977.

Bernard, Richard M. *The Melting Pot and the Altar: Marital Assimilation in Early Twentieth Century Wisconsin*. Minneapolis: 1980.

Bicha, Karl. "Settling Accounts with an Old Adversary: The Decatholicization of Czech Immigrants in America." *Social History-Histoire Sociale*. No. 8 (November, 1972).

———. "The Survival of the Village in Urban America: A Note on the Czech Immigrants in Chicago to 1914." *International Migration Review*. 5 (Spring, 1971).

Bigson, Charles. *Aztecs under Spanish Rule*. Stanford: 1964

Billington, Ray Allen. *The Protestant Crusade, 1800–1860: A Study of the Origins of American Nativism*. New York: 1938.

Bland, Joan. *Hibernian Crusade*. Washington, D.C.: 1951.

Blejwas, Stanislaus. "A Polish Community in Transition: The Evolution of Holy Cross Parish, New Britain, Connecticut." *Polish American Studies*. 35 (Spring-Autumn, 1978).

Bodnar, John. "Immigrants and Modernization." *Journal of Social History*. 10 (Fall, 1976).

Bossy, John. "The Counter Reformation and the People of Catholic Europe." *Past and Present*. 47 (May, 1970).

Boxer, C. R. *The Church Militant and Iberian Expansion, 1440–1770*. Baltimore: 1978.

Bradley, J. F. N. *Czechoslovakia*. Edinburgh: 1971.

Brady, John. "Funeral Customs of the Past." *Irish Ecclesiastical Record*. 78 (November, 1942).

Brakas, Martin. *Lithuania Minor: A Collection of Studies on Her History and Ethnography*. New York: 1976.

Bridenbaugh, Carl. *Vexed and Troubled Englishmen, 1590–1642*. New York: 1968.

Brock, Peter. *The Slovak National Awakening: An Essay in the Intellectual History of East Central Europe*. Toronto: 1976.

Brogan, D. W. *The American Character*. New York: 1956.

Brown, Harold. "The 'Italian Problem' in the Catholic Church in the United

States, 1886–1900." *Historical Records and Studies*. 35 (1946).
Brown, Thomas N. *Irish-American Nationalism*. Philadelphia: 1966.
Buczek, Daniel S. "Ethnic to American: Holy Mass of Jesus Parish, Stamford, Connecticut." *Polish American Studies*. 37 (Autumn, 1980).
Bugleski, B. R. "Assimilation through Intermarriage." *Social Forces*. 40 (December, 1961).

Cada, Joseph. *Czech-American Catholics, 1850–1920*. Chicago: 1964.
Capek, Thomas. *The Czechs (Bohemians) in America*. Boston: 1920.
Carey, Patrick. "The Laity's Understanding of the Trustee System, 1785–1855." *Catholic Historical Review*. 64 (July, 1978).
Caroli, Betty Boyd. *Italian Repatriation From the United States, 1900–1914*. New York: 1974.
Carrillo, Albert. "The Sociological Failure of the Catholic Church toward the Chicano." *Journal of Mexican American Studies*. 1 (Winter, 1971).
Carthy, Mary Peter. *English Influence on Early American Catholicism*. Washington, D.C.: 1959.
Chapman, Charlotte G. *Milocca, a Sicilian Village*. Cambridge: 1971.
Christian, William A. *Person and God in a Spanish Valley*. New York: 1972.
Clark, Dennis. *The Irish in Philadelphia: Ten Generations of Urban Experience*. Philadelphia: 1974.
Clark, Ruth. *Strangers and Sojourners at Port Royal. Being an Account of the Connections Between the British Isles and the Jansenists of France and Holland*. Cambridge: 1932.
Coehlo, Anthony. "A Row of Nationalities: Life in a Working Class Community: The Irish, English, and French Canadians of Fall River, Massachusetts, 1850–1890." Ph.D. dissertation, Brown University, 1980.
Collinson, Patrick. *The Elizabethan Puritan Movement*. New York: 1967.
Conistre, Marie. "Education in a Local Area: A Study of a Decade in the Life and Education of the Adult Italian Immigrant in East Harlem, New York." Ph.D. dissertation, New York University, 1973.
Connell, K. H. *The Population of Ireland, 1750–1845*.
Conrad, Glenn R. *The Cajuns: Essays on Their History and Culture*. Lafayette: 1978.
Cooke, Alistair. *The Americans*. New York: 1980.
Cordasco, Francesco and Eugene Bucchioni. *The Puerto Rican Experience*. Totowa: 1973.
Cornelisen, Ann. *Torregreca: Life, Death, Miracles*. New York: 1970.
Costigan, Giovanni. *A History of Modern Ireland*. New York: 1969.
Cronin, Constance. *The Sting of Change: Sicilians in Sicily and Australia*. Chicago: 1970.
Cross, Robert. *The Emergence of Liberal Catholicism*. Cambridge: 1958.

Culen, K. "The Cult of SS Cyril and Methodius amongst the Slovaks in U.S.A. and Canada." *Slovakia*. 22 (1972).

Curtis, Edmund. *A History of Ireland*. New York: 1968.

Daniel, David P. "The Protestant Reformation and Slovak Ethnic Consciousness." *Slovakia*, 28 (1978–1979).

D'Antonio, W. V. and F. B. Pike, eds. *Religion, Revolution, and Reform: New Forces for Change in Latin America*. New York: 1964.

Davies, Norman. *God's Playground: A History of Poland*. 2 volumes. New York: 1982.

de Beaumont, Gustave. *Ireland: Social, Political, and Religious*. 2 volumes. London: 1839.

DeLeon, Arnoldo. *The Tejano Community 1836–1900*. Albuquerque: 1982.

Devillers, Carole. "Haiti's Voodoo Pilgrimages." *National Geographic Magazine*. 157 (March, 1985).

Dignan, Patrick. *A History of the Legal Incorporation of Church Property in the United States, 1784–1932*. Washington, D. C.: 1933.

Doeppers, Daniel F. "Changing Patterns of Aglipayan Adherence in the Philippines, 1918–1970." *Philippine Studies*. 25 (1971).

Dohen, Dorothy. *Nationalism and American Catholicism*. New York: 1967.

———. *Two Studies of Puerto Rico*. Cuernavaca: 1966.

Dolan, Jay P. *Catholic Revivalism: The American Experience, 1830–1900*. Notre Dame: 1977.

———. *The Immigrant Church: New York's Irish and German Catholics, 1815–1865*. Baltimore: 1975.

Dolley, Michael. *Anglo-Norman Ireland*. Dublin: 1972.

Douglass, William. *Death in Murelaga*. Seattle: 1969.

Douglass, William and Jon Bilbao. *Amerikanuak: Basques in the New World*. Reno: 1975.

Dworaczyk, Edward J. *The First Polish Colonies in America in Texas*. San Antonio: 1936.

Dyrud, Keith P., Michael Novak, and Rudolph J. Vecoli. *The Other Catholics*. New York: 1978.

Easton, George Simpson. *Religious Cults of the Caribbean*. San Juan: 1960.

Eccles, W. J. *France in America*. New York: 1972.

Edwards, R. D. and T. D. Williams, eds. *The Great Famine: Studies in Irish History, 1845–1852*. New York: 1957.

Elkins, Stanley. *Slavery: A Problem in American Intellectual and Institutional Life*. Chicago: 1959.

Ellis, John Tracy. *American Catholicism*. Chicago: 1959.

_______. *Documents of American Catholic History*. 2 volumes. Chicago: 1967.

Eterovich, Francis H. and Christopher Spalatin, eds. *Croatia: Land, People, Culture*. 2 volumes. Toronto: 1964.

Evan, Emyr Estyn. *Irish Heritage*. Dundalk: 1945.

Fallows, Marjorie. *Irish Americans: Identity and Assimilation*. Englewood Cliffs: 1979.

Fennell, Douglas, ed. *The Changing Face of Catholic Ireland*. London: 1968.

Fenton, Jerry. *Understanding the Religious Background of the Puerto Rican*. Cuernavaca: 1969.

Fishman, Joshua. *Language Loyalty in the United States*. The Hague: 1966.

Fitzpatrick, Joseph P. *Puerto Rican Americans: The Meaning of Migration to the Mainland*. Englewood Cliffs: 1971.

_______. "The Role of the Parish in the Spiritual Care of Puerto Ricans in the New York Archdiocese." *Studi Emigrazione*. 7 (October, 1966).

Fitzsimmons, M. A. *The Catholic Church Today: Western Europe*. Notre Dame: 1969.

Fortescue, Adrian. *The Uniate Eastern Churches. The Byzantine Rite in Italy, Sicily, Syria, and Egypt*. New York: 1923.

Gaffey, James. "The Changing of the Guard: The Rise of Cardinal O'Connell of Boston." *Catholic Historical Review*. 59 (July, 1973).

Gallagher, Joseph P. *A Century of History: The Diocese of Scranton, 1868–1968*. Scranton: 1968.

Gallup, Rodney. *Portugal: A Book of Folk-Ways*. London: 1936.

Gambino, Richard. *Blood of My Blood: The Dilemma of the Italian Americans*. Garden City: 1974.

George, C. H. and Katherine George. *The Protestant Mind of the English Reformation*. London: 1961.

Gibbons, James Cardinal. *A Retrospect of Fifty Years*. 2 volumes. New York: 1916.

Gilley, Sheridan. "The Roman Catholic Mission to the Irish in London." *Recusant History*. 10 (October, 1969).

Gipson, Charles. *Spain in America*. New York: 1964.

Glazer, Nathan and Daniel Patrick Moynihan. *Beyond the Melting Pot: The Negroes, Puerto Ricans, Jews, Italians and Irish of New York City*. Cambridge: 1963.

Gomez-Ibanez, Daniel A. *The Western Pyrenees: Differential Evolution of the French and Spanish Borderland*. Oxford: 1975.

Gordon, Milton M. *Assimilation in American Life: The Role of Race, Religion, and National Origins*. New York: 1964.

Graves, Alvin R. "Immigrants in Agriculture: The Portuguese Californians, 1850–1970." Ph.D. dissertation, University of California at Los Angeles, 1977.

Grebler, Leo, Joan W. Moore, and Ralph Guzman. *The Mexican-American People*. New York: 1970.

Greeley, Andrew M. *That Most Distressful Nation: The Taming of the American Irish*. Chicago: 1972.

———. *The American Catholic: A Social Portrait*. New York: 1977.

———. *The Communal Catholic: A Personal Manifesto*. New York: 1976.

———. *The Irish Americans: The Rise to Money and Power*. New York: 1981.

———. *Why Can't They Be Like Us? America's White Ethnic Groups*. New York: 1975.

Greene, Victor. *For God and Country: The Rise of Polish and Lithuanian Ethnic Consciousness in America*. Madison: 1975.

Greenfield, Sidney M. "In Search of Social Identity: Strategies of Ethnic Identity Management amongst Capeverdeans in Southeastern Massachusetts." *Luso-Brazilian Review*. 13 (Summer, 1976).

Griffin, Martin I. J. "The First Mass in Philadelphia." *American Catholic Historical Researcher*. 12 (January, 1895).

Griffiths Naomi. *The Acadians: Creation of a People*. New York: 1973.

Guilday, Peter. *The Life and Times of John Carroll, First Archbishop of Baltimore, 1735–1815*. New York: 1922.

Gulovich, Stephen C. "Byzantine Slavonic Catholics and the Latin Clergy." *Homoletic and Pastoral Review*. 45 (1945).

———. "The Ruthenian Tragedy." *Homelitic and Pastoral Review*. 46 (1946).

———. "The Rusin Exarchate in the United States." *Eastern Churches Quarterly*. 6 (1946).

Halecki, Oscar. *A History of Poland*. New York: 1961.

Hartz, Louis. *The Liberal Tradition in America*. New York: 1955.

Hauberg, Clifford. *Puerto Rico and the Puerto Ricans*. New York: 1974.

Hennesey, James. *American Catholics: A History of the Roman Catholic Community in the United States*. New York: 1981.

Herberg, Will. *Protestant—Catholic—Jew: An Essay in American Religious Sociology*. New York: 1955.

Hermann, A. H. *A History of the Czechs*. London: 1975.

Hida, Peter. *The Metamorphosis of a Social Class in Hungary during the Reign of Young Franz Joseph*. New York: 1977.

Higham, John. *Strangers in the Land: Patterns of American Nativism, 1860–1925*. New Brunswick: 1955.

Horowitz, Michael M. *Peoples and Cultures of the Caribbean*. Garden City: 1971.

Houck, George F. *A History of Catholicity in Northern Ohio and in the Diocese of Cleveland from 1749 to December 31, 1900*. 2 volumes. Cleveland: 1903.

Hudson, William M. *The Healer of Los Olmos and Other Mexican Lore*. Dallas: 1951.

Hughes, Thomas. *History of the Society of Jesus in North America, Colonial and Federal*. 4 volumes. New York: 1907–1917.

Janos, Andrew. *The Politics of Backwardness in Hungary, 1825–1945*. Princeton: 1982.

John, Elizabeth A. *Storms Brewed in Other Men's Worlds: The Confrontation of the Indians, Spanish, and French in the Southwest, 1540–1795*. College Station: 1975.

Johnson, Mary. *Ireland in the Eighteenth Century*. Dublin: 1974.

Jones, Maldwyn. *American Immigration*. Chicago: 1960.

Jones, Peter d'A, and Melvin G. Holli. *Ethnic Chicago*. Grand Rapids: 1981.

Kadic, Ante. *From Croatian Renaissance to Yugoslav Socialism*. The Hague: 1969.

Kann, Robert A. *A History of the Hapsburg Empire, 1526–1918*. Berkeley: 1974.

Kantowicz, Edward R. *Corporation Sole: Cardinal Mundelein and Chicago Catholicism*. Notre Dame: 1983.

———. *Polish American Politics in Chicago*. Chicago: 1975.

Kauffman, Christopher J. *Faith and Fraternalism: The History of the Knights of Columbus, 1882–1982*. New York: 1982.

Kayal, Philip M. and Joseph M. Kayal. *The Syrian-Lebanese in America: A Study in Religion and Assimilation*. Boston: 1975.

Kee, Robert. *The Green Flag*. New York: 1972.

Kennedy, Robert Emmet. *The Irish: Emigration, Marriage, and Fertility*. Berkeley: 1973.

Kiev, Ari. *Curanderismo: Mexican American Folk Psychiatry*. New York: 1968.

Kingsdale, Jon M. "The Poor Man's Club: Social Functions of the Urban-Working Class Saloon." *American Quarterly*. 25 (October, 1973).

Kirschbaum, Joseph M. *Slovakia in the 19th and 20th Century*. Toronto: 1973.

Kleppner, Paul. *The Cross of Culture: A Social Analysis of Midwestern Politics 1850–1900*. New York: 1970.

Knight, Frank. *Slave Society in Cuba during the Nineteenth Century*. Madison: 1970.

Knobel, Dale. "Paddy and the Republic: Popular Images of the American Irish, 1820–1860." Ph.D. dissertation, Northwestern University, 1976.

Kollman, Wolfgang and Peter Marschalk. "German Emigration to the United States." *Perspectives in American History*. 7 (1973).

Krickus, Richard. *Pursuing the American Dream: White Ethnics and the New Populism*. Garden City: 1976.

Kucera, Daniel W. "A Historical Pronouncement: Wisconsin Bishops Protest the Bennett Law." *Social Justice Review*. 31 (December, 1940–January, 1941).

Kuzniewski, Anthony J. *Faith and Fatherland: The Polish Church War in Wisconsin, 1896–1918*. Notre Dame: 1981.

Lahey, Raymond J. "The Role of Religion in Lord Baltimore's Colonial Enterprise." *Maryland Historical Magazine*, 72 (Winter, 1977).

Lamott, John H. *History of the Archdiocese of Cincinnati, 1821–1921*. New York: 1921.

Lannie, Vincent P. "Alienation in America: The Immigrant Catholic and Public Education in Pre-Civil War America." *The Review of Politics*. 32 (October, 1970).

Larkin, Emmet. "The Devotional Revolution in Ireland, 1850–1875." *American Historical Review*. 72 (June, 1972).

———. *The Making of the Roman Catholic Church in Ireland, 1850–1960*. Chapel Hill: 1980.

Laslett, Peter. *The World We Have Lost*. New York: 1965.

Latourette, Kenneth Scott. *The Nineteenth Century in Europe: Background and the Roman Catholic Phase*. Grand Rapids, 1969.

Lengyel, Emil. *Americans from Hungary*. Philadelphia: 1948.

Leonard, Henry B. "Ethnic Conflict and Episcopal Power: The Diocese of Cleveland, 1847–1870." *Catholic Historical Review*. 62 (July, 1976).

Leslie, R. F. *Reform and Insurrection in Russian Poland, 1856–1865*. Westport: 1969.

Lettrick, Jozef. *History of Modern Slovakia*. New York: 1955

Levine, Edward M. *The Irish and Irish Politicians*. Notre Dame: 1966.

Lewandowska, S. T. "The Polish Immigrant in Philadelphia to 1914." *Records of the American Catholic Historical Society*. 65 (June, 1945).

Lieberson, Stanley. *A Piece of the Pie: Blacks and White Immigrants Since 1880*. Berkeley: 1980.

Liebman, Lance, ed. *Ethnic Relations in America*. Englewood Cliffs: 1982.

Liesel, N. *The Eastern Catholic Liturgies*. Westminister: 1960.

Lightfoot, Keith. *The Philippines*. New York: 1973.

Linkh, Richard M. *American Catholicism and European Immigrants (1900–1924)*. New York: 1975.

Liptak, Doris A. "European Immigrants and the Catholic Church in Connecticut, 1870–1920." Ph.D. dissertation, University of Connecticut, 1979.

Lockhart, Audrey. *Some Aspects of Emigration from Ireland to the North American Colonies between 1660 and 1775*. New York: 1976.

Lopata, Helen Z. *Polish-Americans: Status Competition in an Ethnic Community*. Englewood Cliffs: 1976.

Lord, Robert H. *History of the Archdiocese of Boston.* New York: 1944.

Lucas, Isidro. *The Browning of America: The Hispanic Revolution in the American Church*. Chicago: 1981.

Luebke, Frederick. *Ethnicity on the Great Plains*. Lincoln: 1980.

_______. "German Immigrants and Churches in Nebraska, 1889–1915." *Mid-America*. 50 (April, 1968).

MacDonagh, Oliver. "The Irish Famine Migration to the United States." *Perspectives in American History*. 10 (1976).

MacGaffey, Wyatt and Clifford R. Barnett. *Cuba: Its People, Its Society, Its Culture*. New Haven: 1962.

MacManus, Seumas. *The Story of the Irish Race*. New York: 1944.

MacMurtain, Margaret. *Tudor and Stuart Ireland*. Dublin: 1972.

Madsen, William. *Mexican-Americans of South Texas*. New York: 1964.

Magri, Francis Joseph. *The Catholic Church in the City and Diocese of Richmond*. Richmond: 1906.

Marty, Martin E. *Righteous Empire: The Protestant Experience in America*. New York: 1970.

Maxwell, Constantia. *Country and Town in Ireland under the Georges*. Dundalk: 1949.

Maynard, Theodore. *The Catholic Church and the American Idea*. New York: 1953.

Mcartney, Carlile. *Hungary*. London: 1934.

McAvoy, Thomas T. *The Americanist Heresy in Roman Catholicism, 1895–1900*. Notre Dame: 1963.

_______. *The Great Crisis in American Catholic History, 1895–1900*. Chicago: 1957.

McCaffrey, Lawrence J. *The Irish Diaspora in America*. Bloomington: 1976.

McColgan, Daniel T. *A Century of Charity: The First One Hundred Years of the Society of St. Vincent de Paul in the United States*. Milwaukee: 1951.

McGuire, C. E., ed. *Catholic Builders of the Nation*. Boston: 1923.

McManamin, Francis G. *The American Years of John Boyle O'Reilly, 1870–1890*. Washington, D.C.: 1959.

McNally, Robert, ed. *Old Ireland*. New York: 1965.

Mead, Sydney. *The Lively Experiment. The Shaping of Christianity in America*. New York: 1963.

Mecham, J. Lloyd. *Church and State in Latin America*. Chapel Hill: 1966.

Meng, John. "Cahenslyism: The First Stage, 1883–1891." *Catholic Historical Review*. 31 (January, 1946).

———. "Cahenslyism: The Second Chapter, 1891–1910." *Catholic Historical Review*. 32 (January, 1947).

Merton, Thomas. *Seasons of Celebration*. New York: 1965.

Merwick, Donna. *Boston Priests, 1848–1910: A Study of Social and Intellectual Change*. Cambridge: 1973.

Messenger, John C. "Sex and Repression in an Irish Folk Community." In Donald S. Marshall and Robert C. Suggs, eds. *Human Sexual Behavior*. New York: 1970.

Mikus, Joseph A. *Slovakia and the Slovaks*. Washington, D. C.: 1977.

Miller, David. "Irish Catholicism and the Great Famine." *Journal of Social History*. 9 (Fall, 1975).

Miller, Randall and Thomas D. Marzik, eds. *Immigrants and Religion in Urban America*. Philadelphia: 1977.

Miner, Horace. *St. Denis: A French-Canadian Parish*. Chicago: 1939.

Mocha, Frank, ed. *Poles in America*. Stevens Point: 1978.

Monzell, Thomas I. "The Catholic Church and the Americanization of the Polish Immigrant. *Polish-American Studies*. 26 (January–June, 1969).

Moody, T. W. and F. X. Martin. *The Course of Irish History*. New York: 1967.

Moss, Leonard W. and Stephen C. Cappannari. "Folklore and Medicine in an Italian Village." *Journal of American Folklore*. 73 (April, 1960).

Mumchar, Stephen William. "Nationalism, Religion, and the Problem of Assimilation among the Ukrainians in the United States." Ph.D. dissertation, Yale University, 1942.

Nelli, Hubert. *From Immigrants to Ethnics: The Italian Americans*. New York: 1983.

Nemec, Ludvik. *Church and State in Czechoslovakia*. New York: 1955.

———. "The Czechoslovak Heresy and Schism: The Emergence of a National Czechoslovak Church." *Transactions of the American Philosophical Society*. 65 (1975).

Nicholls, Kenneth. *Gaelic and Gaelicized Ireland in the Middle Ages*. Dublin: 1972.

Notestein, Wallace. *The English People on the Eve of Colonization, 1603–1630*. New York: 1954.

Novak, Michael. *The Rise of the Unmeltable Ethnic*. New York: 1971.

Ober, Frederick A. *Travels in Mexico and Life among the Mexicans*. Boston: 1883.

Obidinski, Eugene. "The Polish American Press: Survival through Adaptation." *Polish American Studies*. 34 (Autumn, 1977).

O'Brien, David. "American Catholics and Organized Labor in the 1930s." *Catholic Historical Review*. 52 (July, 1966).

O'Connor, Edward, ed. *Perspectives on Charismatic Renewal*. Notre Dame: 1975.

O'Connor, Thomas H. *Fitzpatrick's Boston 1846–1866: John Bernard Fitzpatrick, Third Bishop of Boston.* Boston: 1984.

O'Faolain, Sean. *The Irish*. Harmondsworth: 1969.

O'Farrell, Patrick. *Ireland's English Question*. New York: 1972.

O'Grady, Joseph P. *How the Irish Became American*. New York: 1973.

———. *The Immigrants' Influence on Wilson's Peace Policies*. Lexington: 1967.

Olson, James S. *The Ethnic Dimension in American History*. New York: 1979.

Orzell, Lawrence. "A Minority within a Minority: The Polish National Catholic Church, 1896–1907." *Polish American Studies*. 36 (Spring, 1979).

Osada, Stanislaw. *History of the Polish National Alliance*. Chicago: 1905.

Ott, Sandra. *The Circle of Mountains: A Basque Shepherding Community*. Oxford: 1981.

O'Tuathaigh, Gearold. *Ireland Before the Famine, 1798–1848*. Dublin: 1972.

Otway-Ruthven, A. J. *A History of Medieval Ireland*. London: 1968.

Pap, Leo. *The Portuguese Americans*. New York: 1981.

Park, Julian. *The Culture of Contemporary Canada*. Ithaca: 1957.

Parot, Joseph John. *Polish Catholics in Chicago, 1850–1920: A Religious History*. DeKalb: 1981.

Phelan, John L. *The Hispanization of the Philippines: Spanish Aims and Filipino Responses, 1565–1700*. Madison: 1967.

Platt, Warren C. "The Polish National Catholic Church: An Inquiry into Its Origins." *Church History*. 46 (December, 1977).

Potter, George. *To the Golden Door: The Story of the Irish in Ireland and America*. Boston: 1960.

Potter, George, May M. Diaz, and Jack Potter, eds. *Peasant Society*. Boston: 1967.

Pounds, Norman J. *Poland between East and West*. Princeton: 1964.

Prockho, Bohdan P. *Ukrainian Catholics in America*. Washington, D. C.: 1982.

Prpic, George. *The Croatian Immigrants in America*. New York: 1971.
Putz, Louis J. *The Catholic Church U.S.A.* Chicago: 1956.

Ray, Mary A. *American Opinion of Roman Catholicism in the Eighteenth Century*. New York: 1936.
Renoff, Richard, and Stephen Reynolds, eds. *Proceedings of the Conference on Carpatho-Ruthenian Immigration*. Cambridge: 1975.
Reymont, Ladislas. *The Peasants: Fall, Winter, Spring, Summer*. 4 volumes. New York: 1925.
Ricard, Robert. *The Spiritual Conquest of Mexico*. Berkeley: 1966.
Ridge, Martin. *Ignatius Donnelly: Portrait of a Politician*. Chicago: 1962.
Riegelhaupt, Joyce C. "Festas and Padres: The Organization of Religious Action in a Portuguese Parish." *American Anthropologist*. 75 (1973).
Rippley, La Verne J. *The German Americans*. New York: 1976.
Rodechko, James P. *Patrick Ford and His Search for America: A Case Study of Irish-American Journalism, 1870–1913*. New York: 1976.
Rodriguez, Richard. *Hunger of Memory*. Boston: 1982.
Rogers, Francis M. *Americans of Portuguese Descent: A Lesson in Differentiation*. Beverly Hills: 1974.
Rolle, Andrew. *The Italian Americans: Troubled Roots.* New York: 1980.
Roohan, James E. "American Catholics and the Social Question." Ph.D. dissertation, Yale University, 1952.
Rothan, Emmet H. *The German Catholic Immigrant in the United States, 1830–1860*. Washington, D. C.: 1946.
Russin, Keith S. "Father Alexis G. Toth and the Wilkes-Barre Litigations." *St. Vladimir's Theological Quarterly*. 16 (1972).
Russo, Nicholas J. "The Religious Acculturation of the Italians in New York City." Ph.D. dissertation, St. John's University, 1968.
Ryan, Joseph Paul. "Travel Literature as Source Material for American Catholic History." *Illinois Catholic Historical Review*. 10 (January–April, 1928).

Schultz, Stanley K. *The Culture Factory: Boston Public Schools, 1789–1860*. New York: 1973.
Seller, Maxine, *To Seek America: A History of Ethnic Life in the United States*. Englewood Cliffs: 1977.
Senn, Alfred E. *The Emergence of Modern Lithuania*. New York: 1959.
Seton-Watson, Robert. *A History of the Czechs and Slovaks*. Hamden: 1965.
______. *Racial Problems in Hungary*. New York: 1972.
Shanabruch, Charles. *Chicago's Catholics: The Evolution of an American Identity*. Notre Dame: 1981.
Sharp, John K. *History of the Diocese of Brooklyn, 1853–1953*. New York: 1954.

Shaughnessy, Gerald. *Has the Immigrant Kept the Faith? A Study of Immigration and Catholic Growth in the United States*. New York: 1925.

Silvia, Philip T. "The 'Flint' Affair: French Canadian Struggle for Survivance." *Catholic Historical Review*. 65 (July, 1979).

Slomka, Jan. *From Serfdom to Self-Government: Memoirs of a Polish Village Mayor 1842-1927*. London: 1941.

Smith, Denis Mack. *Italy: a Modern History*. Ann Arbor: 1959.

_______. *A History of Sicily: Modern Sicily after 1713*. New York: 1968.

Smith, Timothy L. "Protestant Schooling and the American Nationality, 1800–1850." *Journal of American History*. 53 (March, 1967).

Smithers, M. F. *Things Seen in Portugal*. London: 1931.

St. Laurent, Charles F. *Language and Nationality in the Light of Revelation and History*. Montreal: 1896.

Steinberg, David Joel. *The Philippines: A Singular and a Plural Place*. Boulder: 1982.

Steiner, Edward. *On the Trail of the Immigrant*. New York: 1906.

Stoddard, Ellwyn. *Mexican-Americans*. New York: 1973.

Stolarik, Mark. "Lay Initiative in American-Slovak Parishes: 1880–1930." *Records of the American Catholic Historical Society*. 83 (September–December, 1972).

Swiderski, Gregory. "Polish-American Polish National Catholic Bishops." *Polish-American Studies*. 24 (January–June, 1967).

Taylor, Philip D. *Distant Magnet: European Emigration to the U.S.A.* London: 1971.

Thomas, W. I. and Florian Znaniecki. *The Polish Peasant in Europe and America*. New York: 1919.

Thomsen, Samuel H. *Czechoslovakia in European History*. Princeton: 1953.

Tomasi, Silvano. *Piety and Power: The Role of Italian Parishes in the New York Metropolitan Area*. New York: 1975.

Van Kley, Dale. *The Jansenists and the Expulsion of the Jesuits from France, 1757–1765*. New Haven: 1975.

Vardys, V. Stanley. *The Catholic Church, Dissent, and Nationality in Soviet Lithuania*. New York: 1978.

Vassidy, Vela Jr. "The 'Homeland Cause' as Stimulant to Ethnic Unity: The Hungarian-American Response to Karolyi's 1914 American Tour." *Journal of American Ethnic History*. 2 (Fall, 1982).

Vecoli, Rudolph J. "Contadini in Chicago: A Critique of the Uprooted." *Journal of American History*. 51 (December, 1964).

_______. "Prelates and Peasants: Italian Immigrants and the Catholic Church." *Journal of Social History*. 2 (Spring, 1969).

Vigil, James D. *From Indians to Chicanos. A Sociocultural History*. St. Louis: 1980.

Viski, Karoly. *Hungarian Peasant Customs*. Budapest: 1932.

Wade, Mason. "The French Parish and *Survivance* in Nineteenth Century New England." *Catholic Historical Review*. 36 (July, 1950).

———. *The French Canadians, 1760–1945*. Toronto: 1956.

Wakin, Edward. *Enter the Irish-American*. New York: 1976.

Wakin, Edward, and Joseph F. Scheuer. *The De-Romanization of the American Catholic Church*. New York: 1966.

Ward, Charles A., Philip Shashko, and Donald E. Pienkos. *Studies in Ethnicity: The East European Experience*. New York: 1980.

Ward, Fred. *Inside Cuba Today*. New York: 1978.

Warzeski, Walter C. *Byzantine Rite Rusins in Carpatho-Ruthenia and America*. Pittsburgh: 1971.

Weed, Perry. *The White Ethnic Movement and Ethnic Politics*. New York: 1973.

Weeks, Lyman. *Among the Azores*. Boston: 1882.

Wilhoit, Francis M. *The Politics of Massive Resistance*. New York: 1973.

Williams, Eric. *From Columbus to Castro: The History of the Caribbean, 1492–1969*. London: 1970.

Wilson, Robert A. *Mexico: Its Peasants and Its Priests*. New York: 1856.

Winner, Irene. *A Slovenian Village*. Providence: 1971.

Wise, Frank H. *The History of the Philippine Independent Church*. Dumaguete: 1965.

Wittke, Carl. *Refugees of Revolution: The German Forty-Eighters in America*. Philadelphia: 1952.

Woodham-Smith, Cecil. *The Great Hunger*. New York: 1962.

Woytak, Lidia. "Polish Language Textbooks for English-Speaking Students." *Polish American Studies*. 36 (Autumn, 1979).

Wrobel, Paul. *Our Way. Family, Parish, and Neighborhood in a Polish-American Community*. Notre Dame: 1979.

Yans-McLaughlin, Virginia. *Family and Community: Italian Immigrants in Buffalo, 1880-1930*. Urbana: 1982.

Zwierlein, Frederick J. *The Lives and Letters of Bishop McQuaid*. 2 volumes. Rochester: 1927.

Index